THE CHURCHILL COMPLEX

Also by Ian Buruma

A Tokyo Romance: A Memoir

Their Promised Land: My Grandparents in Love and War

Theater of Cruelty: Art, Film, and the Shadows of War

Year Zero: A History of 1945

Taming the Gods: Religion and Democracy on Three Continents

The China Lover: A Novel

Murder in Amsterdam: Liberal Europe, Islam, and the Limits of Tolerance

Conversations with John Schlesinger

Occidentalism: The West in the Eyes of Its Enemies

Inventing Japan: 1853–1964

Bad Elements: Chinese Rebels from Los Angeles to Beijing

Anglomania: A European Love Affair

The Missionary and the Libertine: Love and War in East and West

The Wages of Guilt: Memories of War in Germany and Japan

Playing the Game: A Novel

God's Dust: A Modern Asian Journey

Behind the Mask: On Sexual Demons, Sacred Mothers, Transvestites, Gangsters, Drifters and Other Japanese Cultural Heroes

The Japanese Tattoo (text by Donald Richie; photographs by Ian Buruma)

THE CHURCHILL COMPLEX

THE RISE AND FALL OF THE
SPECIAL RELATIONSHIP

IAN BURUMA

Atlantic Books
London

This edition published by arrangement with Penguin Press,
an imprint of Penguin Random House LLC.

First published in Great Britain in 2020 by Atlantic Books,
an imprint of Atlantic Books Ltd.

Book design by Amanda Dewey

1 2 3 4 5 6 7 8 9

A CIP catalogue record for this book is available from the British Library.

Hardback ISBN: 978-1-78649-465-8
E-book ISBN: 978-1-78649-466-5
Paperback ISBN: 978-1-78649-467-2

Printed and bound by CPI Group (UK) Ltd, Croydon, CR0 4YY

Atlantic Books
An Imprint of Atlantic Books Ltd
Ormond House
26–27 Boswell Street
London
WC1N 3JZ

www.atlantic-books.co.uk

For John Ryle

CONTENTS

One

UNDER THE SIGN
OF VICTORY

———

It seems to me that God, with infinite wisdom and skill, is
training the Anglo-Saxon race for an hour sure to come . . .[1]

• REV. JOSIAH STRONG, 1885

When the war is over we shall live in an Anglo-American world.
There will be other great powers, but the sanctions on which the
West reposes will be the ideas for which England and America
have fought and won, and the machines behind them.

• CYRIL CONNOLLY

saw Winston Churchill. On my seventh birthday, in 1958. My
grandparents took my younger sister and me to see *Peter Pan* at the
Scala Theatre in London. When she wasn't too drunk to perform,
Sarah Churchill played Peter. Quite often she played Peter while
drunk as well. Once, she audibly said "Fuck!" when she landed
awkwardly after flying across the stage unsteadily on a wire.

Nothing like that happened on the afternoon we attended the
play. Or if it did, I can't remember. What I do recall is the moment
Sarah's father arrived. The memory is a kind of audiovisual blur: a
pale face in the spotlight, a pudgy hand emerging from a fur muff to

make the V sign, and everyone around me, including my very patriotic British grandparents, breaking into wild applause. (The fur muff is a detail I know only from the photograph published in the papers the next day.) Being Jewish, my grandparents felt strongly that Churchill had saved their lives. The extraordinary enthusiasm of that moment, the shining eyes and the raucous cheering for an old man in a theater box, has stayed with me; it was a bit like watching adults behave like rowdy children, which fitted the story of Peter Pan in a way, the boy who never grew up.

I must have had only a very vague idea who Churchill was. But reminders of the war were still around us: waterlogged bomb craters all over London, drunken soldiers from the British Rhine army throwing up on the ferry from the Hook of Holland to Harwich, and a steady diet of British comic books featuring dashing Spitfire pilots and beastly Germans. At home in The Hague, where I was born to a Dutch father, I assembled plastic Airfix models of Lancaster bombers. And British people we would meet at family parties in England still spoke to foreigners with the polite condescension that those who had lived through their finest hour still reserved for those who had been defeated.

Recent history was experienced by people of my age—I was born just six years after the war—largely as myth, in which Churchill played an important part. We were allowed a day off school to watch his funeral in black-and-white on television. This was just another reminder that we had been liberated from the Germans by people who spoke English. Canadians finished the job in the early spring of 1945, but American and British troops, as well as Canadians, had already entered the country from the south in 1944 and were dropped in the autumn of the same year along the Rhine in the disastrous Battle of Arnhem. Polish troops had played a heroic part, too, but this was not widely known. The language of freedom was English. Canadian troops were billeted in my paternal grandparents' house in Nijmegen, near Arnhem. The women danced with their liberators to Glenn Miller's "In the Mood." Hershey bars and silk stockings were liberally distributed in return for favors, which in many cases might have been granted anyway. And it was never forgotten that in the "hunger winter" of 1944–45, British and American bombers dropped onto a starving population bags of flour, corned beef, margarine, and chewing gum.

My own perception of Europe's liberation, like that of most people of my age, was largely shaped by the movies. Some of the most powerful cinematic memories bear little relation to artistic quality, or indeed historical accuracy. I still cannot watch *The Longest Day*, Darryl Zanuck's Hollywood reenactment of the D-Day landings, without weeping. All the Anglo-American stereotypes are there: Robert Mitchum, the macho Yankee chomping on a cigar while leading his men onto Omaha Beach; Sean Connery as a plucky Scottish private; Peter Lawford as Lord Lovat, accompanied by his own bagpiper—the very idea of a bagpiper playing under German fire is enough to reduce me to tears; John Wayne, dropped from the sky over Normandy to sort things out; and Kenneth More, the unflappable Royal Navy captain wading through the surf with his bulldog named Winston.

If the ghost of Churchill hovered around my childhood in The Hague, its presence was felt even more keenly in Washington, DC, and it lingered far longer. Presidents from John F. Kennedy to George W. Bush and beyond have hoped to follow the great war leader's example and save the world for democracy. His was the heroic myth they felt they had to live up to.

So tenacious has the aura of Churchill been that a political row erupted in 2016 over his bust in the Oval Office when Donald Trump was about to move in. Trump's people placed a bust of Churchill in the office with great fanfare, claiming that President Obama had replaced it with a bust of Martin Luther King Jr. Boris Johnson— the British politician who expressed warm feelings for Trump, wrote a shallow hagiography of Winston Churchill, encouraging flattering comparisons to the author, and would later become prime minister— attributed this "swap" to "an ancestral dislike of the British Empire."[2] In fact, the sculpture that Obama replaced had been loaned to George W. Bush by Tony Blair, while an older bust of Churchill, once given by Britain to Lyndon B. Johnson, was being repaired. Obama quite properly gave the new bust back once the old one was restored. Now the old bust perches behind the desk of Trump, whose scowl might be mistaken for an attempted impersonation of Churchillian gravitas.

Churchill the man has been more popular in the US than his country ever was. Even presidents who had little time for the British revered Churchill. There are several possible reasons for this. Churchill's own (belated) sentimental feelings for the native country of his beloved mother, Jennie Jerome from Brooklyn, New York, were often expressed in flowery speeches all over the US. His frequent references to "the English-speaking peoples" and Anglo-Saxon "kith and kin" no doubt appealed to Americans of a certain age and class. But Churchill's main attraction, I believe, lies in the same myth that colored my childhood, which ties in closely to the view many Americans have of themselves: the beacon of liberty, the city on the hill, the land of the brave, the exceptional nation that freed the world from dictators. Churchill, although only half-American, became the symbol of this defiance of tyranny. He is the bulldog face of Anglo-American notions of valor.

Another ghost haunts Washington, DC, as well as London, along with Churchill's. Indeed the two are intimately linked. That is the ghost of Munich, the city where the British prime minister Neville Chamberlain signed an agreement with Hitler in September 1938 that allowed Germany to take a chunk of Czechoslovakia with impunity. Chamberlain thought he had bought "peace for our time." Churchill, speaking in Parliament, called it a "total and unmitigated defeat." He thought this "bitter cup" could be averted only once Britain recovered its "moral health and martial vigor" and arose again to take a "stand for freedom as in the olden time."

It is possible, as some maintain, that if Britain and France had taken that stand in 1938, Hitler's ambition of conquering Europe would have been thwarted. Others continue to argue that Chamberlain had no choice, since Britain was not ready to fight a war against Germany, and the US was in no mind to get involved. But the mythical verdict, still repeated in political speeches, and celebrated in the movies, is that Chamberlain was a shortsighted and cowardly appeaser and Churchill the hero. Ever since, whenever a foreign crisis has loomed, from the Suez Canal to the Korean peninsula, from Vietnam to the Falkland Islands, and from Bosnia to Iraq, the specter of Munich is invoked by Anglo-American leaders who want to go down in history as Churchill, not Chamberlain.

Churchill is often credited with coining the phrase "Special Relationship." He certainly made it popular, if only to convince the Americans to come to Britain's rescue in the perilous early years of World War II. Since then, despite Churchill's mythical spirit living on in the White House, the Anglo-American relationship has been more special in London than in Washington. Given the growing gap in relative power and influence between the two countries, this was inevitable. Indeed, as Britain's power waned, clinging to the Special

Relationship was one way for the British to maintain an illusion that the glow of its finest hours under Roosevelt and Churchill had not been totally extinguished. British leaders might have been reduced to playing a steadily diminishing and sometimes demeaning role of impoverished but worldly-wise Greeks in the American Rome, but in their own eyes at least, this still allowed them to sup at a higher table than the other Europeans.

Britain's tortured relationship with the European continent, resulting at this time of writing in acrimonious wrangling over Brexit, is partly the result of Britain's nostalgia for the Special Relationship. Churchill himself spoke out in favor of a united Europe in 1946, even though he was vague about Britain's participation, but his spirit has made it harder for Britain to regard itself as a European nation on par with Germany or France, and to find its proper place in common European political and financial institutions.

There are many ways to chronicle the Special Relationship between Britain and the United States since they joined forces in World War II. One would be to examine the history of close cooperation between the British and American intelligence agencies. Another would be to describe the building of international financial institutions, such as the IMF and the World Bank. One of the promises made by Churchill and Roosevelt in their Atlantic Charter of 1941 was "global economic cooperation." Defeating Hitler, fascism, and the Japanese Empire was an internationalist enterprise. The postwar order, solidified in the Cold War, was set up by Britain and the US to defend democracies against their despotic enemies. If an anti-Communist despot was supported nonetheless, as long as he served Anglo-American interests, this was generally regarded in Washington and London as a necessary form of hypocrisy.

However, this book is not a history of institutions. I have chosen to write about the evolution and erosion of an idea, the Anglo-American myth that I grew up with. All US and British leaders have been touched by the history of World War II, even those who were not yet born when Roosevelt and Churchill drew up the Atlantic Charter. The story of those leaders and how they related to one another is also the story of their respective countries and how they affected the rest of the world, west as well as east.

It is my view that the shared myth has been both magnificent and a curse. History can inspire but also bedevil. How a wartime alliance that defeated Hitler, with the indispensable help of Stalin's Red Army, ended up after more than half a century of peace and prosperity in the West in the dispiriting and dangerous bluster and self-delusion of Trump and Brexit, is a melancholy tale. Britain and the US, despite all their flaws, were once regarded as models of openness, liberalism, and generosity. Even if they by no means always lived up to these ideals, the two English-speaking nations still offered some hope for what the Hungarian-born writer Arthur Koestler once called "the internally bruised veterans of the totalitarian age."

Now, perhaps only for the time being, the internationalist ideals set out in the Atlantic Charter have made way for populist agitation against immigrants, a hugely destructive British divorce from Europe, and an American president whose greatest wish is to build a big wall to keep the tired, poor, huddled masses from entering the US. Enoch Powell, a British Tory politician who held many reprehensible views, said once, quite wisely, that all political lives end in failure, "for that is the nature of politics and human affairs." The same might be said of the hopes of once great nations. That doesn't make those hopes any less admirable.

Two

BLOOD AND HISTORY

*Let not England forget her precedence of teaching nations
how to live.*

· JOHN MILTON (TO PARLIAMENT)

Before World War II, there was not much love lost between the British and Americans. Few people had the means to travel across the Atlantic. Historic wounds—the Boston Tea Party, wars of independence, 1812—were, if not fresh, still remembered in America. True, the US had joined the Allies in World War I in 1917 as an "associated power," and left more than fifty thousand dead on European soil (another sixty thousand died of disease, most because of the flu epidemic in 1918). But German and Irish Americans, and quite a few other "hyphenated" citizens not of British stock, had reason to be bitter about being made to feel like suspect outsiders in their own country. The great American journalist H. L. Mencken, who still spoke German with his parents, was so bruised by this experience that he later refused to see the conflict with Hitler's Germany as anything but "Roosevelt's war."

American Anglophilia existed, of course, but as in Europe, it was mostly a form of snobbery, a kind of mimicry of upper-class manners, popular among East Coast elites, the kind of people who sent their sons to English-style boarding schools and later to the pseudo-Gothickry of Ivy League universities. In his *History of the American People* (1902), Woodrow Wilson, a Southerner of Scots-Irish extraction, and the man responsible for getting his country into the European war, extolled the special virtues of "the self-helping race of Englishmen."[1] This splendid race, he enthused, having outsmarted the wily French, provided the necessary backbone to the New World. In 1918, after the war was won, Wilson was stung by domestic criticisms that he had been too easily swayed by British interests. And so, at a victory banquet given to him at Buckingham Palace by King George V, he tempered his earlier sentiments: "You must not speak of us who come over here as cousins, still less as brothers; we are neither. Neither must you think of us as Anglo-Saxons, for that term can no longer be rightly applied to the people of the United States."[2]

When the British in 1940 and '41, desperate for American help in a war that threatened to overwhelm them, used their finest rhetoric about common values, the shared English language, and the Anglo-American love of freedom, most Americans refused to be drawn in. Many were wary of being outwitted by the silver-tongued British, and suspicious that Britain was fighting selfishly to preserve its empire, for which few Americans felt any affection. In late 1941, General George Marshall, chief of staff, was still not keen to give the British all they wanted. But even he felt that there was "too much anti-British feeling" among his military colleagues—"Our people were always ready to find Albion perfidious."[3]

But many of the British grandees sent out to solicit US help didn't like the Americans much either. When Lord Halifax took up his post as ambassador to Washington in December 1940, he wrote to the former prime minister Stanley Baldwin: "I have never liked Americans, except odd ones. In the mass I have always found them dreadful." Lord Linlithgow, the bungling viceroy of India, the man who would make the horrendous Bengal famine of 1943 so much worse, commiserated: "The heavy labour of toadying to your pack of pole-squatting parvenus! What a country, and what savages those who inhabit it!"[4] John Maynard Keynes was dispatched to Washington in 1917 to secure loans for the British war effort. His impression: "The only really sympathetic and original thing in America is the niggers, who are charming."[5]

Winston Churchill made a great deal of his friendship with Roosevelt, which he regarded as the cornerstone of the Special Relationship: "I wooed Roosevelt more ardently than a young man woos a maiden." But he was often scathing about America in private conversations. In 1928, at a dinner party in his home, he said that the US was "arrogant, fundamentally hostile to us, and [wishing] to dominate world politics."[6] When Roosevelt first met Churchill in 1918, at a dinner in London, he didn't care for him at all. Roosevelt, then assistant secretary of the navy, found Churchill, who was minister of munitions, an intolerable snob. Churchill, in Roosevelt's recollection, had "acted like a stinker . . . lording it all over us."[7] When the two leaders met again in Placentia Bay, Newfoundland, in 1941, Churchill had entirely forgotten their first encounter. Roosevelt had not.

Roosevelt, despite his quasi-aristocratic airs, was never an Anglophile. If anything, he was rather proud of his Dutch ancestry. Like most Americans, he had little time for European colonial empires, but he is said to have made an exception for the Dutch East Indies, even though the Dutch probably behaved worse toward their colonial subjects than the British did. So references to Anglo-Saxon roots and shared bloodlines failed to move the American president's cool and calculating heart.

Churchill, on the other hand, talked about his bloodlines a great deal, and not just out of wartime necessity. Receiving an honorary degree at Harvard in 1943, he told his admiring audience, "You will find in the British Commonwealth and Empire good comrades to whom you are united by other ties besides those of state policy and public need. To a large extent they are the ties of blood and history. Naturally I, a child of both worlds, am conscious of these."[8]

Historians have claimed that Churchill invented the Special Relationship as a necessary move to win the war. This is true, up to a point. The Anglo-American alliance might never have been forged if France were not overrun in the spring of 1940. But Churchill only made the term famous six years later, in his speech at Fulton, Missouri, when he urged the Americans to stand firm against Communism and continue the "fraternal association of the English-speaking peoples." He insisted upon the "Special Relationship between the British Commonwealth and Empire and the United States." To Churchill the idea of the English-speaking peoples, of transatlantic kith and kin, was more than an expedient strategy; it defined him as a man. His relationship with the US was a personal twist on a romantic idea that long preceded him.

Before he died in 1902, Cecil Rhodes established a scholarship at Oxford University for students from the US and the British Empire to nurture a common idea of empire and cement "the union of the English-speaking peoples throughout the world." This matched the imperial sentiments of Rudyard Kipling, who sent his poem *The White Man's Burden* ("Take up the white man's burden— / Send forth the best ye breed . . .") to Theodore Roosevelt in 1899, then governor of New York, to encourage the Americans to bring Anglo-American enlightenment to the conquered Filipinos—"Your new caught sullen peoples, / Half devil and half child."

In that same year, when the British were trying to subdue the Boers in South Africa, Joseph Chamberlain, who was prime minister as well as foreign secretary, called for a "new triple alliance between the Teutonic race and the two great branches of the Anglo-Saxon race." On the other side of the Atlantic, Theodore Roosevelt's supporter Albert J. Beveridge, a "progressive" senator from Indiana, exclaimed, "God has not been preparing the English-speaking and Teutonic peoples for a thousand years for nothing but vain and idle self-admiration. No! He has made us the master-organizers of the world to establish system where chaos reigns."[9]

So the idea that the Anglo-Saxon races were called upon to subdue barbarians and order the world was already current when Churchill and Franklin Delano Roosevelt were still children. It was the kind of thinking that justified colonial rule and resulted in some of Churchill's worst traits, such as his contempt for the people of India. ("I hate Indians. They are a beastly people with a beastly religion.") The inclusion of the "Teutons" in this line of thought might suggest a kind of crypto-Nazism, which would be highly ironic considering the history of the two world wars.

In fact, there actually was more than a hint of this. One of the intellectual fathers of nineteenth-century Anglo-Saxonism was the historian and politician Edward Augustus Freeman, famous for his *History of the Norman Conquest*. His approval of the US was unusual for an Englishman of his time. And he was clearly a racist. Benjamin Disraeli was, in his view, "a dirty Jew." Freeman condoned Russian pogroms, and anti-Chinese riots in California too. After all, he thought, these were "only the natural instinct of any decent nation to get rid of filthy strangers."[10]

And yet, Freeman was not a conservative, but a liberal supporter of William Gladstone. The notion that Anglo-Saxons and Teutons were a superior breed was not so much based on bloodlines as on the claim to a unique love of liberty. This is something that appealed to German romantics as well, the ancient Teutonic spirit of freedom, expressed in German literature, but also, so some Germans claimed, in Rembrandt's paintings and Shakespeare's plays, the "Nordic" greatness of which, they believed, emerged only in German translation. But the idea goes back much further than the age of the great bard. Here is Freeman again, on the victory in 9 AD over the Roman army by a Germanic tribe led by Arminius: "Arminius 'liberator Germaniae,' is but the first of a roll call which goes on to Hampden and Washington."

John Hampden, one of Churchill's heroes, was a politician who fought with the Ironsides in the English Civil War for parliamentary rule and against the absolute power of the king. He was killed in battle in 1643. His, or for that matter George Washington's, link to Arminius is tenuous at best, but it made for a peculiar political conceit.

The name left unmentioned in this pantheon of liberty is that of Pericles, who lived long before the Angles, the Saxons, or the Teutons had even been heard of. But his oration about the exceptional nature of Athens, spoken in 431 BC, after the first battle of the Peloponnesian War, could be read as a kind of blueprint for Anglo-Saxon exceptionalism. He spoke of the laws that afforded equal justice to all men, and of the "freedom we enjoy in our government." The people of Athens, like the imagined English-speaking peoples more recently, "dwelt in the country without break in the succession from generation to generation, and handed it down free to the present time by their valor."

The concept of the English-speaking peoples now has an imperialist ring, promoted in our time by certain conservative historians. Churchill himself told the Americans at Fulton that "70 or 80 millions of Britons spread about the world" (meaning Australia, New Zealand, Canada, and South Africa) stood ready to defend "our traditions and our way of life." What he really meant was spelled out more clearly in a letter to Eisenhower in 1953: "Britain with her eighty million white English-speaking people."[11] But the origins of the term are less blimpish.

During the American Civil War, the main British political parties, as well as much of the upper class, supported the Confederacy. Radical leaders, however, such as Richard Cobden and John Bright, supported the antislavery cause of the North. Their vision of the English-speaking peoples was one of working-class solidarity against the landowning classes in both countries. William E. Forster, a Liberal politician in Gladstone's government, gave his name to what his boss called "Forsterism": the idea that Anglo-American Protestants were called by God to spread democracy to the world's benighted peoples. It was Forster, Cobden, and Bright who first promoted the idea of the common, freethinking, democratic English-speaking peoples, as opposed to the autocratic upper classes from which Churchill sprang.

The radical cause was not something one would associate with Churchill anyway. And he had such a limited interest in Anglo-Saxonism that he poured cold water over a pet project of his adored mother, an expensive magazine called *The Anglo-Saxon Review*. But the Whiggish conceit that the love of freedom was the birthright of

English speakers stretching back, if not to the Teutonic rebellion against Rome then at least to King Alfred, was certainly part of his makeup. Churchill brought this up on some unexpected occasions. When Joseph Chamberlain wanted to strengthen the imperial economy by erecting a tariff wall around British possessions, Churchill rebelled and made a plea for free trade. "The strength and splendour of our authority," he declaimed, "is derived not from physical forces, but from moral ascendency, liberty, justice, English tolerance, and English honesty."[12]

None of this would have impressed Franklin D. Roosevelt. And yet, despite his earlier misgivings about the British politician, Roosevelt sought Churchill out in 1939, a little over a week after Britain had declared war against Germany. Churchill was first lord of the Admiralty then. The letter, addressed to "My Dear Churchill," expressed Roosevelt's wish to be kept "in touch personally with anything you want me to know about." This was an unusual request for a US president to make of a mere British cabinet minister. But the president told his ambassador in London, the egregiously Anglophobic Joseph Kennedy, that Churchill was likely to become prime minister, so Roosevelt wanted "to get my hand in now."[13]

Apart from a flair for aristocratic affectations—the long cigarette holder, the cigar, the top hats—the two consummate political showmen had one important thing in common: a romance with the sea, and thus with naval matters. In Churchill's letters to Roosevelt, he referred to himself as "Naval Person," and after he became prime minister as "Former Naval Person." Roosevelt was a keen student of Admiral Alfred Thayer Mahan's books, and had corresponded with the author. In his book *The Influence of Sea Power Upon History*, written in 1890, Mahan explains how British greatness was due to their mastery of the seas. Like the Dutch, who conquered the seas before, this had to do in Mahan's view with a natural instinct for trade, which, he argued, stemmed from geography, culture, politics, religion, and race. (The English and the Dutch, he claimed, were "radically of the same race.")[14] A bit oddly for an American, Mahan had good things to say about colonialism too: "In yet another way does the national genius affect the growth of sea power in its broadest sense; and that is in so far as it possesses the capacity for planting healthy colonies."[15] The US, he thought, should emulate Britain, if not in planting colonies, then certainly in asserting power over the seas, in "a cordial understanding" with Great Britain, since both nations "are controlled by a sense of law and justice, drawn from the same sources, and deep-rooted in [their] instincts."[16]

Carl Schmitt commented on Mahan, rather favorably, in his book *Land and Sea*, published in 1942. Schmitt was a German legal theorist who joined the Nazi Party in 1933 and provided legal justifications for Hitler's dictatorship. His argument in *Land and Sea* is that Mahan was right: Britain and the US had owed their immense power to ruling the seas, the result of a typically Protestant entrepreneurial spirit. Catholic powers, he believed, were more land bound. What Mahan had not foreseen, Schmitt argued, was that sea power had become obsolete in the machine age, where airplanes had "lifted man high above the plains and the waves."

Roosevelt might not have gone that far, but he did take Schmitt's point. In his State of the Union address in 1940, he acknowledged that most Americans did not want to send their boys to fight in Europe a second time. But he also made it plain that in an age of modern aircraft and long-range battleships, the US could not survive "as a self-contained unit . . . inside a high wall of isolation, while outside the rest of Civilization and the commerce and culture of mankind are shattered." The US government would insist that military actions be banned within a three-hundred-mile zone of the US coast. Naval Person answered Roosevelt's letter of 1939 with the promise that "we wish to help you in every way in keeping the war out of American waters."

But of course Churchill wanted much more than that. He knew that Germany could not be defeated without full American participation in the war. The problem was that despite Roosevelt's opposition to the isolationists, there was not nearly enough political will to comply. Many Americans, including Ambassador Joseph Kennedy, were convinced in 1940 that Britain was losing the war, and didn't see why they should fight for British interests anyway. Roosevelt was also keenly aware of Woodrow Wilson's failure in 1919 to get the Senate to back his foreign commitments, specifically his attempt to build a new world order through the League of Nations. The world order, although something very much on the president's mind, was not of great concern to most Americans.

Within weeks of becoming prime minister on May 10, 1940, Churchill begged the Americans to intervene when France was buckling to the German Blitzkrieg. They did not. He asked for American destroyers to be sent across the Atlantic. The defense of Britain, he said, depended on it. It was "the only hope of averting the collapse of civilization."[17] To keep up British morale at a very bleak time, and perhaps to boost his own as well, Churchill remained optimistic that the Americans would soon change their minds and come in. A collection of Churchill's prewar speeches, entitled *Blood, Sweat and Tears*, was published in the US with the express purpose of convincing Americans to come to the rescue. One of these speeches had been made on American radio in October 1938: "If ever there was a time when men and women who cherish the ideals of the founders of the British and American

Constitutions should take earnest counsel with one another, this time is now."[18]

This bit of rhetoric, too, drew on old ideas about Anglo-American communalities. Not race, or language, but political institutions were the glue that held the English speakers together. Churchill, and others, liked to draw a straight line from the Magna Carta to the Declaration of Independence. Speaking on the Fourth of July, 1918, he claimed that a "similar harmony exists between the principles of that Declaration and all that the British people have wished to stand for, and have in fact achieved at last both here at home and in the self-governing Dominions of the Crown."[19] He tactfully omitted to say that it was American independence from the Crown that was being celebrated on that day.

There were no doubt Americans who were susceptible to this kind of talk. Churchill's wartime speeches were widely broadcast in the US. Roosevelt was, however, too worried about public opinion to be so easily swayed. But the US could still benefit from British distress. Roosevelt agreed in 1940 to lend fifty old destroyers in exchange for the right to use British bases in Newfoundland and the Caribbean. It was, in Roosevelt's own words, "a 'deal'—and very successful from our trading point of view."[20]

The ships were in poor shape and took some time to become operational. Guns, tanks, and planes were also shipped over, but they had to be fully paid for, since the US Neutrality Act made it impossible to lend credit to countries at war. It was hoped that these measures would allow Britain to protect itself without American intervention. But this proved to be such a drain on British finances that Roosevelt devised a scheme in 1941 whereby the US could lend, lease, sell, exchange, or otherwise dispose of military equipment to its allies. The US, in Roosevelt's words, would be "the great arsenal of democracy." But before the Lend-Lease Act was passed in March 1941, Britain had to dump assets in the US for much less than their real worth and hand over South African gold reserves as well. And the loan of war materials still had to be repaid by giving the US rights to British bases overseas. It was a hard bargain, which Churchill delicately but not quite accurately called "the most unsordid act in whole of recorded history."[21]

Roosevelt defended his decision to help American allies in one of his most quoted speeches, the State of the Union address on January 6, 1941. He said the US could not stand aside in the war against dictators. Americans had to be prepared to defend themselves and help the free nations. But he also laid out his vision for the future, which was a mixture of old and new ideas. The mission should be to fight for four essential human freedoms: freedom of expression, freedom of worship, freedom from want, freedom from fear of physical aggression. And these should be defended "everywhere in the world." It was as though the New Deal had become a universal American goal. The speech ended: "This nation has placed its destiny in the hands and heads and hearts of its millions of free men and women; and its faith in freedom under the guidance of God. Freedom means the supremacy of human rights everywhere. Our support goes to those who struggle to gain those rights and keep them. Our strength is our unity of purpose."

The words that would haunt the Special Relationship, certainly while Churchill was alive, were "everywhere in the world." And "the supremacy of human rights" was not traditionally why countries went to war. But the aim to save the world from barbarism and establish a liberal order was rooted in older notions of Manifest Destiny and the proselytizing spirit of Christianity, especially in its Protestant forms. When territorial conflicts between Britain and the

US were resolved in the Treaty of Washington in 1871, an Anglo-American union was briefly proposed, which, in the words of a Washington newspaper, "would enable the English-speaking peoples to give law to the world, and at the same time be the means of increasing and strengthening the people everywhere who are struggling to secure for themselves, and for their children, the inestimable blessing which we now enjoy—the God-given right of self-government."[22] Roosevelt's words were not quite so high flown, and Manifest Destiny was not foremost in his mind, but rhetorically, at least, the Anglo-American relationship was becoming more like the alliance Churchill had been hoping for all along.

Harry Hopkins, New Dealer and confidant to the president, was asked to administer Lend-Lease. In January 1941, Hopkins, a frail man never in the best of health, was sent to Britain to assess the situation. Refreshingly direct in his manner, Hopkins expressed a concern that Churchill disliked Americans, including their president. Churchill replied that this was an entirely false impression, no doubt spread maliciously by that Irish American ambassador, Joseph Kennedy.

After a lavish dinner by candlelight held in Hopkins's honor at Ditchley Park, Churchill gave a rambling speech, designed perhaps to appeal to his guest's New Deal sentiments. Churchill spoke of a new era of freedom and peace, where the humble English worker would feel safe and sound in his cottage home, equal before the law, and without fear of the knock on the door by the secret police. Those, he concluded, were the only British war aims. Hopkins rose to his feet, and drawled in his Iowa accent: "Well, Mr. Prime Minister, I don't think the president will give a damn for your cottagers." He paused, while the shocked company drew its breath: "You see, we're only interested in seeing that goddamn son of a bitch Hitler

get licked." After that, Churchill saw that all was well, and the din-
ers amused themselves by watching a newsreel of Hitler and Mussolini meeting at the Brenner Pass, which one of the guests declared
to be "funnier than anything Charlie Chaplin produced in *The Great
Dictator*."[23]

But the Americans still had not committed themselves to entering the war. Letters went back and forth from Former Naval Person
to President Roosevelt, keeping the president abreast of mostly
disastrous military affairs in North Africa and the Middle East.
Germany launched its war on the Soviet Union in June 1941, and
Churchill told his assistant private secretary Jock Colville that it was
essential to help the Russians. Still a staunch anti-Communist,
Churchill said that if Hitler invaded hell, he would make a favorable
reference to the devil in the House of Commons.

In late July, Churchill finally got his wish to meet Roosevelt.
Harry Hopkins told him the president was now ready to see him.
The second encounter between the two men obviously couldn't be
on neutral US territory, so it took place, quite appropriately, at sea,
in Newfoundland.

Churchill's own account of the war is not always reliable. He
wrote, or at least supervised the writing of, his multivolume *The Second World War*, in the late 1940s and early 1950s. One topic about
which he could not be candid was the patchy Anglo-American relationship. After completing the final volume in 1953, he reassured
President Eisenhower that nothing he wrote would "impair the
sympathy and understanding which exists between our two countries." But there is no reason to doubt the veracity of Churchill's
description of his sea voyage to Newfoundland.

Churchill boarded the *Prince of Wales* on August 4, together with
Harry Hopkins and some of Britain's top military staff. A letter was

sent by Former Naval Person to remind the president that it was "twenty-seven years ago to-day that Huns began their last war. We must make a good job of it this time. Twice ought to be enough. Look forward so much to our meeting."[24] This was assuming a little too much, perhaps, since 80 percent of Americans, according to opinion polls, still opposed any involvement of US troops in the war.

Churchill was full of hope, however, as he settled down in choppy seas to read C. S. Forester's novel *Captain Hornblower, R.N.*, about a Royal Navy captain swashbuckling his way through the Napoleonic Wars. He also watched *That Hamilton Woman*, a movie he had already seen four times (and misnamed *Lady Hamilton* nonetheless). Laurence Olivier plays Admiral Nelson to great effect. The Battle of Trafalgar is shown with much panache. A few months before, the *New York Times* critic had praised the movie in stirring terms: "Now that the spirit of Nelson is again at large upon the deep and the expectations of England are being triumphantly fulfilled, it is altogether fitting that the greatest Admiral ever to lead a British fleet, at this moment should be pictured with profound affection and respect upon the screen."[25]

Churchill made a little speech after the screening: "Gentlemen, I thought the film would interest you, showing great events similar to those in which you have been taking part."

Roosevelt, in the meantime, keen to avoid any impression that he wanted his country to take a direct part in those great events, pretended to go out on a recreational cruise on his presidential yacht. In the open seas he slipped on board the USS *Augusta*, with his most senior military officers, including General George Marshall. Unlike the camouflaged British battleships, the US Navy ships were painted in a pristine gray.

Nearing Newfoundland, Churchill, dressed in the uniform of

Trinity House, a British outfit that administered lighthouses, turned to Hopkins a bit nervously and wondered whether Roosevelt would like him. Hopkins assured him that he would. "You'd have thought," Hopkins recalled later, "Winston was being carried up into the heavens to meet God."[26] The true nature of how the Special Relationship would develop over time could not have been expressed more succinctly.

What followed was a great deal of fraternal pomp, visits, and return visits between the *Prince of Wales* and *Augusta*, mingling of the ships' crews, bands playing national anthems, and discussions between British and American admirals and generals, which didn't really go anywhere: the war-hardened British found the Americans a little wet behind the ears, and the Americans were still wary of British motives. Churchill eagerly awaited a statement from Roosevelt that the US would finally do battle as an Allied nation. But the president had something else in mind: a joint declaration of broad principles, somewhat along the lines of his State of the Union address, and the Four Freedoms.

This was not exactly what Churchill had hoped for. He writes a little defensively in his war memoirs, "Considering all the tales of my reactionary, Old World outlook, and the pain this is said to have caused the President, I am glad it should be on record that the substance and spirit of what came to be called the 'Atlantic Charter' was in its first draft a British production cast in my own words."[27]

Perhaps. There was much in it the two leaders could agree upon: that neither country sought aggrandizement, territorial or otherwise; that no territorial changes would be made against the freely expressed wishes of the people concerned; that people should have the right to choose the form of government under which they would live; that essential produce would be distributed fairly, domestically and between nations; and that international organization would ensure peace in the world and allow people to traverse "the seas and oceans without fear of lawless assault or the need of maintaining burdensome armaments."

There were, however, a few sticking points that revealed fissures in the Anglo-American fraternity (this was still a man's world). The US insisted that there should be free trade in the world "without discrimination." Despite Churchill's own rousing defense of free trade during Joseph Chamberlain's tariff campaign in 1903, he now felt constrained to protect the special trade agreements struck between the dominions and colonies of the British Empire ("imperial preference"). Churchill insisted on taking out the words "without discrimination" and inserting a clause about "existing obligations." He got his way.

More important was the matter of people's right to self-government. Churchill rightly saw this as an attempt to undermine colonialism and the British Empire in particular. He was of no mind to hand independence to British possessions. This might seem hypocritical, given his many speeches in favor of freedom and democracy. But Churchill did not wish to recognize the contradiction. He liked to think of Britain, with its "island race," as the hub of a close-knit family under the British Crown, the members of which freely and gladly pulled together in common purpose. (The fact that Indian nationalist leaders, such as Gandhi and Nehru, did not do so gladly at all was a major reason for Churchill's loathing of the Indians.) When US general Patrick Hurley, the same man who in 1944 spooked the Chinese Communist leaders by greeting them in their hideout with a Choctaw Indian war cry, reported from Iran in 1943 that the British were monopolizing that country's resources to finance their decaying empire, Churchill wrote a furious letter to

Roosevelt: "The general seems to have some ideas about British imperialism, which I confess made me rub my eyes. He makes out, for example, that there is an irrepressible conflict between imperialism and democracy. I make bold, however, to suggest that British imperialism spread and is spreading democracy more widely than any system of government since the beginning of time."[28]

For the British, the great meeting in Placentia Bay ended in anticlimax. Churchill had failed to draw the Americans into the war. Nothing much was achieved apart from a statement of lofty principles. The Atlantic Charter was neither a law nor a treaty. Its main value was symbolic, and Churchill, a master of symbolism, made the most of it. Referring to the last paragraph about establishing in the future "a wider and more permanent system of general security," he lauded its realism and saw in it "a plain and bold intimation that after the war the United States would join with us in policing the world until the establishment of a better order."

On Sunday morning, August 10, a joint church service was held on the deck of the *Prince of Wales*. Roosevelt, in great pain because of his polio-racked legs, walked the length of the ship on the arm of his son and sat down next to Churchill facing the pulpit draped in the British and American flags. Churchill himself had chosen the hymns. British and Americans sang together "Onward, Christian Soldiers" and ended with "O God, Our Help in Ages Past," which the Ironsides had chanted as they buried John Hampden, Churchill's hero who died in 1643 at the hands of the king's army. "Every word," in Churchill's account, "seemed to stir the heart. It was a great hour to live."

Churchill departed on the *Prince of Wales* two days later. The British played "Auld Lang Syne." The band on the American ship responded by playing "There'll Always Be an England." Almost exactly four months later, Japanese bombers sank the *Prince of Wales* off the coast of Malaya. Half the men who sang while pulling out of Placentia Bay died with it. Three days before that, the Japanese attacked Pearl Harbor.

Churchill was having dinner with the US ambassador when news of the attack was announced on the radio. He spoke to Roosevelt on the phone and said, in his own account, "This certainly simplifies things. God be with you."[29] Roosevelt then sent a cable to Churchill with the famous words "Today all of us are in the same boat with you and the people of the Empire, and it is a ship that will not and cannot be sunk."

Quite why Hitler was reckless enough, bogged down as he was in the Soviet Union, to declare war on the US, has never been completely explained. But his view of America was typical both of how dictators often see democratic countries, and of Hitler's specific political and racial prejudices. The US, in Hitler's view, was a decayed country: "My feelings against Americanism are feelings of hatred and deep repugnance. . . . Everything about the behavior of American society reveals that it is half Judaized, and the other half Negrified. How can one expect a State like that to hold together—a country where everything is built on the dollar."[30]

Churchill's visit to Washington in the last days of 1941 was one of the high points of his own special relationship with the US and its president. The military situation was extremely grim. The first British victory in El Alamein was still a year off, and the far more devastating German defeat at the hands of the Soviet Red Army in Stalingrad would occur even later. Many people in Britain felt that the Japanese attack on the US was just deserts for a country that had failed to come to their rescue. But in the eyes of his physician, Lord Moran (Charles Wilson), Churchill was a different man after Pearl Harbor. Full of youthful zest, he roamed the White House day and night, wearing a dressing gown, or less, walking into Roosevelt's bedroom whenever he felt like it. He signed the Declaration by United Nations, spoke at Christmas about "the common cause of great peoples who speak the same language," and gave one of the speeches of his life to the two houses of Congress. The official name for Churchill's visit to Washington was "Arcadia."

Even some of the isolationists in the Senate praised his speech. Once again Churchill reminded his audience of his American bloodlines. "The occasion," he recalled, "was important for what I was sure was the all-conquering alliance of the English-speaking peoples." But Roosevelt's long-term goal went beyond the Anglo-American alliance. On the first day of the New Year, Churchill was just climbing out of his bath when Roosevelt announced to him that the United Nations would be the proper name for the constellation of nations committed to defeating the Axis powers and establishing a new world order. Churchill, along with Maxim Litvinov for the Soviet Union and T. V. Soong for China, signed the joint declaration of twenty-five Allied nations supporting the ideals of the Atlantic Charter.

In his war memoirs, Churchill calls the UN Pact a "majestic document," despite having had great misgivings about sharing global police duties with the Chinese, or anyone else besides the Americans. Still, in his recollection the trip to the US had been a huge success. There is no doubt that Roosevelt was as committed to winning the war as Churchill. And the British had managed to persuade the president, against the wishes of his top military brass, to give the war against Germany priority over the war against Japan. But there were fault lines in the Special Relationship that Churchill rather skates over. And they would soon grow wider.

During Churchill's visit, Roosevelt had pressed him to let the Indians govern themselves. He saw Gandhi and Nehru's aspirations in the light of the American War of Independence against the British Crown. Churchill was absolutely opposed to the idea. He wrote to Clement Attlee, the lord privy seal, that the Indian troops were splendid fighting men, but they owed their allegiance to the King-Emperor: "The rule of the Congress and Hindu priesthood machine would never be tolerated by a fighting race."[31]

This tells us more about Churchill's imagination than about what Indians really thought. And Churchill's observation that American opinion was pretty much on the side of Britain on this matter was equally deluded. Roosevelt wouldn't let it rest. In March 1942, he wrote a letter to Former Naval Person, in which he repeated the analogy with the American Revolution. It was "just a thought," and "strictly speaking, none of my business," but wouldn't it be a good idea to set up a provisional Indian government. After all, this would be in line with "world changes of the past half-century and with the democratic processes of all who are fighting Nazism."[32] All Churchill will say in his memoirs is that this letter is "of high interest" because it shows how hard it is to compare situations in utterly different periods of history.

In fact, Churchill was furious. Not only did he resent Roosevelt's meddling in British affairs but also he was well aware that Britain alone could only ever be a junior partner to the US. To remain on equal footing as a great power, a goal that Churchill clung to with romantic tenacity, Britain had to maintain its empire (and some years later, its own nuclear bombs). And that was precisely what Roosevelt, most of his military and political advisers, and probably the majority of Americans wanted to resist. Preserving the British Empire was not what they thought they were fighting for. Quite the contrary, in fact.

Roosevelt stuck the knife in Churchill in another way too. In the same month that he expressed his thoughts on Indian independence, he sent another letter: "I know you will not mind my being brutally frank when I tell you that I think I can personally handle Stalin better than either your Foreign Office or my State Department. Stalin hates the guts of all your top people. He thinks he likes me better, and I hope he will continue to do so."[33]

Churchill's idea of sorting out the world majestically alongside the Americans was an illusion. Roosevelt made this pretty clear to him on the several occasions when he, Stalin, and Churchill met at summits in various parts of the world. Even though Stalin was always suspicious that his two capitalist allies were ganging up on him, Roosevelt went out of his way to prove the contrary. In the president's mind, he and Stalin had the same ideas about imperialism. This meant that Roosevelt and Stalin sometimes ganged up on Churchill.

In the next two years, the Soviets did most of the fighting in Europe, while Britain lost its Southeast Asian colonies to Japan and much of its treasure fighting a war that was making the Americans stronger all the time. Until the end of 1943, the British still deployed more troops and ships than the Americans. But General de Gaulle, whose Free French were little more than a token force, and whose paranoia about Anglo-Saxon dominance was almost as deep as Stalin's, made a shrewd assessment of Britain's future role very early on. When Japan forced the US into the war, de Gaulle, like Churchill, believed that the end was no longer in doubt. "In this industrial war," he said, "nothing can resist the power of American industry."

Then he added, "From now on, the British will do nothing without Roosevelt's agreement."[34]

This wasn't strictly true. The US had wanted to launch an invasion of France as early as 1942, or 1943 at the latest. The Russians wanted this, too, to relieve the horrendous strain on the eastern front. In some estimates, more than four million Germans died or went missing on the Eastern Front, against about 329,000 in North Africa and Italy.[35] Churchill, haunted by the carnage of World War I, thought an invasion of France in 1942 would be suicidal, remained skeptical of it in 1943, and preferred to put more Allied resources into the battle for North Africa and the Mediterranean. Through a combination of obstinacy and dissembling, which made the Americans even more suspicious of the British, he managed for a time to get his way. In November 1942, the US did send troops to North Africa. And instead of crossing the Channel in 1943, Anglo-American forces invaded Sicily in July and crossed into southern Italy in September.

Photographs of Churchill and Roosevelt at their meeting in Casablanca in January 1943, smiling at one another, Roosevelt whispering into Churchill's ear, suggest the intimacy of a loving couple on a particularly pleasant holiday, even though intimacy was not a quality normally attributed to the US president. There is one picture in particular that reveals something important about their relationship. It was taken on the roof of the American vice-consul's house in Marrakech. Churchill, standing up, looks tenderly, and a little pensively, at Roosevelt, whose eyes are not on Churchill, but gazing into the sunset over the Atlas Mountains.

The presence of de Gaulle at Casablanca also showed the different temperaments of the two English-speaking leaders. Roosevelt could not stand the man. He saw him as a reactionary French autocrat who had no place in his vision of a democratic world order. And de Gaulle did everything to annoy the American. If Churchill was keen to be seen as Roosevelt's equal, so was de Gaulle, who had never been elected to be the leader of the Free French, or of anything else. When Roosevelt reminded him of this fact, de Gaulle replied that Joan of Arc had not been elected either.

Roosevelt found the Frenchman's pretentions absurd. But Churchill, who was often just as annoyed by de Gaulle's haughtiness, did not find them absurd at all. He understood de Gaulle's romantic idea of nationhood. He understood the power of words. That is why he had given him access to the BBC at the beginning of the war, when de Gaulle was just an obscure French army officer in exile, and words of defiance were all he had to restore French pride. In Casablanca, Churchill said, "France without an army is not France. De Gaulle is the spirit of that army. Perhaps the last survivor of a warrior race."[36] Churchill, whose own authority owed so much to his mastery of rhetoric, wept as he paid this tribute to a grandeur that Americans found insufferable.

When the Allied leaders met again, first in Cairo and then Teheran, in November 1943, and finally in freezing Yalta, in February 1945, it was quite clear that British grandeur was no longer what it was, either, especially in American eyes. Churchill would have liked to meet in private with the US president before they saw Stalin in Teheran. Roosevelt turned him down. He didn't want to make the Russians even more suspicious than they already were. Churchill was also forced to be gracious to the Chinese, whom Roosevelt took very seriously. Lord Moran, Churchill's physician, described a dinner given by Churchill in Cairo for Chiang Kai-shek, with Madame Chiang stepping in as translator. In Lord Moran's account, Churchill refused to regard China as a serious power and grudged "the time that Roosevelt has given to her affairs. To the President, China means four hundred million people who are going to count in the world of tomorrow, but Winston thinks only of the color of their skin; it is when he talks of India and China that you remember he is a Victorian."[37]

Churchill's strategy of concentrating forces in the Mediterranean, fighting over Greek islands, aiming to penetrate the Balkans, and dithering over the invasion of France (Operation Overlord), seriously irritated the Americans. Again, Lord Moran is the cold-eyed observer of his patient's relative position in the world. Harry Hopkins, he recounts, "made it clear that if the P.M. takes this line at Teheran and tries again to postpone Overlord the Americans will support the Russians."[38]

In many ways, whatever Churchill thought of Overlord, the Americans had done that anyway. First of all, they turned down the idea of a summit in London. Roosevelt worried that a trip to England would strike people back home as too accommodating to the British. Teheran was not Roosevelt's choice, either, but Stalin insisted. Roosevelt then decided to use the Soviet embassy as his base there. Anthony Eden, the British foreign secretary, later described Churchill's deferential behavior toward Roosevelt as that of a courtier. In return, the prime minister was often rudely snubbed. Instead of conferring with Churchill first about common strategies, Roosevelt had private meetings with Stalin. He felt that they could discuss the future of the world more fruitfully without the Englishman's presence.

A defensive, even peevish tone enters Churchill's own memories of the Teheran conference, despite his care to hide any rifts in Anglo-American relations. Official dinners were normally held at the Soviet embassy. Churchill insisted that at least one should be hosted at the British legation. This, he wrote, "could not well be disputed. Great Britain and I myself both came first alphabetically, and in seniority I was four of five years older than Roosevelt or Stalin. We were by centuries the longest established of the three Governments; I might have added, but did not, that we had been the longest in the war; and finally, November 30 was my birthday."[39]

This apparently trivial little outburst shows more than any account of battles won or lost how Britain's prestige was beginning to lean rather heavily on the past. The US now dominated the western theater, and the Soviets were fighting by far the biggest battles to defeat Nazi Germany. Roosevelt and his military advisers had run out of patience with Churchill's projects in the Mediterranean. Whatever the British wanted, the invasion of France would have to take place in the spring of 1944.

Churchill's attention was usually so focused on winning the war that he gave much less thought to the world's future than Roosevelt or, in his ruthless manner, Stalin. But Teheran did elicit one thought from Churchill that is worth mentioning. Like many veterans of World War I, Churchill was obsessed with the Prussians. He believed that both wars were the result of Prussian militarism, even though it was Prussian officers who made an attempt on Hitler's life in 1944. Nonetheless, Churchill thought that making a "stern but honorable" peace with Germany, including Prussia, was possible. And this should be followed by a re-creation "in modern forms" of what had been the outlines of the Austrian-Hungarian Empire. Here, Churchill wrote, "would be a great area in which not only peace but friendship might reign at a far earlier date than in any other solution. Thus a United Europe might be formed in which all the victors and vanquished might find a sure foundation for the life and freedom of all their tormented millions."[40]

On the fourth of June, 1944, 150,000 troops and 4,000 ships were waiting for a break in the weather finally to launch themselves at the French coast and begin the liberation of Europe. Churchill was in General Eisenhower's headquarters near Portsmouth. He had invited General de Gaulle to join him there so he could be apprised of the Allied invasion plans. De Gaulle had dragged his feet, but when he finally arrived, the first thing he did was demand the right to telegraph his HQ in Algiers in his own cipher. As "the recognized head of a great empire," that was the least he might expect. He also demanded the right to govern France after it had been liberated. Churchill replied that he would not ask Roosevelt to give de Gaulle the title deeds of his country. But the Free French would be recognized as the legitimate representatives of France.

For all his fawning on the Americans and talk of the English-speaking peoples, Churchill was also a Francophile who in the darkest days of 1940 had actually proposed a union of France and Britain. Marshal Pétain rejected the idea out of hand as a "fusion with a corpse." Unlike de Gaulle, many Pétainistes preferred collaboration with the Germans to fighting on with the British. Despite all his vainglory, de Gaulle had actually been treated well by the British. It was thanks to them that France would take its place among the victorious Allied nations. Churchill and Eden secured this at the Yalta Conference, partly in the hope that France and Britain would be able to keep Europe safe from German revanchism without help from the Americans. It was also thanks to Britain that de Gaulle, as head of the provisional French government, could stand in front of the Hôtel de Ville on August 25, 1944, and announce, "Paris! Paris outraged! Paris broken! Paris martyred! But Paris liberated! Liberated by itself, liberated by its people with the help of the French armies, with the support and the help of all France, of the France that fights, of the only France, of the real France, of the eternal France!"

Even so, de Gaulle could never shake his suspicion that the Anglo-Saxons were out to diminish the status of France, even as more than a hundred thousand Allied soldiers were about to risk their lives to liberate it. Exasperated by the general's cussedness, Churchill said something at that June 4 meeting that has been endlessly quoted, not least by de Gaulle himself, to illustrate the divide between Britain and the European continent: "Mark this—on each occasion that we shall have to choose between Europe and the open seas, we will always choose the open seas. On each occasion that I shall have to choose between you and Roosevelt, I will always choose Roosevelt."

But these were not Churchill's last words on the matter. At the University of Zurich in 1946, he would return to the idea he had mentioned in Teheran. With remarkable prescience and indeed generosity, Churchill envisaged "a kind of United States of Europe" in which Germany and France should "take the lead together." A united Europe, he said, would allow people to "enjoy the Four Freedoms of which the great President Roosevelt spoke and live in accordance with the principles embodied in the Atlantic Charter."

And what of Britain's role in the European future? Churchill could see Great Britain and its Commonwealth as a model for European unity. Along with the US and, ideally, the Soviet Union, they would be "friends and sponsors of the new Europe." But friends and sponsors are not members. One thing Churchill could not imagine was Britain without its empire, as one European nation among others, even as a primus inter pares. One could hardly have expected him to. He was a child of the Victorian age. The tragedy is that so many English people of subsequent generations could not either.

Three

THE EMPIRE IS DEAD, LONG LIVE THE EMPIRE

───────

My impression of our rulers is that they are like an acrobat on a tightrope with a large net cozily below them: they know that if they fall into the net (USA) they will suffer a loss of face but not of life.

· ISAIAH BERLIN[1]

Churchill's last meeting with Roosevelt on February 14, 1945, was at sea on the USS *Quincy*, anchored off the Egyptian coast. The encounter lasted less than two hours. Roosevelt looked frail. Churchill felt that he "had a slender contact with life." They still managed to discuss British participation on the atomic weapons program that would result in the bombs that destroyed Hiroshima and Nagasaki. Britain had initiated research into atomic weapons in 1940 and shared information with the US. In 1943, Roosevelt and Churchill agreed to merge British and American research programs, even though the US was pulling well ahead of British efforts, and the Americans were becoming increasingly cagey. Churchill was eager to continue the cooperation after the war, when he fully expected the British Empire to help the US police the world. The president had no objection.

Two months later Roosevelt was dead. The Special Relationship, according to the British historian David Reynolds, never really recovered from that blow.* The personal chemistry between the two wartime leaders had held it together. Most likely, the relationship wouldn't have survived the war anyway, at least not in the same form, since there could no longer be any question of equality, even for show. As Churchill informed the new president, Harry Truman, at Potsdam in the summer of 1945, the war had almost bankrupted Britain. His country couldn't possibly match American industrial strength. And although much of the empire would be recovered for a few more years, Britain would have a hard time suppressing increasingly frequent rebellions by people who had no intention of putting up with British rule for much longer. Churchill might have known this perfectly well, and indeed he lamented to Truman the waning of Britain's influence in the world. But even Churchill could not have foreseen the rate of Britain's decline. Nor did he ever really wish to accept it. In some ways, romantic nationalists in Britain still haven't. And in quite a few British minds, the Special Relationship remained an essential part of their national self-perception, even though very few Americans, if any, would have viewed the relationship as an important part of theirs.

When they had their first lunch at Potsdam, where the Big Three victors of the war gathered to discuss the future of the world, Truman and Churchill got along quite well. Truman had felt a little overawed by Churchill's reputation, and Churchill felt the absence of Roosevelt keenly. But Churchill was sure that he could work with

---

* Reynolds is the best chronicler of the Special Relationship. See in particular his book *The Creation of the Anglo-American Alliance 1937–1941.*

the new president, with whom he had almost nothing in common personally. He told Truman how much he admired the US, and that he intended to love Truman as much as he had loved Roosevelt. Truman thought the two men could be friends, if only Churchill would not lay on the "soft soap" quite so much.

Ten days later, still in Potsdam, Truman was faced with a new prime minister, Clement Attlee. Most British people had no more desire than Britain's colonial subjects to return to the prewar social order after sacrificing so much to win the war. They opted for a welfare state with decent housing, national health insurance, and solid public education, and saw no problem in government control of coal, steel, transport, or even the Bank of England. They admired Churchill as a war hero, but he was obviously a man of the past, and so they voted him out. Instead of having to deal with an aristocratic imperialist with a cigar, the kind of Englishman most Americans viewed with deep distrust, the president now had to come to terms with a socialist, something many Americans distrusted even more.

Truman's first impression of Attlee, and of his burly working-class foreign minister Ernest Bevin, was unfavorable. They were "sourpusses." Attlee struck Truman as less keen than "fat old Winston" and Bevin looked "rather rotund to be a foreign minister."[2] This sounds oddly snobbish for the son of a Missouri farmer. But Truman would soon revise his view of both men. His first impression of Stalin—"I like Stalin. He is straightforward"—also had to be amended later. Stalin reminded Truman of the mobbed-up Kansas political boss, Tom Pendergast, who had given Truman a leg up in politics.

Attlee was a kind of anti-Churchill. Whereas Churchill had appeared at Potsdam in full military regalia, reveling in the pomp that was laid on for the great man, Attlee had the shy demeanor of a middle-ranking bank manager, a quiet pipe smoker who enjoyed his cup of tea and game of cricket. This image was deceptive: Attlee came from the upper-middle class; he had attended a posh private school and was an Oxford graduate. He impressed the inexperienced and provincial Truman with his knowledge of foreign affairs. And he was able to relax enough to sit down at the piano with the president to sing bawdy songs from the first war, in which they had both served as soldiers. (In fact, Attlee had fought bravely in 1915 in the dreadful battle against the Turks at Gallipoli, a debacle that Churchill had contrived from his desk at the Admiralty in London.)

The prime minister was also the opposite of Churchill on one of the main sticking points between the American and British wartime leaders: India's quest for independence. Already during the war, Attlee saw this aspiration as entirely justified. Britain had promised self-government and should follow up on it. He saw this as a patriotic duty. Not every aspect of colonialism was shameful in his eyes. Attlee was a keen reader of Rudyard Kipling. The British Empire, in his view, had brought many good things as well as terrible atrocities. Attlee's goal was to transform the empire gradually to a commonwealth of free nations, which under benevolent British tutelage would uphold the ideals of democratic citizenship.

But he was also a leftist, although not, as he observed to his wife, Violet, "a rabid one." His 1945 party manifesto spelled it out: "The Labour Party is a Socialist party, and proud of it." This would have been alarming to many Americans, who couldn't see how the US could possibly have a close relationship with a socialist country. Attlee had to gain their trust. As it turned out, the Americans had less reason to worry about trusting the British than the other way around. Aside from the question of Indian independence, what was remarkable about Attlee and Bevin was how little they diverged from Churchill's view of Britain's place in the world.

In his first speech to the House of Commons in 1945, Attlee dismayed the left wing of his party by stating that his foreign policy would continue on the same basis that existed under the wartime coalition government in which both he and Bevin had served as ministers. On landing in Potsdam, Bevin remarked that he was "not going to let Britain be barged about."[3] He was thinking of both the Americans and the Soviets. In fact, despite their British version of socialism, or perhaps because of it, Bevin and Attlee distrusted the Soviets, even as Truman still thought Stalin was a regular guy (and Churchill, too, persisted in hoping to thrash things out personally with Stalin, as one great leader with another). Truman also continued a policy set during the war; like Roosevelt he was afraid of giving the Russians the impression that he was conspiring against them with the British.

When Churchill made his famous speech at Fulton, Missouri, less than a year after VE Day, warning that an iron curtain had descended across the European continent, and that peace had to be secured by "a fraternal association of the English-speaking peoples," Truman felt compelled to pretend that Churchill had gone too far and risked upsetting the Russians. In fact, Truman had read the speech and approved of it in advance. Warming to one of his oldest themes, Churchill admonished his audience "to proclaim in fearless tones the great principles of freedom and the rights of man which are the joint inheritance of the English-speaking world and which through Magna Carta, the Bill of Rights, the Habeas Corpus, trial by jury, and the English common law find their most famous expression in the American Declaration of Independence."

Three months earlier, during his visit to the US, Attlee had used almost exactly the same words in his speech to the houses of Congress: "We in the Labour Party declare that we are in line with those who fought for Magna Carta, habeas corpus, with the Pilgrim Fathers, and with the signatories of the Declaration of Independence." The two countries, he predicted, would enjoy an ever closer friendship, since they were united by "the things of the spirit" and a shared belief in the "validity of the moral precept on which our whole civilization is founded."[4]

But before Britain could play the role it aspired to in upholding the Anglo-American spirit, it had to solve what John Maynard Keynes called the nation's "financial Dunkirk." (Dunkirk and Munich—as in Munich 1938—were terms that would be used over and over again in the seven postwar decades, usually quite erroneously, to justify policies that were often quite unjustifiable.) The specter of Dunkirk looked especially ominous after Truman, just five days after Japan was defeated, stopped the Lend-Lease Act that had kept Britain afloat. The British government was worried that it wouldn't be able to feed its own people, let alone enforce a global order.

Keynes had been one of the architects of the Bretton Woods agreement in 1944, establishing a fixed exchange rate system tied to the US dollar. Now he had to beg the Americans for a loan to restore a degree of health to Britain's depleted finances. Sent to Washington to negotiate, Keynes hoped to secure at least $5 billion. As was often the case in Anglo-American relations, all kinds of prejudices had to be overcome, not least those held by Keynes himself. He believed that rootlessness and lack of historical sense made the Americans unsuitable as world leaders. Britain and its empire were far better placed to take care of that, with American help, of course. Many Americans, on the other hand, fretted constantly about being outsmarted and played for suckers by perfidious Englishmen. Dean Acheson, Truman's debonair secretary of state, once remarked how odd it was that although the French gave far more trouble to the US, it was "the more forthright British" who "were suspected of dominating us."[5]

Mutual prejudices had a reinforcing effect. Harold Macmillan expressed the typical British attitude most famously when he was the minister resident in Algiers in 1943. Addressing Richard Crossman, a young intelligence officer and later cabinet minister, he said, "We, my dear Crossman, are Greeks in this American empire. You will find the Americans much as the Greeks found the Romans—great, big, vulgar, bustling people, more vigorous than we are and also more idle, with more unspoiled virtues and also more corrupt."[6]

This image of Americans was popularized in a stream of films and novels, most notably those written by Graham Greene: Alden Pyle, in *The Quiet American*, whose crass naivete causes havoc in Vietnam; or Holly Martins in *The Third Man*, the innocent author of Western novels, blundering into the ruins of postwar Vienna, where the more sophisticated, world-weary British officer tries in vain to warn him about the lethal rackets in the occupied city, one of them run by a very corrupt American. The other side is portrayed in a large number of Hollywood movies, where sinister and infinitely crafty English villains with upper-class accents take advantage of decent but credulous folks. It was no coincidence that the Disney studios in 1967 cast the suave George Sanders in *The Jungle Book* as the purring voice of Shere Khan, the man-hating tiger.

In the winter of 1945, Richard Russell, the senator from Georgia, wondered why Britain needed to be given a loan at all. After all, wasn't Britain a decadent nation?[7] In the event, Keynes secured a loan of $3.75 billion, interest-free for six years. It was something, but not nearly enough, especially since the US demanded free convertibility of the pound sterling to the US dollar and an end to "imperial preference," tariffs protecting the sterling zone. All this in the name of free trade, an ideology often invoked to further US interests. The American loan was wiped out as soon as debtors and sterling bloc partners made a run on the British exchequer and converted their sterling holdings to dollars. Dunkirk loomed again. Only the Marshall Plan would save Britain.

Other blows to British aspirations soon followed. Attlee flew to Washington in November 1945, hoping in the spirit of his predecessor to cement that "ever closer friendship" with the US, and to make sure Britain would remain a fully informed partner in the development of nuclear technology. He believed that Britain should be protected by the atom bomb. Attlee had moved on from the old fixation on sea power and believed that new technology had changed the way wars would be fought. But he publicly played with the idea that nuclear secrets should be shared by members of the United Nations. Churchill had warned him against it; such awesome powers should be kept in the safe hands of Americans, British, and Canadians. The Americans soon decided that safety lay only in American hands. But Attlee's talk of the United Nations during his visit to Washington allowed the US to stall him with polite noises about setting up special committees to further explore the options. When Congress passed the Atomic Energy Act in 1946, to ensure that technological information would not be shared with any foreign powers, Attlee expressed his disappointment to Truman but politely refrained from blaming the president personally. It was yet another sign that flowery British speeches about the Magna Carta and the Declaration of Independence didn't cut much ice in Washington.

Viewed from there, the US relationship with Britain just wasn't so special anymore.

And yet Britain still wielded considerable clout, with a huge navy and large numbers of soldiers stationed all over the world. Attlee's honorable aim of transforming an empire into a common-wealth was not meant to diminish British stature or influence. What he really seemed to want was imperial power and prestige without an actual empire. His desire for Britain to have its own atom bomb was partly to protect the West against Soviet aggression, but also to keep up with the US, perhaps not as an equal, but still as a partner of substance. Keeping the world safe would be a joint Anglo-American enterprise, with the Russians as inconvenient and usually hostile counterparts who were too powerful to ignore. In some places, such as Greece, where Britain backed a conservative monar-chist government in a ghastly civil war against mostly Communist rebels, London badly wanted Washington's help.

In Palestine, still a British mandate, violence between Arabs and Jews and acts of terror against the British were spinning so badly out of control that Churchill, as opposition leader, wanted the Ameri-cans to take over. But instead of helping, Truman insisted that the British allow 100,000 Jews to move to Palestine immediately, in-stead of the 1,500 a month the British were prepared to allow in. The British effort to restrict Jewish immigration for fear of further violence was denounced by its opponents (mostly people of the left) as "the Palestine Munich." Truman no doubt believed that the European Jews had suffered enough and were entitled to find safety in their own promised land. But his decision inflamed an already fraught situation so badly that a political solution became less and less plausible. Bevin's remark that the Americans encouraged Jews to move to Palestine because they didn't want more of them in New York was crass, to put it mildly, but contained an awkward truth.

In the end, the British decided they could no longer cope and gave up their mandate. Since the US wouldn't deal with the intractable problems in Palestine, the question of how to divide the country between Arabs and Jews had to be voted on in the UN. The British believed that dividing Palestine into two states, a solution fiercely opposed by the Arab nations, would unsettle the Middle East for years to come, and chose to abstain. The US, as well as Australia, Canada, New Zealand, and South Africa, voted for the resolution. On this question, among many others to come, the fraternal association of the English-speaking peoples was considerably less harmonious than either Churchill or Attlee might have hoped. The first major Arab-Israeli war broke out a year later.

One of the most common clichés about the late 1940s, when the Cold War began, is that "the baton was passed" from a formal British Empire to an informal American one. This is a crude simplification. Many Americans were fearful of foreign entanglements, and the US was still a diffident actor on the world stage. In Africa, the Middle East, Southeast Asia, and even in Europe, the US was happy to let Britain do much of the policing. Sometimes it was the British who wanted the Americans to carry more of the burden and sometimes it was the other way around. But it was never a plain matter of the US taking over. If anything, the US often belittled Britain's economic difficulties and overrated its capacity to throw its weight around in the world.

When the Soviet government put Berlin under siege in 1948, hoping to drive the other Allied powers out of the city, it was the British, and not the Americans, who initiated the famous airlift, dropping tons of food and fuel to sustain the hungry population. For a year, a continual stream of military aircraft swooped over the roofs of Berlin to drop their cargo over the heads of cheering Berliners. It was one of the last operations run almost entirely by British, American, and Commonwealth forces. But it took Ernest Bevin a great deal of trouble to get the Americans involved in this concerted effort of the English-speaking peoples. This was done, as it would be so often on later occasions, by conjuring up the specter of Munich. Bevin would not be an appeaser. Churchill, too, publicly recalled what had happened when Chamberlain allowed Hitler's army to march into Czechoslovakia.

A year after the Berlin airlift was successfully concluded, the British desperately wanted Americans to help the French stop Ho Chi Minh's Communists from taking over Indochina. The most influential advocate for making this stand was the British commissioner general in Singapore, Malcolm MacDonald, a suave old Asia expert who believed firmly that if Vietnam were to fall into Communist hands, Malaya, Thailand, and the rest of Southeast Asia would follow—the now notorious "domino theory," which would cost countless Asian and American lives two decades later. He, too, was living in the shadow of 1938, when he had taken Chamberlain's side at Munich. Some Americans—Richard Nixon and John F. Kennedy among them—fell under MacDonald's spell. But distrust of European imperialism and diffidence about sending American boys out again to die in faraway countries among people about whom they knew nothing kept US troops out of Vietnam, for the time being.

One year after that, when North Korean troops took the US completely by surprise and almost succeeded in overrunning the South, it was the Americans' turn to ask for British help. Now it was the British who dragged their feet. They were afraid of exposing Malaya, Hong Kong, and other Asian possessions to Communist attacks if they moved their troops north and stirred up Chinese hostility. Attlee's unwelcome advice to Truman was to negotiate a settlement with Communist China, whose government the British formally recognized in 1950. Republicans worried that Britain was conspiring to make America appease "the Reds." But Ernest Bevin, who was always more of a bruiser than his prime minister, recalled for his edification the example of Munich.

In the end, Attlee did send some troops to Korea, including the Argyll and Sutherland Highlanders, who were greeted at the port of Pusan by a US military band of "colored" soldiers playing "God Save the King." The prime minister also promised to beef up the defense budget, although Britain could not really afford it. When a massive Chinese counterattack in the harsh winter of 1950 drove General MacArthur's UN armies back into the South, there was panic in Washington prompting loose talk about the use of atom bombs. This time, the ghost of Dunkirk was evoked, by Dean Acheson, among others. Dean Rusk, then assistant secretary of state for Far Eastern affairs, said the Americans should adopt the "do-or-die attitude" of the British in 1940. Robert Schuman, the venerable French statesman who laid down the first bricks of a united Europe, was in tears when he heard about American resolve to stand firm. "Thank God," he said, "this will not be a repetition of the past."[8]

Attlee decided it was time to fly to Washington to sort things out with the president. He was worried that the US would drag Britain and the rest of the world into a war with China, and he wanted to make sure that Britain would be consulted about any use of atomic weapons. A closer personal relationship with the president would surely clear the air. Acheson saw Attlee as a "Job's comforter"— "persistently depressing." He compared Attlee's thinking to "a long withdrawing, melancholy sigh."[9] Attlee believed that the Allied forces should withdraw from Korea and Taiwan (then still known as Formosa in the West) and give China a seat at the UN. Truman replied that China and Korea were controlled by Moscow. He restated his Truman Doctrine, first expressed in 1947: "The only way to meet Communism is to eliminate it."[10] The doctrine had been devised as a reaction to Britain's withdrawal from Greece. Because the British were no longer able to hold the fort against Communism, so Truman concluded, the US had to start doing it for them.

Attlee's style of negotiation, in Acheson's words, "was that of the suave rather than the bellicose cross-examiner."[11] This had the effect of sometimes drawing Truman into rash promises. Acheson had to stop the president from agreeing to consult the British if he ever chose to use an atomic weapon. In fact, Attlee didn't gain much from his visit to Washington, apart from a vague assurance that the British government would always be kept abreast of events. Attlee took this to mean that the US and Britain would still be partners, "unequal no doubt in power, but equal in counsel." He tried to reassure the British public that atomic power was in safe American hands. A Republican senator from California, however, who was still apoplectic about the way China was "lost" to the Reds, saw in any accommodation to the British "the makings of a Far Eastern Munich."[12]

Truman declared a national emergency and called for a conference of foreign ministers from the Western Hemisphere to discuss the Communist threat "to the entire free world." Once more, the worn old phrases were evoked to meet the latest crisis. *The New York Times* reported on December 17, 1950, that the free peoples of Europe applauded Truman's "no-appeasement" speech, "in which [Truman] pledged to create an 'arsenal of freedom.'" He stressed that "conquest of the world" was the aim of "Communist Imperialism."

A national emergency had not been declared in Britain, *The Los Angeles Times* reported on the same day, because that country "already has stringent price and economic controls, universal military conscription, and the highest taxes in the world." What this meant, in effect, is that British citizens not only were paying higher taxes than everyone else but were kept on food and sugar rations, while other Europeans, including the disgraced and defeated Germans, were not. The Conservatives promised to end rationing, and duly did so after they were reelected in 1951. Attlee explained to Parliament that austerity measures and rearmament were essential to maintain "our own special relationship" with the Americans.[13]

Meanwhile, Britain was stuck in a dilemma that faces all crumbling empires: how to hand over power without creating chaos. When the old source of authority, however oppressive or unpopular it may be, breaks down, vicious civil wars often follow. In 1972, Harold Macmillan was asked on William F. Buckley's television show whether he thought African leaders had been ready for independence in the late 1960s. Absolutely not, he replied. So had it been the right decision for Britain to hand over power? Absolutely, Macmillan said. And he quoted a wise old British diplomat in Africa. If you prolong colonial rule, the best and most intelligent people will be wasting their time in prison. They have to learn how to run a country. After all, Macmillan said, "it is their country, not ours." The right-wing Buckley seemed a little flummoxed by an answer he had not anticipated from a man he much admired.

The late-imperial dilemma, already apparent in Palestine, was demonstrated in the bloodiest possible way when Attlee decided that India should have its independence in 1948, no matter how unprepared or sectarian the Indian leadership was at the time. The prime minister even hoped that Britain's decision to let go would concentrate Indian minds and result in a harmonious solution. Bevin was skeptical and wanted the British to stay in India a bit longer, just as he insisted on British control of the Suez Canal and Iranian oil, to make sure the Russians wouldn't claim these assets. But Attlee refused to change his mind. Hindus and Muslims were fighting over their political status. State boundaries were often hastily and arbitrarily drawn. Years of British divide and rule threatened to blow the country apart. Afraid of civil war, the British pushed the date of independence forward. India and Pakistan became independent nations on August 15, 1947. More than fourteen million people were displaced in the violence that followed, and as many as two million died, in most cases horribly.

It would take another ten years of brutal fighting between British and Commonwealth troops and Communist guerillas before Malaya and Singapore were free from colonial rule. The end of empire in Africa took even longer, and Hong Kong remained as the last imperial outpost until 1997. But by the end of the 1940s, the dusk of empire was beginning to fall. And the idea that the Commonwealth nations would enable Britain to continue as a great global power for very much longer was fanciful, no matter how many different colored troops wearing all manner of uniforms from all over the world marched through the London streets to the sound of muffled drums to mark King George VI's death in 1952. Dean Acheson made his famous remark that Great Britain had lost an empire but had not yet found a role in 1962; he might, with some prescience, have said it ten years earlier. He might also have said, but refrained from doing so, that the role of the US in the world could be just as elusive.

In hindsight it is easy to condemn British leaders, or indeed

perhaps most British people, for not recognizing their country's relative decline sooner. Memories of Britain's Finest Hour were still
fresh. Great chunks on the global map were still painted in British
imperial pink. British industry was still going strong. British exports
were as large as those of France, Germany, Belgium, the Netherlands, Norway, and Denmark combined. The Festival of Britain in
1951 was a proud celebration of British progress in modern architec-
ture, nuclear physics, jet propulsion, radar, and all "the skills that
made the British workman famous." British, in the minds of most
people—not only in Britain—was still best.

What people failed to realize was how quickly the devastated
countries of Europe, especially Germany, were catching up. British industrial production between 1947 and 1951 rose 30 percent,
France by 50 percent, and Germany by 300 percent. It paid to start
from a low point. But the few who saw what was happening were not
allowed to spoil the mood of national self-congratulation. One of
them was a man named Sir Henry Tizard, chief scientific adviser to
the Ministry of Defence. He wrote in 1949: "We persist in regarding
ourselves as a Great Power, capable of everything and only temporarily handicapped by economic difficulties. We are not a Great
Power and never will be again. We are a great nation, but if we continue to behave like a Great Power we shall soon cease to be a great
nation."[14]

Tizard saw the future clearly, but he might have underestimated
the power of British prestige. For, in fact, Britain could have found
a proper role. It was offered with suitable deference in 1950. Two
Frenchmen, Jean Monnet and Robert Schuman, came up with an
audacious plan. If Germany and France would pool their production
of coal and steel, the raw materials of war, under a higher European
authority, another European war would become unthinkable. This

new model of shared sovereignty over vital resources was meant to lay the groundwork for precisely what Churchill had advocated in 1946, a federal European union. The French were keen; the Germans were delighted. They would be joined by Italy and the Benelux countries (Belgium, the Netherlands, and Luxembourg). And Great Britain, as the mightiest nation in Europe, the liberator from Hitler's tyranny, the country everyone looked up to, would be asked as the senior partner to lead Europe into a brighter future.

Dean Acheson, in Paris the day before Schuman announced the plan, thought it was a splendid idea. The US wanted Britain to lead the integration of Europe. Rather than "taking over" the British imperial role, the Americans hoped—in vain, as it turned out—that strong defense and economic institutions in Europe and elsewhere in the "free world" would make American entanglements abroad unnecessary. Hence the Marshall Plan, in 1948, to get Europe "on her feet and off our back";[15] hence NATO, to build a common defense against the Soviet Union. Britain was eager to help set these up, since they would anchor the Americans in Europe. The other advantage, in British eyes, would be that such transatlantic arrangements would enable Britain to remain anchored in the Special Relationship.

When Acheson met Bevin in London on the day Schuman's plan was announced, the British foreign secretary, by then a very ill man who could barely keep his eyes open in meetings, was furious. He had not been properly consulted. This was a Franco-American trick to lure the pragmatic British into some airy-fairy European project. How could a proudly socialist Britain possibly imperil its welfare state by submitting vital industries to supranational institutions? The Labour Party manifesto clearly rejected the idea of European economic integration. Attlee stated in Parliament that he couldn't "conceive that Britain would be an ordinary member of a federal union limited to Europe in any period that can be foreseen."[16]

And so the first members of what would one day be the European Union discussed their future plans in Paris without the British. The Conservatives questioned the wisdom of Britain's standoffishness. Churchill wondered what would become of Britain if France and Germany struck a deal and Britain were to be left out of a common market. Attlee was asked if it was the Labour Party or the government that was deciding policy on such an important question. *The New York Times*, reporting on the parliamentary debate, had a clear view of the real situation. The trade unions were against British participation and this left the Conservatives "in the difficult position of hating what the ruling party says, but fearing to challenge that party's philosophy for fear of losing votes, for despite its doctrinaire parochialism, the party manifesto reflects a good deal of British feeling toward Europe, regardless of party lines."[17]

Parochialism certainly played a part. But it was more than that. As Bevin told Schuman, the British didn't really regard themselves as Europeans. They were used to running the world. Foreign Office mandarins, who had little sympathy for Attlee and Bevin's socialist objectives, had no more desire to join Europe than they did. One such influential figure in the FO, Sir Roger Makins, had already objected to Britain joining a European customs union in 1947, since it would come at the expense of links with the Commonwealth and that would "spell the end of Britain as a world power."[18]

To many British leaders, the European continent, which had abjectly fallen to the Nazis while Britain stood alone, seemed farther away than the US, or perhaps even New Zealand. Churchill wrote in 1930 that Britain had its own dream and its own task: "We are with Europe, but not of it."[19] And he was a cosmopolitan compared to most of his compatriots. When my British mother attended a drinks party in the English countryside with my Dutch father sometime in the 1950s, she tried to make small talk with an Englishwoman she had never met before. Isn't it interesting, my mother remarked, desperate for something to say, that our car was the only one with foreign number plates. "That's nothing to be proud of," the woman snapped, and turned on her heel.

Acheson's verdict in hindsight, delivered with a certain degree of self-regard, was surely correct: "Despite my most earnest arguments . . . Britain made her great mistake of the postwar period by refusing to join in negotiating the Schuman Plan. From the bitter fruits of this mistake both Britain and Europe are still suffering."[20] He wrote this in 1969, three years before Britain finally joined the European Economic Community (EEC). I am writing this at the end of 2019, just as Britain is tormenting itself and everyone else with the terms of its divorce from the European Union. Acheson's words could not be more apt. What is worse, the arguments against "Europe" in Britain, on the sectarian left and on the delusional right, have not changed one bit since Attlee had to defend himself in Parliament in 1950.

Four

THE ROAD TO SUEZ

*Ship me somewhere east of Suez, where the best is
like the worst,
Where there ain't no Ten Commandments an' a man
can raise a thirst*

• RUDYARD KIPLING

October 28, 1951: Winston Churchill was driven to Buckingham Palace to start his second term as prime minister by "kissing hands" (of the king, that is). Attlee had not lost the election by much. But he seemed exhausted, by the Korean War, trouble in the Middle East, and money running out from spending too much on hanging on to the assets of an imperial power. Although increasingly stooped and deaf, Churchill at seventy-six was still Churchill. As Dean Acheson remarked, quoting a British historian, Churchill was as much loved by the English people as "the Great Queen," a somewhat odd comparison, but one gets the point. Perhaps he was even more than that. Churchill tearfully recalled a visit to Liverpool during his election campaign. There was "rapture" in people's eyes, he said. "They brought their children. I'm not conceited, but they wanted to touch me."[1]

Two months later, Churchill was bound for the US on the *Queen Mary* to meet President Truman. He thought it had been a huge mistake that he didn't go to see the president immediately after Roosevelt died. Not that he was under any illusion about Britain's shrinking status, which made him melancholy. The economy was in bad shape. Coal was running short. Horsemeat was doing a brisk trade on the black market. Mohammad Mossadegh, the Iranian prime minister, wanted to drive the British out of Iran, and he nationalized the oil fields, which had provided the Royal Navy with much of its fuel. Egyptian nationalists were challenging British control over the Suez Canal.

"When I have come to America before," Churchill mused to Lord Moran, his personal physician, "it has been as an equal. If, late in the war, they spoke of their sacrifices we could retort by saying that for a year and a half we fought alone; that we had suffered more losses." He sighed, then continued: "They have become so great and we are now so small. Poor England! We threw away so much in 1945."[2]

The Americans were not ecstatic about Churchill's visit. There was a lot of suspicion in Congress that the British would be playing the Americans for suckers once again, asking for more money, and so on. Churchill's party was met in New York with placards that read ENGLAND BLEEDS AMERICANS, or MONEY FOR IMPERIALISTS, BUT NONE FOR VETERANS. Churchill's doctor assumed that the protesters were either Irish or Communists.

But Truman wanted to make the visit a success. He would butter up Churchill with the maximum of symbolism without giving anything much away. Symbols were important to Churchill. He needed the Americans to confirm his own status and that of his country by words and gestures, if nothing else. The trappings of Great British power should still be maintained. After a satisfying dinner with Truman and his senior foreign policy officials on the presidential yacht, Churchill turned to Dean Acheson and said, "Did you feel that around the table this evening there was gathered the governance of the world—not to dominate it, mind you, but to save it?"[3] And just before retiring to his bed, he told his doctor how much he had enjoyed dining with the president: "We talked as equals."

In Churchill's mind the Anglo-American order was still the only one that counted in the world, even if Britain's own role could no longer be what it once was. Keenly aware of American opposition to his imperialist proclivities, he put his views in a universal moral light, which appealed to the Protestant idealism rooted in US history. Holding on to British rights over the Suez Canal, for example, was not to protect British interests. Not a bit of it. It was "for civilization." If only the US could send a brigade to Suez, then Britain's burden could be lightened. It would also be a great help if the Americans could bring Mossadegh to his senses by not sending any more money to Iran.

The Americans politely refused on both counts. Financial aid continued to flow to Iran, and no US troops were sent to help police the Suez Canal. But Churchill was just as unwilling to budge on certain things the Americans wanted, such as the further integration of Western Europe. Churchill had made speeches about the need for a European army, but as with other grand schemes of his to unify Europe, he was coy about British participation. On his visit to Washington, he became rather a bore on the subject of European armed forces, muttering about bewildered French soldiers unable to convey orders to Greeks, Germans, and other foreigners. When it came to plans for the European Defense Community, which General Eisenhower, the first supreme commander of NATO, was very keen on, the British blamed the French for pulling back, for fear of Germans strutting in their jackboots again. But it was the British, not the French, who had sabotaged the EDC first by refusing to commit any of their own troops.

It was easier to compromise on more symbolic matters. Churchill made a great fuss over who was to command the Atlantic fleet; he wanted a British admiral, not an American. After all, he argued, Britain may now be a broken power, but the Royal Navy had sunk more U-boats than the Americans, and the ocean floor was "white with the bones of Englishmen."[4] In the end, it was agreed that consideration would be given to extending British command over the eastern Atlantic. When Churchill wanted the Canadians to restore "Rule Britannia" as the official anthem of the Canadian navy, instead of "Vive la Canadienne," he was promised that the former would be played whenever a British admiral boarded a Canadian ship.

Churchill's heart was further warmed by the hero's reception he received when he gave a speech to the joint session of Congress. He reminded a packed House of Bismarck's words "that the supreme fact of the nineteenth century was that Britain and the United States spoke the same language. Let us make sure that the supreme fact of the twentieth century is that they tread the same path." He was applauded more rapturously than the president himself. Whatever Americans thought about the British, the cult of Churchill showed no sign of waning in Washington, and this would prove to be not entirely a good thing.

The problem with the Special Relationship was that US and

British aims in the world were not always compatible. The wartime generation of British leaders, even as the empire was beginning to fray, still wanted Britain to continue being a global power. And they all resented, some more, some a little less, subservience to the Americans. This was just as true of Labour Party politicians as of Conservatives. One of Attlee's cabinet ministers, Hugh Gaitskell, put his finger on it: "We do not like to admit our relative weakness, because we should then look too much like a satellite."[5] His successor as minister of fuel and power, Philip Noel-Baker, voiced his concern in 1950 that access to Iranian oil might be in peril, for then, he said, "we should no longer be on equal terms with the Americans in the sphere of oil affairs."[6]

Resentful grumbling about the Americans among such grandees as Anthony Eden, the foreign secretary, was so prevalent that Churchill often had to tell him to pipe down. Churchill's chancellor of the exchequer, R. A. ("Rab") Butler, understood this mentality very well. He admired Eden's courage, his wartime record, and the way he stood up for British interests in the world. But these deep-seated sentiments, he ventured, "coalesced only too easily with less generous sentiments: the residues of illiberal resentment at the loss of Empire, the rise of colored nationalism, the transfer of world leadership to the United States."[7]

A few months before Churchill was returned to power, two of the "Cambridge spies," Guy Burgess and Donald Maclean, had absconded to Moscow. There were several possible reasons why these privileged Englishmen had chosen to become Soviet spies. Some felt in the 1930s that Communism was the only serious antidote to the rise of fascism. Some might have enjoyed the secret atmosphere of subversive spying—a bit like being members of a very smart club. Burgess's homosexuality has been mentioned as a reason for resentment, or a talent for secrecy. Another possible motive, often suggested by experts on this inexhaustible subject, was frustration over Britain's shrinking role in the world. These were men who might once have enjoyed running the empire. Now that British dominance was waning, they chose to serve another one. What they all had in common—Burgess, Maclean, Kim Philby, and Anthony Blunt—was contempt for the US, in some cases to a pathological degree.

The common American perception of *their* role in the world was to support "colored nationalism," to oppose colonialism, and to be the city on a hill that would lead the world to freedom and democracy. Colonialism in any form, Truman believed, "is hateful to Americans. America fought her own war of liberation against colonialism and we shall always regard with sympathy and understanding the desire of people everywhere to be free of colonial bondage."[8] Eisenhower—and other US presidents since—sometimes used the word "crusade" to describe the American mission to make the world safe for democracy.

In this endeavor, however, 1941 was as important a date as 1776. On the first day of his presidency, Eisenhower observed that his new task was "like a continuation of all I've been doing since July, 1941—or even earlier."[9] He saw the struggle against Communism as "a war of light against darkness, freedom against slavery, Godliness against atheism."[10] The desire of Eisenhower and subsequent presidents to avoid another "Munich" in this war against the forces of evil was as strongly held, if not more so, than any anti-imperial sentiments evoked at Boston or Concord.

Both the British perception of history, especially in its Churchillian form, and the American one lent themselves to hypocrisies. The British desire to hang on to power was couched in moral terms:

"for civilization." But the real motive was articulated more honestly by Harold Macmillan during the Suez crisis. As chancellor of the exchequer, he was a firm advocate of using force to bring down the nationalist Egyptian leader, Gamal Abdel Nasser. If Egypt could get away with pushing Britain around, Macmillan believed, "Britain would become another Netherlands."[11]

In the American case, when people's desire to escape from colonial bondage stood in Washington's way, especially if Communist influence was suspected, the US was by no means so supportive. Even as Churchill refused to send British troops to Indochina in 1954 to help the French fight off the North Vietnamese Communists at Dien Bien Phu, President Eisenhower was thinking of some very severe methods to stop Ho Chi Minh. "Give the French a few [atomic] arms and spray them around in Indochina" is the way he put it.[12] He was so angry about British lack of cooperation that he accused Churchill, of all people, of "promoting a second Munich."[13] US foreign policy, then as now, could waver unpredictably between fits of moralism and brutal realpolitik; quite often one would be harnessed in service of the other.

One particularly notorious example was the way the US removed the democratically elected president of Guatemala, Jacobo Arbenz, in 1953. Operation PBSUCCESS was a brutal military coup, backed by the CIA. Arbenz was a leftist, whose land reforms and economic policies lifted peasants from near servitude. This cut into the profits of American business, notably the United Fruit Company. Ousting Arbenz, depicted in US propaganda as a Communist, led to decades of dictatorship, violent rebellion, and civil war. This sequence of events became a pattern in US interventions south of its borders. Since the British were rarely involved, they weren't much bothered by these actions.

The US was happy to collude with the British in putting down inconvenient eruptions of "colored nationalism" when it suited its purposes. But this aspect of the Special Relationship usually had to be carefully disguised. If Dean Acheson was an Anglophile, as was widely assumed, he did his best to hide it. When he got wind of a paper drawn up in 1950 by some US and British diplomats in praise of the Special Relationship, he was so furious that he had all copies burned. He explained in his memoirs that he was pro-British. He valued the relationship and recognized the identity of British and American interests in Europe and elsewhere. But, he wrote, his "annoyance came from the stupidity of writing about a special relationship, which could only increase suspicion among our allies of secret plans and purposes, which they did not share and would not approve."[14]

When Anthony Eden, during Churchill's visit to Truman in 1952, brought up the question of Iran, and asked for American help to stop Mossadegh and his nationalists from wresting authority from the British over the exploitation of Iranian oil, Acheson sided with the nationalists. He believed that Anglo-American solidarity in this case would put their respective countries in the position of "a couple locked in warm embrace in a rowboat about to go over Niagara Falls."[15] Truman, later that year, was even more direct: "We tried to get the blockheaded British to have their oil company make a fair deal with Iran. No, no, they couldn't do that. They knew all about how to handle it—we didn't, according to them."[16]

Churchill hoped for more understanding from General Eisenhower, his old wartime friend, who was elected president the following year. But Eisenhower, at first, was no more interested in opposing Mossadegh than Truman had been. Some deft British manipulation was clearly in order. An MI6 agent in Teheran, named Christopher

Montague Woodhouse, explained: "Not wishing to be accused of trying to use the Americans to pull British chestnuts out of the fire, I decided to emphasize the Communist threat to Iran rather than the need to recover control of the oil industry."[17] Eisenhower, and his secretary of state, John Foster Dulles, quickly came around to Eden's view that there might be "alternatives to Mossadegh."

Eisenhower's conviction that "any nation's right to form a government and an economic system of its own choosing is inalienable" began to lose force. The US now backed the British boycott of Iranian oil in order to starve the Iranian economy. American funding to Iran was stopped. CIA agents, including Kermit ("Kim") Roosevelt, Theodore Roosevelt's grandson, were dispatched to Teheran, where they helped the British to stir up violence in the streets. A suitable political alternative to Mossadegh was found in the shape of Fazlollah Zahedi, an army general who had collaborated with the Nazis during the war. A coup was contrived with the help of bribed Iranian officials and the same kinds of thugs hanging around the bazaars that would bring down the shah a couple of decades later. The Anglo-Iranian Oil Company was absorbed in a mostly Anglo-American consortium. Iran received a share of the profits, and money flowed from the US to Teheran once more.

Eisenhower has been disparaged as a lazy and ineffectual figure. "The great golfer," as Gore Vidal called him. This is surely to underestimate a steelier character. In fact, the British made the great mistake of assuming that John Foster Dulles was the real power behind the great golfer, an assumption that would cause them much grief.

By the same token, many people, including Eisenhower himself, underestimated Churchill in his second term. To be sure, even his doctor noted that the old man was no longer as alert as he should be, and was quickly bored with subjects—China, for example—that didn't immediately concern Britain's security. But Churchill could still be sharp about some important issues. He understood the peculiar importance of nuclear arms earlier than Truman or Eisenhower, who spoke about the use of atomic bombs as though they were just much more powerful conventional weapons. Not that Churchill wished to ban the bomb. On the contrary, since possession of atomic arms was deemed to be essential to remaining a serious power, he had been adamant that Britain should have them. But he was quickly aware of the political implications, especially after the development of the H-bomb, which in his view was as far removed from the A-bomb as the A-bomb was from the bow and arrow. Any war with the Soviet Union would now have more-catastrophic consequences than anything ever seen before. A country like Britain could be swiftly wiped out. The British were unsure whether American leaders had fully grasped this.

Churchill's extraordinary self-assurance had been a great boon in 1940, when a German invasion seemed to be imminent. But in the nuclear age, he became almost megalomaniacal. The US was now the greatest power on earth. The difficulty, in Churchill's view, was "how far we ought to go in restraining her from taking risks which we cannot share."[18] He developed what Eden called a "lunatic obsession" with safeguarding the world in a summit with the Russians. He would stretch out his hand "to grasp the paw of the Russian bear." Great things were within his grasp. The direction of the world could be changed. "America is very powerful, but very clumsy."[19]

This was a fine expression of the British belief that the coarser Americans had to be reined in by a dose of old-world sophistication. Eisenhower did not buy it. The Soviet Union, in his opinion, could never be reasoned with, only opposed. Civilization was at stake. And so Churchill decided it was time to go and talk sense into the US president: "I put my paw out to Ike, and it was fixed up at once. My stock is very high. There is a feeling that I am the only person who could do anything with Russia. I believe in Moscow they think that too."[20] They did not, and nor, during their meeting in Bermuda, in December 1953, did Ike.

Fearful once more that the world might suspect Anglo-American collusion, Eisenhower had insisted that the French prime minister, Joseph Laniel, and his foreign minister, Georges Bidault, should be of the party too. Churchill, despite his occasional bouts of Francophilia, treated the Frenchmen with total disdain. When asked at one point what the French thought about his plan to talk to the Russians, he said, "I take no account of them, they are harmless."[21] (On the plane to Bermuda, Churchill had been reading one of C. S. Forester's novels set in the Napoleonic Wars, entitled *Death to the French*.)

Nothing much came from the conference, which is what Eisenhower had anticipated. Churchill and Eden were appalled by the casual way the president talked about using the A-bomb in Asia. American pressure to get serious about the European Defense Community, as part of NATO, went nowhere. The French still worried about German dominance. The British said Germany should be allowed to rearm on its own, if the EDC failed. The Americans threatened to pull their troops out of Europe if the Europeans were not prepared to defend themselves. Churchill lectured Eisenhower about the virtues of imperialism, and how power should never be handed to people who weren't ready to use it responsibly. Eisenhower thought the prime minister ignored that "any attempt by European powers to sustain by force their dominant positions in these territories would have long since resulted in furious resentment, unrest, and conflict."[22] Which is true, but this sat rather awkwardly with Eisenhower's insistence on supplying arms to the French in Indochina. Eden wrote to his wife, Clarissa: "Conference is very hard going now, & I am sad & tired, not so much about details as about this poor world & what I fear lies ahead."[23]

The main problem for Britain, which was also discussed at Bermuda, was the Suez Canal, where, to quote from Eisenhower's thoughts about imperialism once more, "the spirit of nationalism had become rampant and often uncontrollable."[24] To protect the supply of oil from the Middle East, the British had built a vast military base along the canal, as well as in the center of Cairo, with tens of thousands of troops, along with a large number of airfields, depots, and workshops. Even though Egypt was nominally an independent country since 1922, the British still treated it as a protectorate. Already under the corrupt and dissolute King Farouk, Egyptians wanted to drive the imperialists out. Guerilla attacks on the British could be handled with a sharp crack of the imperial whip, but when riots erupted in Cairo and the king was ousted by a group of militant military officers, including Colonel Gamal Abdel Nasser, the situation became more serious. Since the Soviets were keen to exploit the growing animus against British imperialism, a war that could escalate dangerously in an era of nuclear arms was now a serious risk. The British military presence in Egypt was also extremely expensive. And so, in 1954, Anthony Eden decided it would be best to withdraw the troops. Churchill disagreed with his foreign secretary. Ever since Indian independence, which he had seen as a great blunder, Churchill had become allergic to what he called "scuttling"; a great power didn't scuttle away from its vital interests. Eden was also opposed by a number of right-wing Tories known as the Suez

Group, who accused him of appeasing a dictatorship. Eden was depicted in cartoons as Chamberlain. Once again, "Munich" loomed over the proceedings.

As though this were not aggravating enough, Eden was tormented by Churchill, who after several strokes was no longer capable of functioning properly as prime minister but kept postponing the moment of handing over leadership of the Conservative Party. Churchill still had dreams of saving the world by talking to the Russians. Then, finally, with a minimum of ceremony, in April 1955, Churchill gave up his struggle so that Eden could go and kiss the hand of the young queen.

Anthony Eden was in many ways the perfect man to be prime minister at a time of crisis abroad. He was a top student at Oxford in Oriental languages and spoke both Arabic and Persian. Unlike Churchill's, his French was fluent. Although imbued with all the loftiness of an English gentleman born at the summit of British imperial power, Eden felt comfortable with foreigners in a way that few British politicians did, or indeed do. He even managed to be friends with General de Gaulle during the war, when most people shunned the touchy Frenchman as a pompous nuisance. Eden was a great diplomat, a towering figure at international conferences, one of the best foreign secretaries ever. But he turned out to be a disastrous prime minister, whose downfall was inextricably bound to the areas of his greatest affinity, the Middle East and France.

When it came to European politics, the suave and cosmopolitan Eden suffered from the same blind spot as most other men of his class and age. He could not conceive of Britain as a European nation on par with other countries. He had stated his view five years earlier, when Schuman touted his plan in London: "We wish to cultivate the idea of an Atlantic Community based on the three pillars of the United States, the United Kingdom (including the Common-wealth), and Continental Europe."[25] Two months after his election as prime minister, a meeting took place in the Sicilian town of Messina, which would radically change the shape of Europe. The six members of the European Coal and Steel Community—Germany, France, Italy, Belgium, Netherlands, and Luxembourg—agreed to build a common European market, administered by common institutions. The Schuman Plan was no longer an abstraction.

Out of deference to Britain, a draft of the plan was shown to the Foreign Office first, before the meeting in Messina took place. There was not the slightest curiosity in London. British officials dismissed it as woolly nonsense concocted by overexcited foreigners. Messina, in any case, was "too outlandish a place to send a British civil servant."[26] The conference was barely mentioned in the British newspapers. Eden showed no interest at all. Harold Macmillan, then foreign secretary, was in San Francisco. When Rab Butler, as chancellor of the exchequer, was informed after the Messina meeting, he waved it all away as "some archeological excavations" in a remote Sicilian town.[27]

Many reasons have been advanced for this second refusal of the British to be engaged in what was to become the European Economic Community: the vestiges of empire, pride in the Commonwealth, a jealous attachment to the Special Relationship, or plain old-fashioned chauvinism. All these explanations hold some truth. But there was also something else, articulated by a British diplomat named Michael Palliser, who was one of the rare advocates of active British participation in Europe; he married the daughter of the Belgian statesman Paul-Henri Spaak, the man who led the negotiations at Messina. Analyzing British attitudes in a BBC documentary about

British relations with Europe, Palliser said, "We certainly regard ourselves in many ways as superior to the others. At the same time we have the sort of feeling they are cleverer than we are. We may be honest, but not very clever."[28]

This is, of course, precisely what many Americans had long thought about the British, and what the British traditionally thought about the French. It reflects a Protestant prejudice about Catholics. The Protestant Anglo-Saxon may be a little slow and unsophisticated, but at least he is frank and sincere, whereas the wily Jesuits and other papists cannot be trusted. They say one thing and mean something else; behind their silky manners lurks all kinds of deceit. This sentiment is behind the image of John Bull, the honest English yeoman, and new-world views of the old. Old-fashioned English gentlemen were sometimes quite clever, but they knew it was good form to disguise it.

The founding fathers of European unification were almost all Catholics. When the EEC became official with the signing of the Treaty of Rome in 1957, Spaak, gazing upon the Italian capital, said, "There we see what is left of the Roman Empire. . . . We all felt that way. . . . We felt very strongly that we were at home."[29] Spaak was actually the only Protestant among the founding fathers. But he was foreign minister of a largely Catholic country. And the palimpsest of Europe is marked as much, if not more, by the Holy Roman Empire as it is by the ancient Roman Empire. The former held no attraction for most British people whatsoever. When Englishmen of Eden's generation thought about the Schuman Plan and its later developments at all, they were more likely to suspect a sinister plot, possibly emanating from the Vatican itself.

And yet, irony of ironies, when it came to Eden's downfall, it involved a plot hatched by the British and the French, joined by the Israelis, that was kept secret from the Americans. Of course, the ghosts of Munich, once more, had something to do with it.

Even after Britain began to withdraw its troops from Suez in 1954, the Suez Canal Company continued to be run jointly by Britain and France. British civilians still maintained the military base. Colonel Nasser, the new strongman with ambitions to be the reincarnation of Saladin, leading the Arab nations against enemies from the West, stirred up popular hostility to the British in a constant stream of propaganda.

The British first tried to repair relations with Egypt by diplomatic means. In 1955, as prime minister, Eden visited Cairo, where he was oddly obtuse about Egyptian sensitivities. Nasser was invited to dine at the British embassy, a palatial reminder of imperial hauteur, without being reminded to come in evening dress. There is a photograph of Eden, and the British ambassador, both dressed to the nines, sitting on a leather sofa with Nasser between them, looking ill at ease in his simple army uniform. When Eden spoke a few words of Arabic to him, expecting to break the ice, Nasser took this as intolerable condescension.

Hostility swiftly mounted. Guerilla fighters from Egypt probed the Israeli border. Israel, soon to be supplied with French jet fighters, raided the Gaza Strip with commandos, even as Eden was trying to entice other Arab countries into joining a common defense alliance. Nasser saw dark imperialist plots in all these moves. And Eden began to see Nasser as a Mussolini-style dictator, who had to be resisted.

Nasser seemed better disposed toward the Americans. He liked watching films starring Esther Williams, the "Bathing Beauty," and eating (veal) hot dogs. The Americans, eager to be seen as the champions of "colored nationalism," wanted to be friends with him, too, even if this irritated the British. When the British pressed the US to be on their side, Eisenhower, as well as Dulles, refused. Eisenhower wished to avoid giving the impression that an Anglo-American alliance was trying to push Third World nationalists around. However, the US was also anxious that oil supplies continued to be shipped through the Suez Canal. And both Eisenhower and Dulles, although deeply suspicious of British imperialism, were equally suspicious of Soviet plots to bring Nasser to their side.

Unfortunately, the combination in Washington of moral posturing, anti-Communism, and flashes of realpolitik created a great deal of confusion. Dulles, who loathed Nasser as much as Eden did, tended to side with the British on Egypt, even though his distrust of British imperialism frequently clashed with his equally fervent hatred of Communism. Eisenhower was more firmly on the side of the Egyptians. Even when he backed British attempts to safeguard the oil, he wanted to avoid any impression of a united Anglo-Saxon front. Eden never felt comfortable with Americans, and he despised Dulles as a moralizing, Presbyterian prig. So both sides often found themselves at cross-purposes.

When Nasser decided to buy arms from the Soviet bloc, after being turned down by Britain and the US, American anti-Communism came into play. Nasser's request for US and British funds to pay for the very costly Aswan dam over the Nile was initially granted, but then, in a fit of pique (Nasser had recognized Communist China), Dulles suddenly withdrew the offer. Nasser first heard about this on the radio, and he was crushed by what he called the "insultive" nature of the refusal. A few days later, Nasser gave orders to seize the property of the Suez Canal Company, nationalize the company, and put the canal zone under military law.

He instantly became a Third World hero, lending pride to millions who felt humiliated by Western arrogance. Egyptian crowds flocked to his speeches, as though he were a holy man. Leadership of the Arab world seemed to be in reach. Dulles was furious. But Eisenhower understood. Nasser, he said, "embodies the emotional demands of the people of the area for independence and for 'slapping the White Man down.'"[30]

The French and British wanted to intervene. Eden spoke on television about the dangers of appeasement: "We all remember all too well what the cost can be in giving in to fascism." He was careful not to compare Nasser to Hitler, but the name Mussolini frequently popped up in his conversations. Dulles hinted that he might back a Franco-British action. Eisenhower never did. The British, deluded by the image of Eisenhower as a lazy golfer, chose to listen to Dulles.

There was, however, not much the French or British could legally do about Nasser's move, since the Suez Canal was in Egypt, and the strongman had not done anything illegal. But he was a maddening reminder of the shrinking boundaries of British power. Eden wrote to Eisenhower that this was the most dangerous crisis that Britain had known since 1940: "We have many times led Europe in the fight for freedom. It would be an ignoble end to our long history if we tamely accepted to perish by degrees."[31] It sounds histrionic now, but Eden was expressing feelings that were no doubt common among men who had fought on the victorious side in two world wars.

When Dulles suggested forming the Suez Canal Users Association as a way out, the British, desperate to keep the Americans onside, and the French, albeit more reluctantly, agreed. Each country would supply its own pilots to navigate the canal, and an adequate fee would be paid to the Egyptians. The association would be the

Suez Canal Company under a new name. Eden made it clear that if the Egyptians should interfere with the association, armed force might have to be used.

The seriousness of this threat should have been clear to Eisenhower. It certainly was to Dulles. But when Eisenhower considered the possible consequences of using force, he suddenly backed off. There was no way the US would shoot its way through the canal. Without the US, SCUA was effectively dead. Both the British and French felt let down by the Americans. And their bitter feelings led to an act of madness.

Eden fell for a mixture of sordid tricks and peculiar delusions that would become a familiar feature of more recent Middle Eastern conflicts, unleashed by far-less-sophisticated men. British secret agents plotted ways to murder Nasser. Eden convinced himself that Egyptians would surely be cheering in the streets if the British could rid them of their dictator. And, incredibly, he agreed to a French scheme to bring Nasser down with help of the Israelis.

Meeting in secret at a house in a Parisian suburb that had been used by the Resistance during the war, French, British, and Israeli officials hatched a plan. The atmosphere was tense. The British foreign minister, Selwyn Lloyd, treated the Israelis with distaste, as though they were riffraff from the streets. The Israelis, already distrustful of the British, found him a pompous snob. Christian Pineau, a Resistance leader during the war who had been tortured by the Gestapo and had barely survived Buchenwald, represented France. The plan was for Israel to attack Egypt, and thus to provoke a military confrontation. The French and British would then demand a cease-fire. If the warring parties refused, Franco-British troops would occupy the canal zone.

And so it happened. On October 29, 1956, the Israelis attacked.

Colonel Ariel Sharon, the future Israeli prime minister, made a hash of an impetuous raid in the Sinai and lost thirty-eight men in an ambush. But, on the whole, the operation was a success. Paris and London issued their ultimatum. Eden assured Eisenhower that any action he might take had nothing to do with old colonial ways, and he hoped that the Americans would help him to strengthen "the weakest point in the line against Communism."[32]

Nasser, despite buying weapons from the Soviets, was in fact not a Communist, or even a fellow traveler. But British secret service men cooked up false intelligence, supposedly from an agent inside Nasser's circle, code-named Lucky Break, alleging that Nasser was about to overthrow the monarchies in the Middle East and align Egypt with the Soviets. Eden chose to believe it. Eisenhower was not impressed, and he replied quite politely that he was deeply concerned about the ultimatum. In fact, he was fuming about having been kept in the dark, and the sheer recklessness of the military operation: "I can't believe they would be so stupid as to invite on *themselves* all the Arab hostility to Israel." There were no better people than the Brits to have as allies in a war, "but *this* thing! My God!"[33]

Apart from venting his anger, however, Eisenhower had no clear policy on the Middle Eastern crisis. He was distracted by the Hungarian uprising, which had been egged on by American anti-Communist propaganda. But when it erupted in October, the US had no intention of giving the Hungarians any active support— another case of empty moral rhetoric.

The Israelis refused to back down and took much of the Sinai and the Gaza Strip. British and French troops landed on the beaches of Port Said, as though reenacting a shabby version of D-Day. Egyptian airfields were bombed. Egyptians were killed without mercy.

"To us," recalled one British paratrooper, the Egyptians were "wogs. They were less than human." Once more, Eden went on television to speak to the British people. "All my life," he said, "I've been a man of peace. . . . But I'm utterly convinced that the action we have taken is right. Over the years I've seen, as many of you have, the mood of peace at any price. Many of you will remember that mood in our own country, and *how* we paid for it!" He promised that Commonwealth troops were forthcoming and soon the Americans would join in too.

In fact, none of this happened. And public opinion in Britain was deeply split. Huge anti-war demonstrations were held in London. Friendships were lost and families divided. French and British troops were almost at the canal. The Soviet premier, Nikolai Bulganin, threatened to intervene with force if the fighting didn't stop. Finally, Eisenhower decided to act. With the pound under severe pressure, the British had to dig into their gold and dollar reserves to maintain its value. The US refused to lend money, as long as the British continued the war. A loan from the IMF was blocked. The French wanted to fight on. Macmillan, once the great advocate of a war against Nasser, now was the first to back down. "There has been a serious run on the pound," he said, "viciously orchestrated in Washington."[34] The British, as ever, felt unable to defy American demands, and agreed to a cease-fire. When Eden pleaded with Eisenhower to allow British troops to clear the canal and remain to keep the peace, Ike wrote him a blunt message: "If you don't get out of Port Said tomorrow, I'll cause a run on the pound and drive it down to zero."[35]

The consequences, for Eden personally, but especially for European relations with the US, were enormous. Not for centuries had a British leader, presiding over a great empire, been spoken to like this. Eisenhower's message relegated Britain to the status of a secondary power. This process had already begun in the later years of World War II, but for the sake of politeness, old memories, Winston Churchill, and the occasional paranoid overestimation of British imperial might, American leaders had pretended not quite to notice. Now they did. Macmillan reflected that Suez had been the last gasp of a declining power. In two hundred years, he said, the Americans would know how the British felt.

The French felt betrayed by the Americans, as well as by the British. For Charles de Gaulle, who was no longer in power, Suez confirmed that the Anglo-Saxon powers could not be trusted, that NATO would not safeguard French interests, and that Britain, faced with the choice between the European continent and the colossus on the other side of the Atlantic Ocean, would always opt for the latter.

Eden was a broken man. Already plagued by illness, made much worse by a botched operation on his gallbladder, he stepped down. But just before he did so, he accepted an invitation to recuperate in a country house in Jamaica called Goldeneye. The house belonged to Ian Fleming. He was writing *From Russia, with Love*, one of his first novels, while Suez was going on, featuring the perfect imaginary hero for his time: a suave English operator, accustomed to command, the savvy heir to great imperial power, perfectly groomed by the finest tailors—a little like Anthony Eden, in fact. This was obviously a fantasy; real power was slipping away. But here was a man who could use all his extraordinary skills to teach the less-polished cousins across the ocean how to save the world from villainy. His name, of course, was Bond, James Bond.

Five

AN ANGLO-
AMERICAN BOND

Most of our people have never had it so good.
· HAROLD MACMILLAN

arold Macmillan knew he was a bit of a ham. He once observed that being a politician was like being an actor. His act was to look and sound like an Edwardian grandee, happiest when prowling about a Scottish grouse moor in tweed plus fours, or when making the driest of quips in the slow drawl of a gentleman who is used to being heard without ever having to raise his voice. Macmillan's languid response at the United Nations to Nikita Khrushchev's noisy temper tantrum, when the prime minister politely requested a translation of the Russian's desk banging, was vintage Macmillan. His manner suggested generations of aristocratic breeding in fine country houses and the best private schools. The "effortless superiority" of his education at Balliol College, Oxford, gave him an air of elegant amateurism. Behind this carefully honed facade, however, was a shrewd politician who could be quite ruthless when it suited him. When he saw that Anthony Eden was on his last legs, battered by the Suez misadventure for which Macmillan was partly responsible, he pretended to be imminently retiring from politics, only to shove his potential rivals aside and ease his own way into 10 Downing Street in 1957.

Far from being an aristocrat, Macmillan was the son of Maurice Macmillan, a London publisher, and the rather overwhelming Helen "Nellie" Belles, from Spencer, Indiana. Like Churchill, Macmillan was proud of being half-American. His great-grandfather was a simple Scottish crofter. He was also tougher than he appeared. His shuffling gait, making him look prematurely old, was the result of multiple wounds received in 1915 as a Grenadier Guards officer in the Battle of the Somme. Shot in the leg and pelvis, he spent twelve hours in a shell hole, giving himself doses of morphine while reading Aeschylus with enemies all around him.

Everything about Macmillan suggested an England that hadn't changed since the Great War, a world that had fossilized in the comic exaggeration of a P. G. Wodehouse novel, even though his own taste ran more to Anthony Trollope and Jane Austen. And yet, as prime minister, nicknamed "Supermac," Macmillan presided over more than six years associated with frantic economic development: modern buildings replaced hastily torn down Victorian railway stations and Georgian terraces; homes were newly furnished with washing machines, refrigerators, and television sets. This was the age of anti-austerity and get-rich-quick schemes. Young people born during or just after the war were listening to rock 'n' roll hit records presented by disc jockeys on Radio Luxembourg. *Look Back in Anger*, John Osborne's play about disaffected youth, was Britain's answer to James Dean. The Oxford historian Hugh Trevor-Roper deplored the new age as a "vulgar, jolly, complacent, materialist social-democracy," the kind of society that "triumphed in America."[1]

Macmillan himself appeared to celebrate it in his most often quoted speech: "Let's be frank about it: most of our people have never had it so good."

He actually said this less in a spirit of celebration than as a warning that it might not last, with fast-rising prices and the possibility of high inflation. In any event, Britain was changing rapidly into a country that bore little resemblance to the one Macmillan grew up in. It was, as Trevor-Roper rightly observed, becoming more like America.

Unlike Anthony Eden, and more like Churchill, whom he admired enormously, Macmillan felt comfortable in the US, and got on well with two presidents who couldn't have been less alike: Eisenhower and Kennedy. Of the two, he was closer by far to John F. Kennedy, the stylish, younger man, who projected a dynamic, modern, hedonistic, open America. Kennedy—but certainly not Macmillan—was a keen reader of James Bond novels. The endless partying with young girls, the sharp suits, the slightly louche glamour, as well as some of the more bizarre exploits under his watch— trying to get rid of Fidel Castro with an exploding cigar—could have sprouted from Ian Fleming's lurid imagination. Kennedy actually had dinner with Fleming once in New York and gratefully received some tips on how best to deal with the Cuban leader.

Macmillan's first task as prime minister was to clear up the mess of Suez and mend relations with the US. The last time he had met Eisenhower, as foreign secretary in the midst of the Egyptian crisis, he had to be smuggled into the White House through a side entrance to avoid unwelcome press attention. The Americans were still angry about British actions in a foolish war started behind Eisenhower's back, and the British were still smarting from the way the US, after sending confusing signals, twisted their arm to end it.

Prime minister and president decided to meet in March 1957, on British territory in Bermuda. As old wartime comrades, personal relations between the two men were considerably warmer than they had been in Anthony Eden's time. Even though Eisenhower found the British fixation on Colonel Nasser tiresome, he enjoyed having "bull sessions" with Macmillan, discussing the future of the world in their pajamas at the Mid-Ocean Club. Macmillan, sensing the loneliness of the US president ("half King, half Prime Minister"), described their meetings as "being not at all like an experience in the modern world. More like meeting George III at Brighton."[2] The comparison was slightly eccentric given King George's difficulties with the American colonies, but this nicely sums up the difference in his attitude with that of his predecessor. Macmillan didn't mind bending his knee to a superior sovereign. He once remarked to a Labour Party minister, "Europe is finished. It is sinking. It is like Greece after the second Peloponnesian war. . . . If I were a younger man, I should emigrate to the United States."[3]

They decided to let bygones be bygones. All would now be well with the Special Relationship. Eisenhower thought the Bermuda meetings had been "the most successful international conference that I had attended since the close of World War II."[4] The two men discussed common interests in European defense. The Americans were eager for European integration (much more so than most British politicians, even Macmillan); Eisenhower committed the US to take an active part in defending countries in the Middle East against Communism, as part of what became the Eisenhower Doctrine; and both countries would strive toward German reunification. But what made the conference most successful, from the British point of view, concerned something of a British obsession: the nuclear bomb.

Like other British prime ministers since the war, Macmillan firmly believed that Britain needed its own nuclear weapons if it were to continue as a serious power. This is why the McMahon act in 1946, ending nuclear cooperation between the US and its allies, had been such a blow to British prestige. The act was amended in 1954 so that British bombers could at least carry US nuclear arms in wartime. In Bermuda, Eisenhower promised to place sixty intermediate Thor missiles in Britain. The British thought this would lead to nuclear independence, even though the Americans didn't quite see it that way, and it fueled French suspicions of Anglo-American collusion. But Macmillan came away from his meeting with Eisenhower feeling very pleased that his country would continue to "punch above its weight," in the words of a British foreign secretary many years later.[5]

Nuclear cooperation with the US, even if Britain had to be the junior partner, lay at the heart of what the British especially still saw as the Special Relationship. Macmillan's idea of Britain's role remained that of the ambivalent and skeptical Greek among the rampant Romans. He very much wanted the US to have such nuclear superiority that the Soviets would not be tempted to go to war with the West. But he also believed it was his duty to rein in the Americans when they got too wild. Already in 1944, he wrote in his diary about the American tendency to "intervene in a pathetic desire to solve in a few months problems which have baffled statesmen for many centuries. . . . We have got to guide them both for their own advantage and ours and for that of the future peace of the world."[6]

Like Churchill, then, or indeed like several generations of thinkers in Britain, and to some extent the US, Macmillan was convinced that the fate of mankind, or at least that of the West, would best be vouchsafed in the Anglo-American order. But the problems of being a junior partner soon became painfully evident in the Eisenhower years.

China had already become a bit of a problem between Britain and the US during the war. Roosevelt annoyed Churchill by insisting that the Chinese generalissimo Chiang Kai-shek attend the Cairo and Teheran conferences. Unlike the Americans, Churchill didn't take the "Chinaman" seriously. After Chiang lost the civil war in China, and retreated to Taiwan in 1949, Mao Zedong's Communists took over. Britain established diplomatic relations with the People's Republic of China one year later, much to the irritation of the US, which saw the PRC as a formidable enemy in the worldwide struggle against Communism.

In August 1958, the People's Liberation Army started shelling two tiny islands just off the Chinese coast that were claimed by Chiang's government in Taiwan. The British rather took the Chinese view that they belonged by right to the PRC. Chiang, who was neither a liberal nor a democrat, asked the US to defend them. Eisenhower dispatched the Seventh Fleet. Dulles, in a letter to Macmillan, expressed a willingness to use nuclear force. This would be "an unpleasant prospect, but one I think we must face up to because our entire military establishment assumes more and more that the use of nuclear weapons will become normal in the event of hostilities."[7]

Macmillan was suitably appalled. And so was Churchill, who was briefed in London by Dulles. When Churchill voiced his alarm about the use of nuclear weapons, Eisenhower responded by saying in a news conference that A-bombs could be used as you use a bullet. As for the British position that a few tiny specks in the Taiwan

Strait were not a good enough cause for war, Eisenhower reached for that old standby in crises and evoked the specter of "Munich."

Macmillan described the British dilemma in a way that sums up much of the history of the Special Relationship since the end of World War II: "If we abandon the Americans—morally, I mean, they need no active support—it will be a great blow to the friendship and alliance which I have done so much to rebuild and strengthen."[8] The price for keeping the relationship alive, and with it British pretensions to "great power" status, has been, with very few exceptions, compliance with US policies, as active participants or at least as loyal cheerleaders.

A somewhat similar dilemma occurred four years later, when the nuclear arms race between the two superpowers was well under way. Macmillan was faced at home with a strong Ban the Bomb movement, whose sentiments were more inclined to be anti-American than anti-Soviet. The prime minister himself found the arms race "so barbarous, as to be almost incredible."[9] But when John F. Kennedy was looking for a secluded spot to test nuclear bombs without alarming Americans with pictures of the mushroom cloud, Macmillan offered him the use of a remote Commonwealth dependency in the Indian Ocean. In exchange, he hoped for an agreement to share scientific and technical knowledge. "Much would be lost," he informed his cabinet, "by declining to make the facilities at Christmas Island available. . . . This would not prevent the United States Government from deciding to resume testing, and the United Kingdom would lose what power they had to influence that decision and to be brought into consultation."[10]

In fact, even before Kennedy tested his bomb over the Indian Ocean, Britain became the third thermonuclear power in the world by dropping its own H-bomb, named Grapple 1, over Christmas Island. This was in the spring of 1957. A bit more than a year later, the US also gave the British what they wanted, and agreed to share nuclear secrets between the two nations. Eisenhower might have acceded to this wish anyway, against the advice of some of his closest associates, but American minds were concentrated by one of those periodic eruptions of existential panic to which the US is prone. The Soviets launched an unarmed satellite called Sputnik into orbit on November 3. The Joint Chiefs of Staff were in a frenzy. Senators wondered when the US would be hit by Soviet missiles. Calls went out to radically expand the military budget. Underground bomb shelters were hastily built. And Democrats, as well as Republicans, were frightened by what they saw, erroneously as it turned out, as "a missile gap" that greatly favored the Russians.

Macmillan must have sensed his chance. He quickly sent a letter to his "dear friend" in the White House, wondering what we are "going to do about these Russians," and suggested going further toward "pooling our efforts."[11] He left for Washington, where he noted that Sputnik had been the biggest shock to the US since Pearl Harbor: "The American cocksure-ness has been shaken."[12] Eisenhower, who had remained calmer than many of his compatriots, reached out to Britain as an ally in a crisis and, to the astonishment of Macmillan, effectively tore up the McMahon act. Henceforth, British and American scientists and engineers would cooperate on the development of nuclear weapons.

The British prime minister thought how pleased his mother would have been to see her son discussing weighty affairs with the US president in the Cabinet Room. And the Declaration of Common Purpose was drawn up. This was a kind of Atlantic Charter of the Cold War, in which collective defense would provide security "for the free world" and "the danger of Communist despotism" would "in due course be dissipated," and "a just and lasting peace" achieved. An attack on one NATO member would be regarded as an attack on all. The US and Britain, as the two allied nuclear powers, would see to that.

Macmillan was delighted with this outcome, even though the French, who wanted their own nuclear deterrent, felt left out. Some British Foreign Office officials did consider the risks of giving the impression that Britain would be nothing but an American satellite. They predicted that in such a case, "we shall damage our relations with our other friends, particularly the Europeans" and "we shall lose influence with the Americans themselves, because this depends upon the extent of our influence elsewhere."[13]

These worries would be realized quite soon, when Macmillan saw his efforts to join the EEC slapped down by de Gaulle, who regarded Britain as a threat to French dominance on the Continent. Since he couldn't quite state this reason directly, de Gaulle argued that Britain was too close to the US, and British membership would mean that Europe would be "drowned in the Atlantic."[14]

Before Macmillan's application to the EEC, however, the Eisenhower Doctrine of using US military force to stop Communism was first tested in a somewhat comical manner in the Middle East. Camille Chamoun, president of Lebanon, was a Maronite Christian and a keen Western ally. He was a frequent target of Muslim agitators and leftists. When Egypt and Syria merged into one nation called the United Arab Republic, Lebanese Muslim crowds cheered, but Macmillan and Eisenhower suspected a Nasserite plot to turn the Middle East into a Soviet sphere of interest. It was, however,

Macmillan who first reached for the "Munich" analogy. Syria, in his view, was "Austria," and the Lebanese would end up like the Sudeten Germans in 1938. Iraq, as "Poland," would soon follow.

Chamoun asked for American military protection. The US hesitated and then entangled itself and its allies in a mixture of confusion, ideology, and ignorance of local politics that would be a common feature of future interventions. This one, as it happened, would be relatively bloodless. Eisenhower was inclined to intervene, prompting Macmillan to say, with some satisfaction, that the US president "was doing a Suez," but then backed off again. Then, on July 14, 1958, the young King Faisal II of Iraq, an Old Boy of Harrow, Churchill's old school, and a staunch Western ally, was gunned down and hanged from a lamppost in a violent military coup. This was the "Poland" scenario Macmillan had feared. Chamoun was getting desperate. The Americans came off the fence, but then decided that going in with the British so soon after Suez would look bad, and so the Sixth Fleet was sent to Lebanon, while British troops were dispatched to defend Jordan. US Marines waded ashore south of Beirut, to be met by astonished sunbathers and small boys selling ice cream and Coca-Cola.

There never was any evidence that Nasser was setting up an Arab Third Reich, let alone a Soviet satrapy, in the Middle East. The Americans hung around Beirut for a few months before packing up and going home. Hardly anyone was killed. Relative normality was restored in Lebanon, at least for some time, partly through the good offices of Dag Hammarskjöld, secretary general of the United Nations. It is easy to blame political leaders, British and American, for their misperceptions in retrospect. But the Lebanese intervention was much like a farce that preceded many tragedies. Too often, nationalism, in this case Pan-Arabism, was mistaken for a global conspiracy to foment evil, and local despots were seen as the incarnations of Hitler. The shadow of 1938 would stretch well into the twenty-first century.

Even though it didn't happen by design, there was something sadly symbolic about the fact that Macmillan was in Bermuda repairing the Special Relationship at exactly the same time that six European nations signed the Treaty of Rome to formally establish the European Economic Community. This was when the Belgian statesman Paul-Henri Spaak saw a new European home arise in the ruins of the Roman Empire.

A united Europe was always what the Americans had advocated in the hope that this would enable US allies to defend themselves in the struggle with evil powers. Part of this hope was that Britain would play a leading role on the continent to which most Americans believed their English-speaking cousins belonged. Macmillan did not wholly disagree. Certainly, compared to many of his colleagues, and perhaps much of British public opinion, he was pro-European. As a well-traveled man who spoke decent French, he had often defended de Gaulle during the war when the Frenchman was heartily detested in London and Washington.

Like Churchill, Macmillan was given to lofty visions of European unification. In his televised interview with William F. Buckley in 1972, he claimed that, with Europe, Britain would be one of the great powers of the world. By itself, he explained, Britain had only been a great power for one hundred years, in between the Battle of Waterloo and the outbreak of World War I. "The people in the Old Europe," he continued, "having twice in my lifetime almost destroyed themselves in a kind of internecine war, like the Greeks did in the Peloponnesian War, must now get together. If they can work together . . . not only economically, but spiritually, politically, they can play a role similar to that of the US, and much more valuable, to the peace and fortunes of the world."

He said this a year before Britain finally joined the EEC. That it took so long had much to do with French intransigence, but also with British equivocation, including Macmillan's. He was still a child of empire and felt a deep attachment to the Commonwealth. When Macmillan was invited to join European foreign ministers in Holland in 1955 to discuss the progress of European integration, he instructed his staff to make an excuse and say that he was "busy with Cyprus." Despite his pro-European instincts, he could never quite bring himself to accept that Great Britain should share its hard-defended sovereignty with nations that had been ruled so recently by fascists and Nazis. He once told colleagues in London that supranationalism was attractive only to three groups: "the Jews, the Planners, and the old cosmopolitan élite."[15] These words might easily have been spoken by right-wing populists on both sides of the Atlantic in 2016, people whom Macmillan would of course have abhorred.

When de Gaulle returned to power in 1958, as a kind of national savior who might rescue France from pending military coups and a bloody colonial war in Algeria, Macmillan went to see him in Paris. With a remarkable lack of tact, he warned the French leader that the EEC was "the Continental System" all over again, as though the specters of Napoleon and Hitler were still hovering over Paris, and that Britain might have to go to war once more if the Continentals persisted on their dangerous course. As an alternative to the EEC, Britain set up the European Free Trade Association (EFTA) with the Scandinavian countries, as well as with Portugal, Austria, and Switzerland.

And yet Macmillan continued to fret that Britain might one day be abandoned by a less friendly US, and isolated from what he called the Empire of Charlemagne, led by France now, but quite possibly by a rampant Germany later. Two state visits to Britain in 1959 and 1960 showed how much perceptions of power had shifted in the decade since the war. First came Eisenhower, who was invited by Macmillan to boost his own chances of being reelected to Downing Street. Huge crowds lined the streets in London to greet the old war hero (more than would later turn out for the popular Kennedy). A fireside chat was orchestrated for television, with the two leaders sitting side by side in formal dinner jackets. Anglo-American relations, Macmillan intoned to a vigorously nodding Ike, were "as close . . . closer than ever before."

But de Gaulle's visit in the following year put Eisenhower's in the shade. De Gaulle had vowed never to come back to Britain except as president of France. In 1944, he was pushed into the background. To his enormous chagrin, the Allies had not allowed him to participate in the conference at Yalta in 1945. But this time, the cross of Lorraine was lit up in fireworks outside Buckingham Palace. De Gaulle, in his general's uniform, reviewed the Household Cavalry, an honor, the sonorous voice on British Pathé News announced, never accorded to a foreign head of state before. "La Marseillaise" resounded in Westminster Hall, where de Gaulle spoke to all the grandees of Britain, including the royal family and a tearful Winston Churchill. The world, he said, would be saved by the wisdom and firmness of Great Britain and France.

It was a triumph for de Gaulle, who reveled in tributes to the grandeur of France. His dream was to lead Europe and gain independence from the Anglo-Saxon powers. Macmillan's dream, as the empire was unraveling and British military might rapidly waning, was to be the great peacemaker who could persuade the leaders of the world to sit down and talk. He became as preoccupied by the idea of summits as Churchill had been. British wisdom might still prevail, or so he liked to believe.

And so, rather reluctantly, a month after de Gaulle's visit to Britain, the leaders gathered in Paris to discuss nuclear disarmament. This is where Macmillan would be in his element. Alas, however, it ended in a disaster. An American spy plane, the U-2, had been shot down over the Soviet Union. Khrushchev was furious and refused to spend any more time talking about disarmament. Macmillan, apparently with tears in his eyes, implored the leaders to be flexible. But the summit was essentially over. Glancing at the ill-tailored Soviet delegates, Macmillan remarked in passing that the Russians clearly were better at making Sputniks than trousers. Eisenhower insisted that Macmillan accompany him for a drive through Paris in an open car. Macmillan noted, "If Khrushchev must break up the Summit Conference there is no reason to let him break up the Anglo-American alliance."[16]

Macmillan's private secretary later recalled that he had never seen his boss more depressed: "This was the moment he realized that Britain counted for nothing; he couldn't move Ike to make a gesture towards Khrushchev, and de Gaulle was simply not interested. I think this represented a real watershed in his life."[17]

In August 1961, Macmillan told Parliament that Britain was applying for membership of the EEC. The statement was met with cries of "shame!" from some MPs. Hugh Gaitskell, the opposition leader, told his colleagues at the Labour Party conference that such a move would mean the end of one thousand years of proud independence. But the US wanted it, the Germans and the smaller member states wanted it, Macmillan now very much wanted it, and most British citizens could be persuaded that they wanted it. Edward ("Ted") Heath, the future prime minister, was sent to negotiate in Brussels because he was thought to be "good with the Continentals."

One of the canards espoused by British "Eurosceptics" to this day is that the British were duped by the Europeans and their British fellow travelers into thinking that joining Europe was a purely economic decision, with no political consequences. It was, after all, the European *Economic* Community and not a federal state in the making. But, in fact, Macmillan's motives never were purely economic. He was most concerned about security. The EEC, like NATO, was one of the institutions that would protect the Western nations in the struggle with Communism. The question of national sovereignty, which exercised some British politicians on the left more than on the right, was conveniently left aside.

Although he didn't say so directly—a fact that would leave a not entirely false impression of deviousness—the one European leader who never wanted Britain to join was Charles de Gaulle. He spoke about incompatible national traditions, about Britain's attachment to the Commonwealth, and its dependence on the US. Macmillan came away from meetings with de Gaulle thinking that the Frenchman was driven by jealousy and an implacable hatred of the Anglo-Saxons. But in certain fundamental ways, Macmillan and de Gaulle were in perfect agreement. De Gaulle never believed in supranationalism either. Like British nationalists—and perhaps like

Macmillan—he thought that nations had their own souls, and it would be "intolerable that a great state confide its destiny to the decision and action of another state, however friendly it may be."[18]

He was thinking of the US. But he had no more desire than Macmillan of diminishing national sovereignty in a European community. As long as France could be "the only cock in the barnyard," he could live with it. Indeed, he once told a French minister, "Europe is the chance for France to be what she has ceased to be since Waterloo," the only power to rank with the US and the Soviet Union. "The English console themselves for their decline by saying that they share in American hegemony. Germany has had her backbone broken."[19]

De Gaulle in 1958 remained what he always had been: vain, stubborn, grandiose, and morbidly oversensitive to slights, especially from the Anglo-Saxons. His analysis was harsh, and his subsequent treatment of the British underhanded, but it contained a large degree of truth. And he had no intention of letting Britain upset French privileges in what then seemed like a cozy European club. As a last sneer at poor Macmillan, de Gaulle paraphrased Edith Piaf's famous song: "Ne pleurez pas, Milord," "Don't cry, Milord."

That Macmillan and Kennedy would get on so well was by no means obvious. Macmillan's first impression had been of a "cocky young Irishman." But as the much older man, he was also self-conscious about being seen as a square in comparison. And he had loathed Kennedy's father, Joe, as an Anglophobic appeaser of the Nazis. In fact, however, the two leaders had a great deal in common. Having "had a good war" was important to Macmillan. Both men still suffered from war wounds; Kennedy's chronic back problems had been made worse by a violent encounter with a Japanese destroyer in 1943. There was a family connection: Kennedy's sister Kathleen had been married to the nephew of Macmillan's wife, Lady Dorothy. And the two leaders shared a sardonic sense of humor. Although Kennedy's remark that going without sex for more than three days gave him a headache might have seemed a little presumptuous to an old Edwardian cuckold who probably had not had sex for years, Macmillan quite liked the company of raffish characters.

They also shared a patrician idea of economics that sought to distribute wealth more equitably. Margaret Thatcher would later characterize this as "wet." Bill Clinton and Tony Blair would call it the Third Way. Macmillan actually wrote a book in 1938, entitled *The Middle Way: A Study of the Problem of Economic and Social Progress in a Free and Democratic Society*. And Kennedy's thesis at Harvard was about the Munich crisis, later published as *Why England Slept*. Kennedy's idealism about the US mission to spread democracy and fight the despots might be seen as a rebuke to his father's appeasement in the late 1930s. Macmillan admired him for it, and saw himself as the older and more experienced adviser who could knock the rougher edges off the young president's enthusiasms. This is where the Greek could really come into his own.

Macmillan was born when Queen Victoria was still on the throne. Kennedy was the first US president born in the twentieth century. He inherited the zeal of his predecessors to fight the forces of evil, and his first action was an even more farcical affair than Eisenhower's invasion of Lebanon. Unnerved by Fidel Castro's revolution in Cuba, and worried about Soviet influence in the US sphere, Eisenhower had made plans for an invasion to stir up an anti-Communist revolt. Macmillan was not unsympathetic. He wrote to

Eisenhower that Castro was "the very devil," indeed he was America's Nasser. Nothing happened, however, until Kennedy, without consulting Macmillan (there was no reason why he should have, of course), was persuaded to unleash Operation Bumpy Road.

Kennedy insisted that the US should not be identified as the aggressor. So 1,400 Cuban desperados, secretly trained by the CIA, came ashore at the Bay of Pigs on April 17, 1961, after a number of B-26 bombers, rather ineptly disguised as Cuban planes flown by defectors, had bombed Cuban airfields without much effect. There was never any chance of a popular rebellion. The Cuban military was much too formidable for the ragtag invaders. Kennedy refused to use overt US military force to save the invasion. Bumpy Road soon ended in a ridiculous failure.

Macmillan was not especially fazed. He rather approved of the way Kennedy took responsibility for his blunder. The risk of American interventions in Asia worried him more. Eisenhower had already alarmed Macmillan by meddling in Laos, where a CIA-backed but weak military leader named Phoumi Nosavan was fighting off a Communist insurgency (the Pathet Lao) backed by North Vietnam and China. Phoumi was calling for military help from US and anti-Communist allies in the Southeast Asian Treaty Organization (SEATO), the Asia Pacific version of NATO. Laos, it was thought, would be the place to make a stand against the Communist menace, lest other dominoes fall.

Britain had already divested itself from most of its Asian colonies: India and Burma in 1947, Sri Lanka (still called Ceylon) in 1948. And the same thing was happening in Africa, where Macmillan made his famous speech in 1960 about "the wind of change . . . blowing through this continent." Macmillan, although as wary of Communism as the Americans, was inclined to advise US presidents, if asked, to stay out of Asian conflicts. But his response to Eisenhower's plans for Laos was in line with the usual British reactions to dilemmas thrown up by US interventions: "This is a most dangerous situation for us. If SEATO intervenes (Thais, US and ourselves) it will cause trouble in India, Malaya and Singapore. If we keep out and let US do a 'Suez' on their own, we split the alliance."[20]

Following Eisenhower, Kennedy also toyed with the idea of stopping Communism in Laos. His undersecretary of state, Chester Bowles, made a common argument for war. The US, he advised, was "going to have to fight the Chinese anyway in 2, 3, 5, or 10 years, and it was just a question of where, when, and how."[21] When Macmillan heard that Kennedy might be persuaded that the US should move into Laos if SEATO refused to act, he responded in a meeting with the president in Key West with one word: "Don't." But he was concerned, as always, about a rift in the Special Relationship. Which is why he was also convinced that Britain should support the Americans, whatever they decided to do, "if we are to have influence in future with the President and the new administration."[22]

In the end, Kennedy decided that Phoumi's Laotians were too half-hearted to be viable partners in the struggle against Communism. Laos would not be the right domino to start defending with military force. The proper place should be South Vietnam. Ngo Dinh Diem, the Catholic president, would be America's man. Unlike the Laotians, the Vietnamese were considered to be real fighters. In May 1961, Vice President Lyndon B. Johnson visited Saigon. He concluded from his trip that the loss of Vietnam would force the US to "fight on the beaches of Waikiki." Diem, he said, was "the Winston Churchill of today."[23]

Even as American minds were focused on Southeast Asia and Cuba (in "Operation Mongoose," the CIA was engaged in all kinds of bizarre scams to get rid of Castro), Macmillan was more concerned with trouble brewing in Berlin. As long as there was still freedom of movement, East Germans, and often the brightest and most enterprising among them, kept moving west in large numbers. In the summer of 1961, Walter Ulbricht, the German Communist leader, backed by Khrushchev, decided to build a wall to stop this human hemorrhage. Moscow threatened to hand over Berlin to the East Germans, which would upset the status quo and could push the Western allies out of the city. Hard-line advisers in Washington, including Dean Acheson, the former secretary of state, advocated sending tanks down the autobahn to confront the Communists. Macmillan was in favor of negotiations, a response that provoked cries of "Munich" from his right-wing critics in Britain and the US. Only a month before the wall went up, Macmillan himself had said that Western rights in Berlin should be defended, because "we have not forgotten the lessons learned so painfully in the thirties and we are not prepared to accept acts of force."[24]

"Munich" kept popping up in the oddest ways. One reason that Kennedy was so jumpy about Berlin was that he had been browbeaten by Khrushchev at a meeting in Vienna that was not quite a summit, but more a testing of wills, in June 1961. Khrushchev thought of Berlin as the "balls of the West." Kennedy was keen to show he knew how to protect the Western testicles, but he failed to convince the Soviet leader that he was more than an inexperienced, pampered son of a rich man. Flying to London from Vienna, Kennedy, suffering from excruciating back pain, was feeling low and demoralized. Macmillan, in a letter to the queen, wrote that Kennedy's efforts in Vienna reminded him "in a way of Lord Halifax or Mr. Neville Chamberlain trying to hold a conversation with Herr Hitler."[25]

Kennedy was inclined to agree with Macmillan that a wall was better than war. But German politicians, including Willy Brandt, the left-wing mayor of Berlin, as well as de Gaulle, denounced this diffident attitude. They feared that Germany was being sold out by Anglo-American appeasement. The wall went up and military conflict was averted. But tensions in the Western camp increased the apparent divide between "the Anglo-Saxons" and the Continentals. That Macmillan was always suspicious of the Germans, including Chancellor Adenauer, whom he should have had on his side in Britain's attempt to join the EEC, did not help.

The Cuban missile crisis in October of the following year, although once again a very dangerous war was avoided, might have unintentionally made the rift between Anglo-Americans and Continental Europeans even wider. The US had received hints already in the summer of 1962 that the Soviet Union was up to something in Cuba. Missile convoys were detected at sea. There were intelligence reports about rocket installations. One of the first people to whom Kennedy showed aerial photographs of Soviet nuclear missiles on Cuba in October was the British ambassador and the president's personal friend, David Ormsby-Gore. Macmillan was told on the same day, before members of Kennedy's cabinet were informed.

Macmillan, as was his wont, counseled caution and favored talking to the Russians. Kennedy's military advisers urged the president to strike the Soviet bases at once. The sinister air force chief Curtis LeMay, the destroyer of almost every city in Japan in World

War II, argued that any other course would be "almost as bad as the appeasement at Munich."[26] Many civilians in Kennedy's cabinet agreed. Kennedy, however, was more circumspect. He decided on a blockade to stop Soviet ships from reaching Cuba. If the ships refused to turn back, the situation could escalate into a nuclear war. Macmillan said in private that a blockade was probably illegal, but he expressed his warm support of the president in daily telephone calls. Much of the British press was highly critical of what they saw as reckless American brinkmanship, creating an atmosphere that Macmillan described as just "like Munich."[27] In the end, a deal was struck. Washington and Moscow stepped away from catastrophe. Khrushchev agreed to dismantle the missiles on Cuba in exchange for which NATO missiles would be withdrawn from Turkey.

Whether Macmillan's fatherly advice to Kennedy throughout the crisis amounted to much is debatable. Other Western allies were kept informed as well. But there was far more consultation with the British. Kennedy expressed his thanks in a letter to his "dear friend" in which he wrote, "Your heartening support publicly expressed and our daily conversations have been of inestimable value in these past days."[28] Kennedy also said that Macmillan was the only leader he felt comfortable taking into his confidence: "The others are all foreigners to me."[29] Macmillan noted in his diary with satisfaction that his government "had played our part perfectly. We were 'in on' and took full part in (and *almost responsibility*) for every American move. Our complete calm helped to keep the Europeans calm."[30]

This last claim may or may not have been true. But the peculiar intimacy of the Anglo-American hotline cannot but have strengthened the impression in Paris, Bonn, and other capitals that Britain's gaze was still fixed firmly on the Atlantic. This may be why de Gaulle, rather to Macmillan's consternation, liked to remind the prime minister of Churchill's 1944 remark to that effect.

On January 14, 1963, after sixteen months of painstaking negotiations, conducted in good faith by Britain and its European interlocutors, de Gaulle vetoed British entry into the EEC. He was never keen to begin with, of course. Ill feeling went back to World War II. But there had been an accumulation of more-recent events that closed his mind to British membership: the sense of betrayal after the joint invasion of Suez, the perception that the British were prepared to make a deal with the Soviets over Berlin, evoking memories of Yalta, when the Anglo-Americans, in the mind of de Gaulle (and conservatives in the US), sold out Eastern Europe. But the deciding issue, once more, had to do with the bomb—who had it, and when.

In 1960, Britain had been offered a long-range US missile called Skybolt, which could be fired from bombers. There had also been talk—taken by the British as a promise—of a submarine-launched missile called Polaris, which the US had already deployed for its own forces in Britain. Some of Kennedy's advisers—the "Europeanists"—were unhappy about this. They saw no point in Britain's privileged status. It would be better for the US to have more equal relations with Germany and France. Kennedy, despite his love of London society gossip and familiarity with the British prime minister, was a kind of Europeanist. He took the same view of European integration as Roosevelt had of decolonization. Both men applied US history to the outside world. On the anniversary of US independence, Kennedy made a speech in Philadelphia, calling for a European "Declaration of Independence," after which the US would "discuss with a United Europe the ways and means of forming a concrete Atlantic partnership."[31]

A common European defense force was suggested, which the British thought was nonsense. But Kennedy's feelings about the European continent remained ambivalent. He had told Macmillan earlier, in 1961, that he had come to believe that "it would be undesirable to assist France's efforts to create a nuclear capability."[32] Not because Kennedy was anti-French, but because he worried that Germany might demand nuclear weapons, too, a prospect that alarmed him. Complicating matters further was a meeting between Macmillan and de Gaulle in 1962, from which de Gaulle concluded that Britain had promised nuclear collaboration with France. Then, Secretary of Defense Robert McNamara, who had little time for independent nuclear forces outside the US, outraged the British by saying that Skybolt had technical flaws and would be scrapped, leaving the British with the impression that they had been deceived, or worse, were being edged out of the special nuclear relationship, thus upsetting the Special Relationship itself.

It was clearly time for another Anglo-American get-together, in Nassau this time, which was still a British territory. Macmillan was in a somber mood. He had reacted badly to Acheson's gibe about Britain losing an empire and looking for a role. One should never denigrate the British, he wrote in an open letter. A similar error had been made by another bunch of foreigners, including Louis XIV, Napoleon, and Hitler.

Kennedy's party was greeted at the airport by a band striking up the tune "Oh, Don't Deceive Me." Kennedy himself, once again suffering terrible back pain, was pumped full of drugs. Still, he managed to accompany the prime minister for a long walk under the palm trees. Macmillan lectured Kennedy on the specialness of the Special Relationship, and the history of nuclear cooperation going back to Roosevelt's time. Kennedy saw a good political reason, though not a military one, to mollify the British, and offered to pay half of the costs to develop Skybolt just for them. Macmillan then insisted on Polaris instead. Again, Kennedy gave in, much to the dismay of the Europeanists in his entourage.

One month later, de Gaulle said no to Britain's EEC membership. As already noted, his motives were varied, but Britain's special Polaris deal certainly must have contributed to his sense of being left out once again—even though Kennedy did actually offer him a similar deal. The French had in fact already tested their own atom bomb in 1960, and they would explode their first H-bomb eight years later.

This was not quite the end of bomb-related matters in the Kennedy-Macmillan years. Still bent on bringing the world leaders together to discuss ways to avoid a nuclear catastrophe, Macmillan succeeded in pushing for a summit in Moscow in 1963, which led to a treaty banning nuclear tests in the atmosphere, space, territorial waters, and the high seas. Khrushchev, shocked by the Cuban crisis, wanted this from the beginning. So did Kennedy, but Congress needed a lot of persuading. The treaty was signed by the US, Britain, and the Soviet Union. Lord Hailsham, representing Britain, described the event as "the last time that Britain appeared in international negotiations as a great power."[33]

The French remained aloof from the proceedings. When Kennedy wondered whether an attempt should not be made to get them on board, Macmillan wrote to his "dear friend" that de Gaulle should be stopped from ruining any understanding with the Russians by making intemperate remarks from the sidelines. Macmillan may well have been right about de Gaulle's stubborn obstructiveness, but his moment of triumph cannot have helped Britain's chances to enter Charlemagne's old empire.

The last meeting between president and prime minister took place in the prime minister's private country house, Birch Grove, in West Sussex. (Rather weirdly, around the corner from the house there is an establishment now called Munich Legends, a specialist in BMW cars.) It was the summer of 1963. The hedonistic spirit of the 1960s was fast catching up with Macmillan; his war minister, John Profumo, got himself tangled up in an affair with a "good-time girl" called Christine Keeler, who had also allegedly slept with the Russian naval attaché. The popular press, adopting its usual tone of scornful prurience, made the most of the scandal, involving drugs, black men, spies, and high-society sex parties. Profumo, having lied about his affair to Parliament, had to resign. Macmillan looked out of touch, evasive, and hapless.

Kennedy landed on the lawn at Birch Grove in a helicopter. Macmillan, dressed in an old tweed suit, made tea for the president's foreign policy team. Kennedy entertained a young typist in his bedroom, singing Irish shanties while he dangled her on his knee. The visit was a success. Macmillan wrote to Kennedy that their relationship had become as warm as Churchill's relations with Roosevelt. Four months later, Macmillan, in poor health, exhausted, and discredited by Profumo and yet another spy scandal, resigned as prime minister. One month later, on November 22, Kennedy was assassinated.

Even though Macmillan was succeeded for a short time by the aristocratic Alec Douglas-Home, the end of his premiership could be seen, at least superficially, as the end of upper-class rule in Britain. The Edwardian airs affected by Macmillan were fading from mainstream politics. "The grouse moor image," as Harold Wilson, leader of the Labour Party, described it, was doomed. Profumo's relations with the barely educated Keeler might suggest a break with old rules of social propriety, launching "Swinging London" and the new decade of sex, drugs, and rock 'n' roll. But there was a sting in the scandal that revealed a more complex reality.

The scapegoat in the whole affair was a man-about-town named Stephen Ward, who took pleasure in introducing his well-connected friends to willing playmates. Persecuted in the press, denounced by politicians, and swiftly abandoned by his grand cronies, he was blamed for the scandal and tried in court, despite evidence to the contrary, as a pimp. Before sentencing, he committed suicide. However, the men who brought Ward and Profumo down were not old-fashioned scolds from the fusty upper classes, but Labour Party politicians who appealed to class resentment. Harold Wilson made a moralizing speech, calling the scandal "a corrupted and poisoned appendix of a small and unrepresentative section of society." What the country needed, he said, was "the replacement of materialism and the worship of the golden calf by values, which exalt the spirit of service and the spirit of national dedication."[34] And so the second era of social democracy that would greatly increase social mobility in Britain began in a fit of priggish opportunism.

Lyndon B. Johnson was by no means a prig, but he was a far rougher character than the man he succeeded. He, too, would preside over changes in society that were for the better. In domestic politics, both Wilson and Johnson sped up social reforms already started by their predecessors. But, despite all their undoubted flaws, it is hard not to feel a twinge of nostalgia for the Kennedy-Macmillan duo that gave the Special Relationship a sense of style it would never recover.

Six

THE CLOSE
RELATIONSHIP

—————

Now, let me hold your hand
I wanna hold your hand
· LENNON AND MCCARTNEY, 1962

Neither Lyndon B. Johnson nor Harold Wilson had been leading figures in World War II. There was no wartime camaraderie to fall back on. Johnson had been a congressman and a naval officer, and Wilson served as a director of statistics at the Ministry of Fuel and Power. Both men came from relatively humble origins: Johnson from the rural Hill Country of Texas, and Wilson from a middling town in Yorkshire. Both made the most of their provincial accents. In Wilson's case, this was quite a fashionable thing to do in the 1960s, when a new generation of actors and pop stars, rebelling against the stuffiness of BBC norms, proudly flagged their working-class origins, and sometimes exaggerated them. Although his carefully nurtured image of the pipe-smoking everyman was hardly the epitome of cool, Wilson received a lot of mileage out of opening up 10 Downing Street to the Beatles.

Tony Blair called Wilson Britain's first modern prime minister. Quite what Blair meant by "modern" was left vague. But Wilson linked his idea of socialism to the "scientific revolution." Britain, he told Labour Party members in 1963, would be forged "in the white heat of this revolution." Lyndon Johnson, too, came to power in an ebullient mood. He told an aide in 1964, "I'm sick of all the people who talk about the things we can't do. Hell, we're the richest country in the world, the most powerful. We can do it all."[1] Not only would he build the Great Society of racial equality, prosperity, and clean rivers and skies, but he'd stop Communism in Vietnam, or anywhere else for that matter, regardless of how much it might cost.

Before his election in 1964 as the first postwar socialist prime minister since Attlee, Wilson had been told by a close adviser that Johnson would be happy to welcome his partnership, more so than when "that Eastern aristocrat, Kennedy was in charge."[2] Wilson wanted to believe this. He didn't like aristocrats any more than LBJ did. Although he emerged from the left of the Labour Party with strong reservations about US Cold War politics, Wilson, like Ernest Bevin before him, strongly believed in Britain as a world power, and he took the traditional British view that continuing in this role meant cozying up to Washington. He once bragged that Britain's "frontiers were on the Himalayas."[3] This opinion was not shared by all his colleagues on the left, but then, according Roy Jenkins, Wilson's home secretary, the prime minister was more of an operator than an ideologue. Access to the White House, which Wilson always craved, sometimes to the dismay of the Americans, boosted his prestige at home, or so he thought.

This was one reason for Johnson to distrust Wilson. Johnson hated the idea of foreigners using him for their own domestic political advantage. It made him feel like a sucker. In fact, he didn't particularly care for foreigners in general, and made no exception for the British, even though, like many US presidents, he liked to invoke the hallowed legacy of Churchill. Foreigners who didn't want to be just like Americans made no sense to him. Anglophilia was something for namby-pamby members of the East Coast elite, most of whom Johnson despised. One other reason why Johnson took rather a dim view of Wilson was distinctly strange; he had heard rumors that Wilson was cheating on his wife by having an affair with his secretary, Marcia Williams. The rumor was almost certainly false, and Johnson, as a compulsive adulterer, was hardly in a position to moralize on this score.

Much more than Europe, it was the Pacific region, and Southeast Asia in particular, that engaged the US president's attention. One of the oddities of his years in power was the American insistence, after years of decrying British imperialism, that Britain continue to play an important military role "east of Suez," that is to say in the Persian Gulf, Hong Kong, Singapore, and in Malaysia, where roughly fifty thousand British troops were assisting the former colony in its confrontation with Indonesia, whose president, Sukarno, flirting with Communists at home and backed by China and the Soviet Union abroad, was seen as a serious enemy in the Cold War. Without British help to police the East, Johnson was worried that the US, drawn ever more deeply into Vietnam, would be left on its own, exposed to domestic as well as worldwide opprobrium. And this could spur the American isolationists back into action.

Continuing to be a world power, even as a junior partner of the US, had been draining British government resources for years. With the pound under constant pressure, and a huge government debt, Britain could not afford to carry on like this for much longer without American financial help to keep afloat. This is why important figures to the left of Wilson, such as Richard Crossman, the minister of housing, saw Wilson's policy as an extravagant form of hubris that should be abandoned. He wrote in his diary in January 1965 that Wilson had been "responsible for an over-commitment in overseas expenditure almost as burdensome—if not more burdensome—than that to which Ernest Bevin committed us in 1945, and for the same reason: because of our attachment to the Anglo-American special relationship and because of our belief that it is only through the existence of this relationship that we can survive outside Europe."[4]

Wilson thought that surviving outside Europe was a goal worth pursuing, certainly in the early years of his government. When Britain applied for EEC membership in 1961, Wilson had claimed that if it came to a choice between the Commonwealth and Europe, "we are not entitled to sell our friends and kinsmen down the river for a problematical and marginal advantage in selling washing machines in Dusseldorf."[5] He ridiculed Edward Heath, the British negotiator in Brussels, for rolling on his back like a spaniel every time the French made encouraging noises.

But if the British were divided over their proper post-imperial role, then so were interested American observers. The Europeanists, whom Johnson had inherited from the Kennedy administration, saw no merit in British nuclear independence, or indeed in the Special Relationship. George Ball wrote a memo to President Johnson in September 1965 that repeated what he had been saying for years: "Britain must recognize that she is no longer the center of a world system but that she can nevertheless play a critical role by applying her talents and resources to the leadership of Western Europe. We, on our part, should face the fact that it is basically unhealthy to encourage the United Kingdom to continue as America's poor relation, living beyond her means by periodic American bailouts."[6]

These eminently sensible words would not have impressed Harold Wilson on his first trip to Johnson's White House in December 1964. He craved a bigger stage. Some saw this as the delusion of grandeur of a "Yorkshire Walter Mitty."* Wilson's original suggestion for the December summit in Washington was to travel by warship as Churchill had done during the war. The idea was quickly dropped as impractical.

Johnson had been less keen to see Wilson than vice versa, and he began proceedings by haranguing the prime minister about the effrontery of his predecessor, Alec Douglas-Home, in selling British buses to Cuba. But there was a good reason for the president to be relatively civil. He very much wanted British support in Vietnam, preferably by sending British troops, even if they were just a token bunch of bagpipers in kilts; the important thing was to have the Union Jack flying in Saigon alongside the Stars and Stripes.

Wilson, to his great credit, continued to resist this idea. His excuse was that British military forces were already overstretched in Malaysia. And an active British presence in Vietnam would cause him great political damage, since he would lose the left wing of his own party. Johnson was enough of a political professional to see Wilson's predicament, and he didn't push him too hard on this occasion. But he never let go of the issue, either, and as he became increasingly obsessed by the war, Johnson was not averse to grabbing Wilson by the lapels, metaphorically at least, while hinting that US support of the pound should be repaid with more concrete support

---

* Walter Mitty was a fantasist with delusions of grandeur invented in a short story by James Thurber, which was made into a film with Danny Kaye in 1947, and remade with Ben Stiller in 2013.

in Vietnam. Wilson, squeezed between the anti-war Left at home and a bully in the White House whom he desperately wanted to please, never wavered from his policy of backing the Vietnam War in words, without sending even one soldier to help the Americans fight it.

The other topic of discussion was the American plan for a Multilateral Force (MLF). In this proposal, warships and submarines, manned by international crews from the various NATO countries, would be equipped with Polaris ballistic missiles. This would allow the Germans to play a bigger role in defense of the West. The idea had already been discussed when Churchill came to visit Eisenhower. Churchill then became tiresome on the subject of international forces getting hopelessly tangled up in Babylonian confusion. Wilson's socialists didn't like the prospect any better, precisely because they didn't want Germans anywhere near a nuclear button, and preferred to keep Polaris to themselves. They also worried about unduly irritating the Russians. What they were prepared to do instead was to help build an Atlantic Nuclear Force (ANF), with British and American nuclear submarines operating under the NATO umbrella. But they insisted that the US should retain its veto power on the use of force, lest Europeans do something rash. This never came to anything. But the MLF, too, was quietly ditched, to great British relief.

What the British and American leaders really thought of the Special Relationship in 1964 cannot be easily gleaned from the speeches and toasts that were meant to celebrate it in public. Wilson may have had the reputation of a wily fence-sitter and a less-than-trustworthy operator, but his speech was the more straightforward. He stressed a close relationship, rather than a special one, which would no longer be based "on our past grandeur." Johnson, on the other hand, sprinkled his state dinner speech with the usual guff about "kinship," "Saxon times," the "Magna Carta," "our comradeship in two world wars," and common efforts to build "lasting peace." It was weirdly Churchillian for a hard-nosed Texan whose interest in and love for things English had always been limited.

Indeed, Johnson often said that he felt closer to Germany than to Britain, and his meetings with the rotund German chancellor Ludwig Erhard seemed quite a bit warmer than his encounters with Wilson, who appeared too often either with cap in hand or offering unwelcome advice. Johnson's sentiments might have been personal, but more likely they reflected the relative power of nations, which was quickly shifting, certainly in economic terms, in Germany's favor.

The great satirist Peter Cook warned at the time that England was about to "sink giggling into the sea." Maybe. But British popular culture, spearheaded by the Beatles, reached a global eminence in the Wilson era that was unequaled before or since, not least in the US. British rock musicians excited young white Americans (and outraged their elders) by emulating black musical moves, often with a stylish twist of English humor. In essence, the British exported music, hairdressers, and fashion to the US, and imported a culture of protest back: giggling went one way and anger the other. The Vietnam War divided the political elites but brought a generation together (or at least part of a generation; one should not exaggerate the numbers). The English-speaking pop influence reached everywhere, from London all the way to Tokyo, and was fetishized at the height of the Cold War in countries controlled by the Soviet Union and its proxies.

In any case, Johnson and his team were fairly satisfied with Wilson's visit. At least he hadn't sold buses to Cuba. And the president had done his best to be tactful and did not press US advantage in what Johnson's national security adviser, McGeorge Bundy, called "a power play against a weak opponent." But Bundy also felt that Johnson's "generosity" should not be "misunderstood," for then it would not last long.[7] Wilson, once back in London, declared his meetings with the president as "one of the most important international discussions since the war." They showed, in his view, that Britain was still wanted at the "top table."[8] Indeed, he said, "we are now in a position to influence events more than ever before for the last ten years."[9]

This, as soon became clear, was not really the case. At home, Wilson was coming under more and more pressure for his support of the Vietnam War. It wasn't that he was gung ho for a military solution. He preferred to be a peace broker, bringing the various parties together at summit conferences, making sure that Britain could still play a constructive global role. But when he did support US bombing, he wanted Washington to give him a plausible excuse that it had been the inevitable response to North Vietnamese aggression.

One of Anthony Eden's achievements as foreign secretary was the signing of the Geneva accords in 1954, when the former French Indochina was divided into independent states: Democratic Republic of Vietnam (North), the State of Vietnam (South), Laos, and Cambodia. Elections to unify Vietnam were slated for 1956. Britain and the Soviet Union were co-chairs of the conference. To reach this agreement was already quite a feat, even though the outcome was flawed. While Eden pressed for a diplomatic solution, the French, backed by the US, were still threatening to thwart Communist ambitions with force. Since there was no agreement on who would supervise the general election in 1956, South Vietnam and the US refused to sign the accords.

Wilson, who liked to boast that he knew how to talk to the Russians as well as to the Americans, was very keen to chair a second Geneva conference to see whether peace in Vietnam could be negotiated. But Wilson's enthusiasm as a peace broker tended to get on Johnson's nerves. The president never thought the Vietnamese Communists could be trusted, and if any country should find a way to end the war on satisfactory terms, it should be the US.

In February 1965, these terms were nowhere in sight. US military action in Vietnam was escalating, with more and more troops being mobilized. The use of napalm and gas caused particular outrage in Britain. Fifty Labour MPs signed a motion to push the British government into putting active pressure on the Americans to achieve a cease-fire. A guerilla attack by South Vietnamese Communists (Vietcong) on a US barracks, costing the lives of thirty American servicemen, was likely to trigger even more violence. Wilson's instincts were like Attlee's when Eisenhower mentioned the use of nuclear arms in Korea; he needed to meet the US president right away, to talk sense into him. The White House expressed no desire for such an encounter. So Wilson called Johnson on the hotline on the night of February 11.

He got the full Johnson treatment. There was absolutely no call for "flapping around the Atlantic with our coattails out" whenever there was a problem. Wilson said he just wanted to talk. Johnson pointed out that that was what telephones were for. But Wilson was having serious problems in the House of Commons over Vietnam. Johnson said he had his own problems with Congress, and he saw no need to drag Wilson into it. Why didn't Wilson send troops? Surely, said Wilson, a trip to Washington would be a good idea. Johnson: "Why don't you run Malaysia and let me run Vietnam!"[10]

Wilson later recalled that never in the history of the Anglo-

American relationship had a leader spoken "in language one-tenth as abusive" as this. But his alarming phone conversation with LBJ didn't weaken his resolve to support US policies in Vietnam, at least in words. This was in marked contrast to General de Gaulle, who never passed up an opportunity to criticize the war. In 1966, he went out of his way to annoy the Americans by making a speech in Cambodia demanding the withdrawal of US troops from the region.

Wilson did, however, continue to press for negotiations with the North Vietnamese. One of the people who urged Johnson to hold firm was Eisenhower. Wilson, the old general told Johnson, had no experience with this kind of problem. The Americans had learned that "Munichs win nothing," and so the answer should be "not now boys."[11]

Pressure on Wilson at home did not come from just the Left. On April 30, 1965, the cover of the satirical magazine *Private Eye*, hardly a leftist journal, showed a cartoon of a cringing, doglike Wilson, pulling down LBJ's pants to lick his behind, with the US president thinking, "I've heard of a special relationship, but this is ridiculous."

Wilson was in a serious fix. As long as he wanted Britain to continue playing a role east of Suez, he needed US help to prop up the pound and avoid financial disaster. The reason he continued to think this role was vital for British fortunes was not just personal vanity or loyalty to "friends and kinsmen" of the Commonwealth, but because in the words of the British diplomat Paul Gore-Booth, "a British withdrawal would inevitably change the whole nature of our relationship with the United States and drastically reduce our influence on them."[12]

There was another reason for Wilson to stick to Washington at the risk of looking like "President Johnson's Poodle."[13] British

Commonwealth attachments, still a source of sentimental national pride, and not just among members of the royal family who enjoyed touring among the natives abroad, were being severely tested by events in Rhodesia, the country that would later become Zimbabwe. White British planters in Rhodesia were trying to stave off black majority rule in the former colony by forming a white supremacist government in Salisbury (later Harare) under an old RAF fighter ace named Ian Smith.

Smith and his friends were the kind of people Wilson loathed: coarse reactionaries, and keen supporters of apartheid. British prestige, not least among other members of the Commonwealth, especially in Africa, rested on the government's capacity to put a stop to Smith's plans. Ironically, African leaders were hoping for a British military intervention on their continent. But Wilson, always averse to military force, knew that Britain no longer had the wherewithal or the stomach for a war in Rhodesia. His great mistake was to make this perfectly plain to Smith so that even the threat was taken away, allowing the white Rhodesians to declare independence without risk in 1965.

All Wilson could do about it was to organize an economic boycott. Imports from Rhodesia were banned and oil supplies halted. Since oil companies outside British jurisdiction, in South Africa and elsewhere, failed to comply, this solution never really worked well. And without US support the embargo would not work at all. It didn't have to be spelled out to the British that American help in dealing with this postcolonial headache meant continued British backing for US wars in Southeast Asia. Rhodesia, for Wilson, became almost as much of an obsession as Suez had been for Eden, and Vietnam was for Johnson. It showed only too painfully the limitations of British power.

This awareness is also why Wilson slowly decided to get off the fence about Europe. This, and the constant pressure on the pound. Devaluation might be needed to revive the British economy, but it would make Britain's east-of-Suez position impossible to sustain. Wilson's colleagues were split on the question whether Britain should try again to join the EEC. Denis Healey, the secretary of defense, preferred to stay out and expected de Gaulle to veto British membership anyway. The position of George Brown, foreign secretary, was simple: "We've got to break with America, devalue and go into Europe."[14] Richard Crossman wavered, but was mostly in favor of a proudly socialist "Little England"—out of Asia, out of the Middle East, and aloof from the US, as well as the EEC. And if Britain should join after all, it should be a Gaullist Europe of sovereign nation-states. Anthony Wedgwood Benn, later named "Tony" Benn, leader of the party's left flank, still took the view that America was closer to Britain than Europe.

But most British politicians, Tory and Labour, came around to a common opinion that for economic reasons Britain could not afford to stay out of Europe. And some, including Wilson himself, now followed a line long promoted behind the scenes by pro-European Foreign Office mandarins, namely that Great Britain's best chance of remaining great was to be a leading power inside Europe. This is what the Europeanists in Washington had been urging the British to do for a long time as well.

And so, against the advice of some of his leading cabinet ministers, Wilson decided to go on a tour of European capitals in the first months of 1967 to sound out foreign leaders and see under what conditions they might let Britain in. Some saw this as a humiliating enterprise. And some saw it as another typical démarche of the Yorkshire Walter Mitty, banking on the vain hope that personal chemistry would do the trick. When Wilson was asked whether this "probing" exercise might not best be left to professional diplomats, Wilson said: "I *am* a professional."[15] Upon being reminded of de Gaulle's conviction that Britain's entry was like a Trojan horse from across the Atlantic, Wilson said he knew how to handle de Gaulle. He would play it by ear.

George Brown, Wilson's travel companion, was a bright and energetic foreign secretary, but he also had a chip on his shoulder about class (which is partly why Wilson chose him), and was prone to drunken outrages, yelling at ambassadors' wives, or shouting incoherently at colleagues after long boozy dinners. In the end, drink got the better of him, and Brown had to be quietly edged out of his job. But as foreign secretary he was at least a convinced European. His Continental interlocutors took his eccentricities in their stride.

On January 23, Wilson made a remarkable speech at Strasbourg. It was first of all a noteworthy piece of salesmanship, projecting his vision of Britain's revolutionary white heat onto the European scene. British innovation in science and technology would free Europe from its dependence on the US, he argued. A modern European economy, guided by British know-how and get-up-and-go, would save Europe from its "industrial helotry." But the most interesting thing about the speech was buried under the clichés, which might now seem disingenuous. But in fact they are a poignant illustration of Britain's struggle to find an identity somewhere between America and Europe.

Sentiments about the kith and kin of the Commonwealth seemed instantly forgotten. Instead, there in Strasbourg, there was another England, whose democracy was shaped by "forms of law, brought to England 900 years ago by men from France, themselves of Scandinavian origin." Indeed, a "thousand years ago, the name England itself, reflected the community of invaders and settlers." And had not Churchill, in 1940, suggested a union between Britain and France? Of course, Wilson's desire to liberate Europe from economic slavery to the US should not let people think that the US no longer mattered to Britain. He stressed that the US, too, was "a creation based on European diversity."

The speech was a transparent, rather plodding attempt to dissolve the old barriers between the Anglo-Saxon and Continental worlds. De Gaulle's initial response was polite and noncommittal. The general had the impression, he said, of an England that wished to "moor itself alongside the continent."[16] In Wilson's typically rosy interpretation, de Gaulle's reference to "mooring alongside" was a historic breakthrough. It was not.

Back in Britain, Wilson's continued backing of the Vietnam War was turning the first modern British prime minister into a hate figure for the growing number of anti-war protesters. Wilson was often pelted with eggs and tomatoes or called a "fascist pig" whenever he visited a university, and his honorary membership to the Cambridge University Labour Club was taken away from him. In December 1965, he had still been awed by the invitation to help light the Christmas tree on the White House lawn, the first such honor, he noted with pride, to be bestowed on a British prime minister since Winston Churchill in 1945. Now he was treated at home as an accomplice of war criminals.

One thing Wilson refused to do was to endorse US bombing of North Vietnamese cities. When the US did just that in the summer of 1966, in Operation Rolling Thunder, aimed at fuel depots in Hanoi and Haiphong, Wilson was forced to formally disassociate the

British government from the bombing. But he immediately sent an apologetic note to Johnson, assuring him that although he was forced by political circumstances to make a statement on the bombing, this by no means implied a weakening of Wilson's support for the war.

Wilson was once again eager to meet Johnson in person so he could explain himself further. But American diplomats advised that the president had been very upset by Wilson's decision to disassociate Britain from American bombing tactics. It was understood on the American side that the prime minister had to make such statements from time to time so as not to be seen as a stooge. But if Wilson wanted to come to Washington, he should make sure not to antagonize the White House any further. Anti-war sentiment in Britain was making the Special Relationship very hard to maintain for Wilson, but he had one advantage of coming from the left. The Americans were well aware that receiving support from a Labour prime minister was more valuable than from a Tory. They agreed to receive Wilson in July.

The trip proved to be an unexpected success. Wilson did everything to reassure the US of Britain's goodwill. Naturally, his support for the war was as firm as ever. Britain would continue to play its role east of Suez, and also keep a military presence in Germany. And the balance-of-payments problem would surely be solved. Wilson repeated in Washington the cocky slogan he would later use on his tour of European capitals: "We mean business." Johnson was duly reassured. And what promised to be a frosty encounter became a slightly bizarre Anglo-American lovefest, capped by a hastily written lunchtime speech by the president, in which he not only dredged up Shakespeare and Milton but also expressed the following astonishing sentiment: "In World War II, Mr. Prime Minister, England saved herself by fortitude and the world by example. You personally are asking of the British people today the same fortitude—the same resolve—that turned the tide in those days."

Wilson modestly told colleagues that the effusiveness of Johnson's words and the comparison to Churchill were a trifle embarrassing. Not all his colleagues took him at his word. Wilson said something else on the same occasion, recorded in Richard Crossman's diary: "What I have fixed with LBJ is enough to make de Gaulle foam at the mouth. We needn't really worry now about any possibilities of going into Europe."[17] This is astounding if one considers that Wilson's European tour would begin only six months later. In that same year, even as the Beatles' performance of "All You Need Is Love" was broadcast live from the Abbey Road studios by satellite to 350 million viewers all over the world, the British government decided to devalue the pound, give up its military bases east of Suez (except for Hong Kong), and reapply for EEC membership.

Once again, General de Gaulle resolutely turned the British application down. He cited the parlous state of the British economy. He might also have said something along the lines of his first veto, namely that England didn't amount to much anymore. But the chief thing in his mind was that Britain was still an "Anglo-Saxon" country, too close to the US and unable to fit into a common European home (run by France, of course). This was a nasty blow, but considering what Wilson had told his ministers, flush from his last visit to Washington, there was an element of just deserts.

Of all Britain's radical moves in 1967, it was the planned abdication of responsibility east of Suez that upset many Americans in government most. Some members of Wilson's cabinet, such as the defense secretary Denis Healey, tried to cut the defense budget while still hoping to keep Britain's bases in Asia and the Persian Gulf open. But this would only result in making promises the country could no longer afford to keep. That is why it was thought best to cut British losses and retreat. President Johnson saw this as the final confirmation that Britain was withdrawing from world affairs. The structure of peacekeeping, in his view, would be "shaken to its foundations" and "our own capability and political will could be gravely weakened if we have to man the ramparts alone."[18]

In fact, however, Johnson had already lost confidence in Britain after Wilson's public disassociation from the bombing of Hanoi and Haiphong. Even though Wilson still expected to be fully informed, if not always consulted, about US military moves as the reward for supporting LBJ's war, this was no longer the case. Being kept out of the loop almost caused a serious rift in Anglo-American relations in the early months of 1967. The Soviet deputy premier Alexei Kosygin was visiting Britain in February. Wilson saw this as a perfect opportunity for another peace-finding exercise. He would act as the intermediary between the US and the Soviet Union. Then the Russians could persuade their Asian friends to stop fighting, if the US would halt the bombing.

Partly to keep Wilson happy and onside, the Americans let him go ahead. Kosygin seemed forthcoming too. There was talk of another Geneva conference co-chaired by Britain and the Soviet Union. In private, Wilson informed Kosygin of the American conditions for a halt to their bombing of North Vietnam. They would do so once they were assured that the Vietnamese would stop infiltrating troops and weapons into the south. Kosygin wanted this in writing so he could pass it on to Hanoi. Wilson thought a great diplomatic coup was in the making. Then, on the night of February 10, shortly before Kosygin boarded an overnight train to Scotland, everything fell apart. Without informing the British or even their own representatives in London, the Americans had submitted a very different demand to the Vietnamese: assurance was not enough; the bombing would be halted only once infiltration had actually stopped. A new document had to be hastily dispatched to the railway station and thrust into the Russian's hands just as he was boarding his train. The deal went nowhere.

Wilson was furious. Johnson was furious. And when Chester Cooper, who had been sent to London by the CIA, complained to Walt Rostow that he and the British were left looking like idiots, the national security adviser shouted down the phone, "Well, we don't give a goddam about you and we don't give a goddam about Wilson. . . . You damn well change it!"[19]

Even more damning was Cooper's own later comment on the sorry affair. He said that Wilson had always been far too optimistic, and that "the US administration regarded Wilson at best as marginal, at worst as a nuisance and did not bother to keep him informed of their own thinking even when he thought he was negotiating on their behalf."[20]

And so the war went on, ever bloodier, with Johnson, looking exhausted and defeated, gazing out on crowds at the gates of the White House shouting, "Hey, hey, LBJ, how many kids did you kill today?" He now knew that the US could not "do it all." His Great Society was being severely undermined by the sheer expense of a war he could not win. Walter Cronkite, America's fatherly newscaster, concluded in February 1968, after Vietcong had managed to fight their way into the US embassy grounds in Saigon, that "we've been too often disappointed by the optimism of the American leaders."

Wilson began the year of youth revolts all over the world with a diminished currency, a vetoed application to join the EEC, the soon-to-begin withdrawal of British troops from east of Suez, and a clear lack of influence in the nation he had spent so much of his political capital to defend. A State Department assessment made note of the fact that the British prime minister was portrayed in the British press as a discredited, broken, pathetic little man. The least the leaders of Britain and the US, on the eve of Johnson's departure from the scene, could do was to be nice to one another.

Wilson asked to see the president in Washington one more time. They didn't have much of importance to say. The atmosphere was cordial. Friendship was toasted. But Wilson cannot have pleased his host with words about Vietnam aimed perhaps at an audience more than three thousand miles from Washington: "I have said a hundred times that this problem will never be solved by a military solution."[21] The strangest note in this great year for Anglo-American rock 'n' roll was a musical one. Wilson was greeted on his arrival at the state dinner by an orchestra striking up a fine musical rendering of an English poem first heard in 1907:

Ship me somewhere east of Suez, where the best is like the worst.

Seven

TO EUROPE
AND BACK

While preachers preach of evil fates
Teachers teach that knowledge waits
Can lead to hundred-dollar plates
Goodness hides behind its gates
But even the president of the United States
Sometimes must have to stand naked

· BOB DYLAN

Richard Nixon promised voters that he would end the war he had inherited from the Johnson administration. But his views on the second major American war in Asia since the defeat of the Japanese Empire were not substantially different from Johnson's. Eisenhower had already reminded LBJ of "Munich," as a fate to be avoided at all costs. Nixon thought that American goals had not been spelled out clearly enough to "the American people." Like so many presidents, Nixon, too, was guided by the legend of Churchill. This is what he wrote in his memoirs:

After the Munich Conference in 1937 [*sic*],* Winston Churchill warned the House of Commons that "the idea that safety can be purchased by throwing a small state to the wolves is a fatal delusion." What had been true of the betrayal of Czechoslovakia to Hitler in 1938 was no less true of the betrayal of South Vietnam to the Communists advocated by many in 1965. The fall of free Vietnam to outside aggression would have sent shock waves throughout Asia. As I put it in many of my speeches, "If America gives up on Vietnam, Asia will give up on America."

That really was the point. American prestige as guardian of the free world was at stake. Saving the South Vietnamese was a secondary concern. Nixon's conclusion: "To me the choice lay not, as many doves thought, between *this war* and *no war*—but between *this war* and a *bigger war later* when the Communists would be stronger and more confident."[1]

Nixon became president in January 1969. It would take almost six more years for the US to get out of Vietnam. More than twenty thousand Americans died there while Nixon was in power. We don't know exactly how many Vietnamese were killed during that period, hundreds of thousands at least. Equally hard to know is exactly how many Cambodians died as the result of a secret bombing campaign in Cambodia, called Operation Menu, starting with Operation Breakfast in March 1969, followed by Lunch, Snack, Dinner, and Dessert, and ending in May 1970. Some claim about one hundred thousand. Some say many more.

The only European leader to back Nixon's policies in Indochina, including the bombing campaigns, was the British prime minister Edward Heath, who took over from Harold Wilson in the summer of 1970. Heath subscribed to Nixon's idea that the US had to end the

---

* Nixon actually gets the date wrong. The conference was concluded on September 29, 1938.

war "with honor." A hasty retreat would be a disaster. This was one of the few issues upon which Heath was out of step with his European colleagues. In almost every other way, he deliberately turned his back on the Special Relationship and tried to transform Britain into a thoroughly European nation.

Harold Wilson was different. He had been happy to flatter even Richard Nixon just to be close to the US. When Nixon, at an official dinner in London, decided to overlook the fact that John Freeman, the former editor of *The New Statesman* and Wilson's new ambassador to Washington, had once published a hostile article about the president, Wilson slipped Nixon an obsequious note praising him for his extraordinary generosity: "Just proves my point. You can't guarantee being born a lord. It is possible—you've shown it—to be born a gentleman."[2]

Nixon was quite prepared to get along with Heath, however, and he positively revered the former prime minister and now foreign secretary Alec Douglas-Home. For a lower-middle-class Californian who feared and loathed the old East Coast elites perhaps even more than Johnson did, Nixon was oddly partial to the British, not for their style so much as for their sophisticated know-how—the Athenians in his Rome. Britain, as Nixon observed to the ambassador in Washington, "knew her way around."[3] The suave Old Etonian Douglas-Home, in his eyes, was the consummate Greek. So he was delighted when Heath's Conservatives won the election in 1970.

Heath and Nixon should have gotten along, since they were rather alike. Prickly about their modest backgrounds—Nixon's in suburban Southern California, where his father ran a gas station, and Heath's in a seaside resort in Kent, where his father worked in the building trade—both men were socially awkward but highly ambitious and intellectually gifted. The Conservatives had picked

Heath as their leader precisely because of his humble origins; they needed him to challenge the folksy Wilson. Unlike Wilson, however, Heath used his scholarship at Oxford to cover his provincial accent with a peculiar plummy way of speaking, which never endeared him to the common man or convinced any upper-class Tories. Like Nixon, despite his background, Heath lacked the popular touch. It was easier to admire some of their achievements than to like these two men. But that didn't mean they liked each other very much.

Normally, the first task for a fresh British prime minister was a quick trip to Washington. Heath chose to break with this tradition. His aim was to get Britain into the EEC as soon as possible, and he didn't want the French in particular to get the wrong idea. He saw all the flimflam around the Special Relationship as a bore and a hindrance. And so, feeling rather put out by Heath's apparent snub, Nixon made a trip to Britain first. Heath received the president at Chequers, the prime minister's official country residence, but because the queen was also invited, nothing of substance was discussed. Neither leader being strong on social niceties, it proved to be a stilted encounter. Heath, in his memoirs, rather glosses this over with vague talk about Nixon's "pleasingly human side."[4]

When Heath visited Washington later that year, he stated that references to a "special relationship" would upset other countries in Europe. There should be a "natural relationship" instead. This was of course what the Europeanists in US administrations had been saying for years. But it took the Nixon government by surprise. Henry Kissinger later recalled that Heath "dealt with us with an unsentimentality totally at variance with the 'special relationship.'" As a result, Nixon's relationship with Heath "was like that of a jilted lover."[5]

Heath was a patriotic Englishman who spoke very bad French,

but his attachment to Europe was deep and started early. In this respect, he was an unusual British politician. He visited Paris as a schoolboy in 1930. He was in Spain during the civil war, and traveled in Hitler's Germany as a student, where he actually met some of the Nazi leaders at an SS cocktail party on the Rhine. He could recall Himmler's "wet, soft, flabby handshake."[6] At an Oxford Union debate, Heath argued against Chamberlain's appeasement policy. During the war, he served as a lieutenant in the army, and was shocked by the devastation he witnessed on the European continent. He was also a spectator at the Nuremberg war crimes tribunal. All these experiences haunted him. He wrote, "Europe had once more destroyed itself. This must never be allowed to happen again. . . . Reconciliation and reconstruction must be our tasks."[7]

The Cold War and security had persuaded Macmillan to apply for membership in the EEC. Wilson dithered, but then decided that Britain could not afford to be isolated from European economic progress. With Heath it was the memory of war. (One of his closest friends at Oxford was a relative of mine, a Jewish refugee from Germany.) That is what made Heath a truly European politician, whose outlook was shared by Continental leaders. His finest hour came on May 21, 1971, when he finally managed to get Britain into Europe. It couldn't have happened under Charles de Gaulle. But the new French president, Georges Pompidou, took a less rigid view of the Anglo-Saxons. Sitting next to a beaming Heath at the Élysée Palace, in the same room where de Gaulle had vetoed British entry before, Pompidou reminded the press corps how many people used to believe that Britain was not European and did not wish to be. However, "ladies and gentleman, you see tonight before you two men who are convinced to the contrary."[8]

Whether most people in Britain felt that way is doubtful.

Right-wing members of Heath's party were opposed, as was the Left of the Labour Party. The question of parliamentary sovereignty came up, there were some television debates on the consequences of having to abide by laws executed by unelected supranational institutions. This was an important matter, which ought to have been taken more seriously. Heath fudged it by claiming there would be no erosion of "essential national sovereignty." What "essential" meant in this case was deliberately left vague. But after years of haggling with Europeans over sugar, butter, and other economic matters, earning him the nickname "Grocer," Heath managed to cobble together enough votes from pro-Europeans in both major parties to get British entry approved by Parliament. Typically, while his colleagues celebrated this considerable feat at boisterous festivities all over town, Heath repaired alone to 10 Downing Street, where he played a Bach fugue on his clavichord.

That Britain's membership in the EEC was not just an economic move but also very much a political one was left in little doubt by the Grocer. But Britain in 1971 had changed a great deal from the Britain in 1945. The unquestioned sense of superiority was no longer as much in evidence. An endless succession of financial crises had made the British feel vulnerable. Inflation was harming consumers. The pound was under constant siege. Unemployment was increasing. And the member states of the EEC had risen from the ashes of war very swiftly to become a major economic force in the world. This is precisely what made the US nervous. The European allies, although still dependent on the US for their security, could no longer be treated as needy vassal states. Their combined economies now began to compete seriously with the US economy. Heath had to reassure Nixon that Europe would be competitive but not confrontational. Which didn't stop the Americans from imposing a surcharge of 10 percent on imports and suspending convertibility of the US dollar to gold. This threatened to upend the agreement made with US allies at Bretton Woods in 1944, when the dollar became the world's reserve currency pegged to the price of gold. There were signs that Americans were beginning to chafe at some of the international institutions they had once created themselves.

Even though the prime minister finally achieved what US officials had been urging Britain to do all along, the Americans didn't necessarily like what they had wished for. Heath was in some ways more European than the Europeans. He suggested pooling British nuclear technology with France and establishing a Franco-British nuclear force that would become the core of European defense. It never happened, of course. The French were keen to hang on to their own nuclear force de frappe. And the British defense establishment was no more enthusiastic. Kissinger, who was appalled by the idea, recalled in his memoirs how Heath's scheme was received in Washington: "We faced in Heath the curiosity of a more benign British version of de Gaulle."[9]

There were other frictions. Although Heath was happy to support the American war in Vietnam, he had no desire to follow the US in the Indo-Pakistani War of 1971, when East Pakistan became Bangladesh after hundreds of thousands, and possibly many more, civilians were massacred by Pakistani troops and Muslim militants. India came to the rescue of the Bengali nationalists. Nixon and Kissinger backed Pakistan. They saw India as a Soviet proxy and needed Pakistan to help "open China." Heath thought Nixon and Kissinger were trying to use the Special Relationship to "land Britain in it as well." He saw his open disagreement with the US administration as a great step forward. Relations had changed. He admonished Americans to get used to it. He later wrote, "Now, there are some people who always want to nestle on the shoulder of an American president. That's no future for Britain."[10]

The Watergate hearings, which would bring Nixon's presidency to an end, began on May 17, 1973. Henry Kissinger decided to designate that same fateful year as the Year of Europe. His intention was to rethink American relations with Western Europe in light of renewed European economic strength and what was beginning to look like political cohesion. This, he argued, had "radically altered a relationship that was originally shaped in an era of European weakness and American predominance." What was needed, in his view, was a new Atlantic Charter. Kissinger made these remarks in a speech to the Pilgrims of Great Britain, traditionally the kind of occasion for venting much hot air on Milton, Magna Carta, liberty, and Churchill. But in the Heath era, there was a new twist, expressed by Kissinger: "The United Kingdom, we believe, is in a unique position. We welcome your membership in the European Community—though the loosening of some of our old ties has been painful at times. But you can make another historic contribution in helping develop between the United States and a unifying Europe the same special confidence and intimacy that benefitted our two nations for decades."[11]

Heath's response, though not exactly untrue, and certainly in line with his thinking, was typically somewhat lacking in grace. As he recalled it: "I said to him, 'Now you've done this, we must have a year of the United States. Who are you to propose that there should be a Year of Europe? You're not part of Europe.'"[12]

Heath never understood Kissinger. He thought the secretary of state was oblivious to European concerns, which Heath thought was strange for a man born in Germany. Kissinger, as Heath saw it, was so determined to be American that he refused to speak German to reporters in his own native country: "It was this lack of sensitivity which led to his mistaken creation of the 'Year of Europe.'"[13] In fact, it is probably Heath who was being obtuse. Both men were marked by the war, Kissinger perhaps even more so than the British prime minister. His family had to escape from persecution and mass murder. That is why he made a fetish of US power. But he didn't really get Heath either. Heath's attitude seemed perverse to Kissinger, who valued informal ties with America's closest traditional ally so much that he asked British Foreign Office mandarins to draft an agreement on nuclear defense instead of his own State Department officials. Kissinger couldn't fathom how "for the sake of an abstract doctrine of European unity . . . something which had been nurtured for a generation was being given up."[14] No doubt, many people in high places in Britain would have agreed with him.

And yet, Heath's distrust of Washington was not entirely misplaced. Despite all the rhetoric about mutual respect and traditional ties, in a crisis the US wanted the European allies, very much including Britain, to behave as American acolytes. This led to some very high-handed behavior.

When Egypt and Syria attacked Israel on the Day of Atonement (Yom Kippur) in October 1973, hoping to recover the territories occupied by Israel since the Six-Day War in 1967, the US immediately took Israel's side. The Americans demanded a full retreat by the Arab nations from land that used to be theirs. There was a great deal of political pressure in the US, then as now, to be on Israel's side in any conflict. And Middle Eastern politics to Kissinger were part of the great chess game in the Cold War. The Europeans, who were more dependent on Middle Eastern oil than the US, and in any case less sympathetic to the continued Israeli occupation of Arab land, took a different view. Britain, France, and Germany refused to allow the Americans to use bases in their countries to supply the Israelis. Kissinger was furious and saw this as a betrayal of the Atlantic alliance. He assumed that American and European interests were the same, and expected Europeans to show their loyalty to "the great goal of Atlantic cooperation." Heath, once again, chose to be on the side of Europe, even though the European countries were not completely united. The Dutch, still highly sensitive when it came to Jewish affairs, since the Germans sent about 75 percent of Dutch Jews to their deaths with the help of local collaborators, did allow the US to use American bases in Holland.

When the Israelis pushed back against Egyptian and Syrian armies, President Anwar Sadat asked for Soviet and American help to separate the warring sides and save Egypt from a disaster. The Russian leader, Leonid Brezhnev, said he was prepared to send troops, even if the US did not. Nixon was too drunk and preoccupied with Watergate to decide what to do. Without waking the president from his alcoholic slumber, Kissinger told the American military to be ready for war. Nuclear weapons forces were put on high alert. None of the European allies were consulted. Only Britain was told an hour before. That much was still left of the Special Relationship. So much for the Year of Europe.

Before Heath came to power, the British argument for backing Washington, regardless of the merit of US policies, was simple; it was the only way to retain British influence. Heath turned this around. In 1970, after his election, a top Foreign Office official wrote to Alec Douglas-Home: "We shall wish to keep our special links with the United States, e.g. in the intelligence and nuclear fields, so far as we can, but must recognize that unless we can find a new power base in Europe our influence in Washington is bound to decline and it will be necessary on occasion to demonstrate that for us Europe has priority."[15]

After Heath, such occasions became increasingly rare, and British policy reverted to its traditional mode. Alas for Heath, that moment came rather soon. Oil prices were jacked up by the Organization of the Petroleum Exporting Countries to punish nations for being insufficiently supportive of the Arabs in the Yom Kippur war. Then miners' strikes led by militant trade unions plunged the country into a dark and freezing "three-day week." Heath called an election in February 1974, asking who was running the country, the trade unions or his government? The result showed that it was unlikely to be any government under Heath. His general unpleasantness had left him without many friends. He was unable to form a new government. One of the few Tory politicians to speak kindly of this worthy but flawed figure was Margaret Thatcher, MP, a woman Heath would heartily loathe until the day he died. Four months later, Richard Nixon resigned in disgrace.

Members of the new administration under Gerald Ford were seriously worried about the new Labour government, once again led by a now less robust Harold Wilson, who didn't last in his job for more than two years. Americans feared that Labour would be taken over by leftists, such as Tony Benn, who were anti-American in a way that Heath never was. Heath actually believed that a strong European Britain would bolster the Atlantic alliance. But Labour left-wingers were thought to be unreliable members of NATO.

They might easily turn against nuclear defense. A *Wall Street Journal* commentator described England under Wilson as "John Bull with horns and a forked tail."[16] Two years later, Brent Scowcroft, President Ford's national security adviser, would claim that the condition of Britain was "considered by us to be the greatest single threat to the Western world."[17]

This worry was totally overblown. Wilson had never felt at home in Europe in the way Heath did. He didn't even like the food, especially the Mediterranean variety. His holidays were invariably spent pottering around a bungalow on the Scilly isles off the coast of Cornwall. In Wilson's own words: "I have never been an emotional European. I don't stand on the South coast, look towards the continent and say there's the new Jerusalem. . . . I am an emotional Commonwealth man."[18] And he never fawned on European leaders in the way he did on occupants of the White House. Left-wing members of his party may have been instinctively anti-American, but certainly not Wilson, or his foreign secretary, James Callaghan, who was a confirmed Atlanticist and talked often about the special cultural and historical ties between the great English-speaking peoples. "Sunny Jim," a man of even humbler origins than Wilson, got on famously with Henry Kissinger. When Wilson was reelected in 1974, Callaghan summoned British ambassadors to London, and told them, "I want you to understand that all this European enthusiasm is not what we are in business for."[19]

The first thing Wilson did, with great fanfare, later to be replicated by Margaret Thatcher, was to indulge in a fit of petulance and renegotiate the terms of British membership of the EEC. The newest member of the EEC was not just throwing its weight around but wanted to be seen to be doing so, especially at home. Shuttling back and forth to Brussels, Callaghan complained that Britain was paying too much money to the EEC, and that the Common Agricultural Policy was biased toward French farmers (which it was). The Europeans were keen enough for Britain to remain a member to allow UK representatives to grandstand at their expense. But they gave little away. It didn't really matter. Wilson, although never a Euro-enthusiast, wanted Britain to stay in the EEC. Left-wing skeptics in his party, however, still did not and asked for a national referendum. To appease them, Wilson needed to show that he could wring concessions from the Europeans, however trifling. And the first national referendum in the history of Britain was held in June 1975.

When Churchill suggested holding a referendum to extend his wartime coalition government in 1945, his then deputy prime minister Clement Attlee rejected the idea out of hand: "I could not consent to the introduction into our national life of a device so alien to all our traditions as the referendum which has only too often been the instrument of Nazism and Fascism."

In 1975, British voters were asked the same question as in 2016: In or out? While the wily Wilson publicly sat on the fence for a time, pro-European Tories and Labour politicians campaigned to stay in, and Wilson discreetly backed them. Again, the question of parliamentary sovereignty and the impact of the European "project" on democratic institutions came up, but never got much traction. The case was made that it was in Britain's interest not to be left out of Europe. What was distinctly lacking, even among most pro-Europeans, was a truly positive case for European integration. European idealism never quite made it across the Channel. Heath was unusual. Wilson and Callaghan were not.

Nonetheless, 67 percent of British voters said they wished to remain in the EEC, against 32 percent who said they didn't. Idealism didn't play much of a role in this outcome, and nor did any sense of common culture. The common culture of Western Europe was becoming more and more American anyway, and Britain was the most Americanized culture of all. To the intense annoyance of the French, English would gradually become the European lingua franca. Highly educated members of the generation of Anthony Eden and Harold Macmillan were still steeped in the classics of Greece, Rome, and nineteenth-century Europe, but that cut little ice with most people even in their time, and much less in 1975.

Jim Callaghan, first as Wilson's foreign secretary and then as prime minister, between 1976 and 1979, was finally persuaded that Britain was best off as a member of the EEC, but he remained, like so many British politicians on the left and the right, a lukewarm European. In a talk at the Labour Party conference in 1975, he expressed pride in Britain's role in the United Nations, but then said, "I always feel uneasy about some of the rhetoric used about the future of Europe." The German chancellor Helmut Schmidt was probably right when he claimed "the European vision" never meant much to Callaghan and that he was mired in Britain's historical role. Valéry Giscard d'Estaing, the French president, also found him "too English" with "a non-continental attitude."[20]

There are, of course, two ways of looking at this: that Britain would never fit into an integrating Europe and should have stayed out so that others could get on with it; or that Britain's democratic skepticism about pan-national arrangements was a welcome corrective to technocratic utopianism. My own view tends toward the latter. What is clear, though, is that the Americans correctly saw Callaghan as a traditional postwar British leader. In a Carter administration briefing book for the prime minister's visit to Washington in 1977, Callaghan was described as "well disposed towards the

United States" and "totally pragmatic" in his "commitment to Europe."[21]

So keen was Kissinger on Callaghan that when the latter was honored by the city of Cardiff, which he represented in Parliament, Kissinger flew over specially to join in the celebration. Huge numbers of demonstrators came to the city from all over Britain to protest against Kissinger's alleged crimes in Vietnam, Cambodia, Chile, and so on. Callaghan wasn't fazed. The protesters' feelings were not shared by the good people of Cardiff, he said. And he might well have been right.

When it suited them, Kissinger and Ford consulted Callaghan as the worldly elder statesman who could guide the Americans by his expertise, especially in Middle Eastern affairs. There were some disagreements, to be sure. A military coup in 1974, sponsored by the odious military junta in Greece, which was backed by the Nixon administration, toppled Archbishop Makarios, the president of Cyprus. Nixon was about to resign, and Kissinger was distracted. The Turks invaded Cyprus. Callaghan blamed the US for not doing more to stop them. Kissinger, despite his support of the Greek colonels, was wary of alienating Turkey, an important member of NATO, and didn't take kindly to being criticized by the British. A war between Greece and Turkey seemed imminent. In the end, a cease-fire was negotiated, and the junta, which had tormented Greece for seven years, was forced to make way for a democratic government in Athens.

Then there was the small matter of Belize, formerly British Honduras. This self-governing British protectorate was claimed by Guatemala, a US client state, whose democratically elected leader Jacobo Arbenz had been overthrown in 1954 by a CIA-orchestrated coup. Wanting to keep brutal but staunchly anti-Communist strong-men in Central America happy, Kissinger was content for Guate-mala to have Belize. So, over lunch, he asked Callaghan whether this could be arranged. Callaghan replied that it could not.

But on the whole, Callaghan succeeded in restoring some of the coziness of Anglo-American relations that Heath had deliberately disrupted. This continued under President Carter, even though the British found him harder going than the genial Gerald Ford. Cal-laghan might have found some common ground with Carter. Both came from puritanical Baptist backgrounds. Callaghan could never shake off a sense of guilt imbued by his Sunday school teachers about human sinfulness, quotations from the Gospels came readily to his lips, and he took a stern view of the loose sexual mores of Anglo-American youth culture.

Certainly, Callaghan did everything he could to court the new president. Indeed, he had already expressed his enthusiasm for the Special Relationship to Carter when he was still governor of Geor-gia. Trips were arranged in England, where Carter was treated to a joint visit to Newcastle. He was greeted there by the traditional chants of the local soccer team and presented with the autobiogra-phy of a famous trade union leader. Although difficult to imagine, this might have melted the ice. Callaghan was a former trade union negotiator, a skilled practitioner of the backslap and glad hand. But Carter's earnestness and priggish demeanor made him difficult to warm to. White House dinners, where the guests were asked to hold hands while Carter said grace, were a trial even for the Baptist PM. Still, both men, like most politicians, had a healthy dose of vanity. Callaghan had suits designed with pinstripes consisting of tiny Js and Cs, the letters of his monogram. His gift of a bolt of this precious cloth to be made into a suit for Carter, who shared the same initials, was apparently greatly treasured by the president.[22]

From Carter's religious beliefs came a devotion to human rights. Many imprisoned dissidents and persecuted people all over the world benefited from this. And standing up for human rights was no doubt admired in London, at least as an abstract principle. But Carter's moral zeal caused tensions, too, especially when his attention to human rights came too close to home, as for example in Ireland.

Carter was under some domestic pressure from groups, such as the Irish National Caucus, whose Washington director, F. B. O'Brien, wanted the president to raise the matter of human rights in Ireland with Callaghan (whose father, a sailor, was actually Irish). O'Brien wrote to Carter's national security adviser Zbigniew Brzezinski: "British patterns of torture do not seem to change much over the centuries; one need only travel to Charleston, South Carolina and view where the British tortured Americans in their own wine cellars."[23] Many more people have been tortured in South Carolina, of course, and not just by the British. But this missive does suggest the special flavor of Irish American sentiment.

As home secretary under Harold Wilson, Callaghan had actually handled Northern Irish affairs with some skill. He stood up to Ian Paisley and his fire-breathing Unionist Protestants. The notorious Protestant paramilitaries were being phased out, the Royal Ulster Constabulary was disarmed, the British army appeared to have mastered the situation, and Callaghan, ever the jovial negotiator, enjoyed quite good relations with both Catholics and Protestants in Northern Ireland. But things started sliding badly out of control after 1970, when the Conservatives were back in power. The "Provos" (Provisionals) of the Irish Republican Army, generously funded by sympathizers in the US, began a brutal campaign on the British mainland, with bombs placed in public buildings and railway stations, and gory assassinations of public figures. British paratroopers killed thirteen men and boys on January 30, 1972, known as "Bloody Sunday," in Londonderry.

To see the violent political divisions in Northern Ireland entirely from the perspective of human rights was a trifle naive. But that is what Carter did in his campaign speeches. To a group of Irish Americans he said that it was "a mistake for our country's government to stand quiet on the struggle of the Irish for peace, for the respect of human rights, and for unifying Ireland." It was certainly rude of James Molyneaux, the Unionist leader in Northern Ireland, to refer to Carter's utterances as the "irresponsible opportunism of this peanut politician."[24] But Carter might have been a bit more circumspect when he spoke just months after scores of people were badly injured from an IRA bomb set off at an exhibition center in London.

In fact, Carter's words were just that, words. He never actually did much about Northern Ireland. The president was advised by leading members of Congress that it was "extremely difficult to be critical of the British actions in Northern Ireland because of our traditional ally relationships with the United Kingdom."[25] Similar messages came from the State Department, which only strengthened its reputation among pro-Irish activists in the US as a place of effete Anglophiles. All Carter did was promise that the US would in one way or another be involved in finding a solution to the Troubles in Ireland. This didn't seriously affect his good relations with Callaghan. They were certainly better than Carter's relations with the German chancellor, Helmut Schmidt.

Schmidt despised Carter as an erratic provincial American bungler who was out of his depth in foreign affairs and whose lecturing on that subject not only was annoying but also undermined the national interests of other countries. Germany and France had signed contracts to sell nuclear reactors to Brazil and Pakistan. Carter, concerned about nuclear proliferation, especially to military dictatorships like Brazil, effectively put a stop to that. Ill feeling between the chancellor and the president was entirely mutual. Carter noted in his diary that "Helmut" was "somewhat unstable . . . postures and drones on, giving economic lessons when others are well aware of what he was saying."[26]

Tensions between Carter and his European counterparts, especially Schmidt, were less about who was right or wrong about any given issue than about the growing anomaly of economically very powerful countries being totally dependent on the US for their security. The postwar American order that once served as a model of freedom and generosity to Germans in particular now began to seem almost humiliating. This explains the erratic nature of Schmidt's own policies. In private he spoke to the Americans like a hardened Cold War warrior, asking for short-range nuclear missiles to be deployed in Europe to counter new Soviet weapons. But in speeches in Germany, he would pander to anti-American feelings and ask for a moratorium on nuclear arms in Europe. Carter pointed out that Schmidt himself had asked for the missiles. And when he warned that Schmidt's public posturing would weaken the Western alliance, Schmidt claimed to be deeply insulted.

Britain was torn as usual between its aspirations to continue to be America's special ally and its common interests with other Europeans. Callaghan tried to act as "the bridge" between Europe and the US. He actually got on well with Schmidt and explained in a letter to the US president that "Helmut is the man you must win back. Giscard will always go his own way, but Helmut is a strong

Atlanticist, moody and tempestuous, but basically on the side of the angels. If I may say so to you, I think it is vital that you give the impression of listening carefully to his views, of weighing them and of seeking agreement wherever you can."[27]

The word "impression" is telling and reflects the reality of Britain's own relationship with Washington. European dependence on its much more powerful patron, at least in military affairs, could not be expressed more clearly. To avoid humiliating its dependents, the US had to give the impression of listening to and taking seriously what they might have to say. The difference between Schmidt and most British prime ministers is that his frustrations were expressed in temper tantrums, whereas the British were more eager to please. But then Germany was in many ways a more powerful country than Britain now, and the gap would continue to grow.

One thing Britain did still have, unlike Germany, was a nuclear weapon. But if Schmidt had a problem juggling his Atlanticism with the instinctively anti-American left wing of his Social Democratic Party, so did Callaghan. The Polaris weapon system was very expensive and getting old. Important members of the Labour Party, backed by a strong civil antinuclear campaign, wanted to get rid of the weapons altogether. Callaghan was not so convinced of their military use himself, but still he decided they needed to be replaced by a new nuclear deterrent. Spending the money on strengthening conventional forces, which many Labour politicians advocated, might have made more sense, but Callaghan argued, in line with all his predecessors since the war, "To give up our status as nuclear weapon state would be a momentous step in British history."[28] Doing so, he believed, would mean a loss of influence in the US.

The decision to continue with a national nuclear defense was not just informed by an illusory attachment to the Special Relationship.

Germany, too, wanted Britain to have the bomb. Otherwise France would be the only European nation to have one. The German chancellor also insisted that he would permit American missiles on German soil only if they were deployed in other European countries too. With two national nuclear deterrents, Europe would seem a little less puny in relation to the US.

This was the general state of affairs when Callaghan, during a summit conference in Guadeloupe in January 1979, walked over to the hut where Carter was resting to discuss replacing Polaris. It is said that Callaghan surprised the president, who was just settling down in his underpants. The prime minister put it to Carter that on balance he thought it would be best for European defense if Britain evolved to the Trident submarine-launched system. Carter agreed that this would be a good idea. Costs could be discussed between experts later.

Britain alone would continue to have access to US nuclear technology. Intelligence would continue to be exchanged. In this sense, the relationship was still special. But for the rest it was largely symbolic. And the enormous cost of a nuclear defense system came at the price of neglecting more-conventional forces, which would soon cause a serious problem for Callaghan's successor, Margaret Thatcher, a figure whom Carter disliked at first sight. Whether people wanted this or not, Britain was now firmly embedded in Europe, important but no longer primus inter pares. Callaghan, perhaps more than his successor, was well aware of this fact. At a dinner in Bonn, hosted by Helmut Schmidt, Callaghan observed, "The mistake we made was to think that we won the war."

Eight

AN EXTRAORDINARY RELATIONSHIP

―――――

"'There are mad people in every nation who want war.' But especially nations which remember wars as victories rather than miseries, which fancy they are still islands. An Italian villager can imagine another nation as a liberator. An English football crowd, it seems, sees nations as game-cocks—bred only to fight."

· NEAL ASCHERSON, *THE OBSERVER*, 1985

James Callaghan had been a naval officer during World War II. Jimmy Carter was in training to be one. Neither Margaret Thatcher nor Ronald Reagan, their successors, took an active part in the war. She was a student at Oxford when the war ended, and he was stuck in the US in a motion picture unit. Reagan's relatively passive role was a bit of an embarrassment to him, but it wasn't really his fault. The army rejected him because of poor eyesight and deafness in one ear.

Possibly because neither Reagan nor Thatcher ever saw action, the war loomed large in their imaginations. Thatcher was the most self-consciously Churchillian of postwar British prime ministers, who was not above reminding fellow Europeans that "we" saved their skins, or that "we won the Second World War" (this was actually in response to reforms in the British health care system).[1] When she moved to 10 Downing Street, Thatcher hung a portrait of Churchill, which had been in her chambers at Westminster, in the Cabinet Room.

Reagan was known to sometimes confuse actual experience with the movies. He told the Israeli prime minister Yitzhak Shamir that he had witnessed the horrors of Nazi concentration camps in 1945, whereas in fact he had seen only film footage of the camps in a studio in Burbank, California. But he was not confused about his grand ambitions, which he laid out to the British Parliament—"a moment of kinship and homecoming in these hallowed halls"—less than two years after his election in 1980.[2] Liberally quoting from Churchill's defiant speech in Washington in 1941—"What kind of people do they think we are?"—Reagan spoke about "a crusade for freedom that will engage the faith and fortitude of the next generation."[3]

He was responding to an equally rousing talk by Margaret Thatcher, given during lunch on that same day, when she quoted General Eisenhower, "also much loved in this, our country," who "put it so well when he said, 'One truth must rule all we think and all we do. The unity of all who dwell in freedom is their only sure defense.'"[4]

This set the tone of the Reagan-Thatcher years: Churchill, kinship, freedom. The adversary was Communism, and the Soviet Union in particular, and not Nazis, but the sentiments harked back to earlier glory. Efforts, associated with Henry Kissinger, to reduce tensions through a policy of détente with the Soviets, were now considered weak-kneed. One of Thatcher's advisers, George Urban, later noted that he had added "some 'Churchillian' words and metaphors" to a speech she gave in the US, because he believed that Thatcher "was the most persuasive and eye-catching representative of the new Western determination to stop the Soviet Union."[5]

Fine speeches about kinship should of course not be taken at face value. Reagan was a Californian, born into a poor Midwestern Irish family whose ties to old Europe were tenuous at best. And Thatcher, more often than not, aligned British interests with those of Europe rather than with those of the US. But their respective projects, often joined, at least in sentiment, and often in practice, were to restore greatness to their nations, which had been battered in recent years by economic crises, imperial retreat, and humiliating military disasters in faraway countries, such as Vietnam and Iran.

Margaret Thatcher and Jimmy Carter, who had the ill luck to preside over some of those national humiliations, never really got along. The first time Carter met Thatcher at the White House, before she became prime minister, he was so irritated by her hectoring on foreign policy that he told his aides to keep her away from him. She claims in her memoirs to have admired Carter for being a pious Christian and "a man of obvious sincerity," and supported him in 1979 when Islamic revolutionaries held fifty-two American diplomats hostage in Teheran. The unintended consequences of Anglo-American shenanigans in Iran had finally come to a head: the pro-Western shah, restored to his throne in 1953 with the help of British and American intelligence services, was overthrown.

Always quick to spot Russian dangers to the West, in and outside Europe, Thatcher was less surprised than Carter apparently was when Soviet troops invaded Afghanistan in the same year: "I knew the beast."[6] She thought Carter's analysis of the world was "deeply flawed." His chief flaw, in her view, was that he underestimated the threat of Communism and was too critical of right-wing dictators who supported the US.[7]

Ronald Reagan impressed her much more than Carter ever had when he visited London in 1975 as a radical conservative ex-governor of California with presidential ambitions. Few took Reagan seriously then, especially in Britain, where people tended to view him as a simpleton. But Thatcher did. She received him in her office at Westminster in the presence of Winston Churchill, MP, the great man's grandson, whom she liked to trot out for visits by American politicians. She liked Reagan's ideas on shrinking the role of government, fighting socialists and Communists, and restoring American greatness. To her mind, as she recalls in her memoirs, he not only advocated American ideals, he "embodied them." Reagan was "the American dream in action."[8]

Thatcher was in many ways predisposed to admire the American dream. Her father, Alfred Roberts, a grocer and local Methodist preacher in provincial Lincolnshire, instilled in his daughter a distrust of foreigners who didn't speak native English, and a pull-your-socks-up work ethic that made her contemptuous of languid upper-class Englishmen who took their privileges too much for granted. Thatcher praised "the puritan morality of the founders of America."[9] Despite her affected way of speaking, contrived, like Edward Heath's, at Oxford, and polished through elocution lessons, Thatcher was not a social snob. She felt comfortable with the Jewish businessmen in her North London constituency who had often worked their way up from very little, and many of them admired her in return. The fact that at one point she had appointed five Jews to her cabinet elicited the rather characteristic remark from Harold

Macmillan that "the thing about Margaret's cabinet is that it includes more Old Estonians* than it does Old Etonians."[10]

I once had the chance to visit the mock-Georgian mansion of Leslie Wexner, an American textile magnate, near Columbus, Ohio. His Jewish parents had owned a clothing store. The very grand house was filled with fine paintings. There were horses on the grounds, rather like at an old English country house, as if in wait for men in pink coats to go riding to hounds. And there was Margaret Thatcher's thick autobiography picked out by a discreet spotlight on a small antique table in the hall, like a precious objet d'art. This seemed entirely fitting. She would have warmed to the self-made American quasi aristocrat much more easily than to most English noblemen living in real Georgian houses. Like Reagan, he embodied the American dream. (In fact, I was informed that the lady had indeed visited the house recently and had left the autographed copy herself.)

There was, however, a peculiar paradox built into the Reagan-Thatcher project to restore the greatness of their respective nations. Convinced, in George Urban's phrase, that Britain and the US were "in a state of declining moral health," their rhetoric was soaked in nostalgia for victories of World War II when Anglo-American power and prestige were at their zenith.[11] Churchill's ghost was constantly beckoned to promote their joint crusade for freedom from foreign tyranny. And yet, their zeal to bring back a radical form of economic liberalism meant a profound break with the postwar order that emerged from the Allied victories against Hitler and fascism.

The aim after 1945, in Britain, and in the US, too, was to ensure greater social and economic equality, a course already set by

---

* The fact that Estonia was not where most Jews came from is irrelevant; the name fitted the bon mot.

Roosevelt's New Deal. Clement Attlee's socialist government took this further than any American Democrat, let alone British Tory, would have done. But even Churchill, despite his hysterical comparison of Attlee's reforms to the work of the Gestapo, advocated a relatively moderate form of capitalism, which Thatcher would have dismissed as hopelessly "wet."

John Maynard Keynes, who advocated public spending, especially during a recession, to help keep people employed, remained the most influential Western economist until the late 1970s. Richard Nixon, a staunch Republican, was prepared to risk high inflation to keep unemployment down. But inflation in Britain caused such a run on the pound in 1976 that the British economy had to be bailed out by the International Monetary Fund. The demands of trade unions, often led by militant left-wing leaders, had brought down the governments of Heath, Wilson, and Callaghan. The Carter years were darkened by the twin ills of high inflation and low growth. Keynes's influence began to wane. The postwar consensus started to crack. And Reagan and Thatcher came to power with big ideas on how to remedy the situation.

Tax cuts, deregulation, unfettered free trade, "supply-side" economics, and the "rollback" of state intervention and union power were the stated recipe for restoring national greatness. Reagan put it this way in his inaugural address in 1981: "In this present crisis, government is not the solution to our problem; government is the problem." Margaret Thatcher put it another way seven years later: "Society. There is no such thing! There are individual men and women, and there are families, and no government can do anything except through people and people do things for themselves first."[12]

A correction of Keynesianism may have been sensible, but this demolition of the postwar economic order that the US and Britain had done so much to set up was not at all conservative. It did more to bring down traditional arrangements and institutions than any socialist government had ever attempted. Fortunes would be made on the London stock market when public utilities, such as telecommunications, transport, and gas, were put into private hands. Tax cuts made the wealthiest citizens even wealthier. Some people did very nicely when public housing was put on the market. But the human cost in old industrial towns and mining communities was immense. Large numbers of people lost their jobs, leaving them in a rage that would last well into the twenty-first century, with catastrophic consequences. Thatcher saw her conflict with the trade unions as a war. She treated miners who went on strike like traitors.

Thatcher and Reagan habitually presented themselves and one another as embodiments of their great nations, she a kind of Boudicca of the British tribe, and he a rugged individualist of the West. They prided themselves on standing up for old Anglo-Saxon values—robust free enterprise versus French- or Japanese-style statism. But the main inspiration behind their fervor to unleash the markets from the kind of state intervention advocated by the very British Keynes was actually a product of the Austro-Hungarian Empire.

One of Thatcher's favorite authors was Friedrich August von Hayek, the Viennese economist, who held that big government and planned economies were always ruinous. His argument, developed during World War II, which Thatcher bandied about to anyone within earshot, was that socialism led straight to serfdom. Hayek's version of economic liberalism became part of the Anglo-American crusade for freedom. Many hands might have gone into writing Thatcher's memoirs, but her tone is unmistakable:

As the years went by, the British example steadily influenced other countries in different continents, particularly in economic policy. But Ronald Reagan's election was of immediate and fundamental importance, because it demonstrated that the United States, the greatest force for liberty that the world has known, was about to reassert a self-confident leadership in world affairs.[13]

On the question of how and where the US should assert leadership, Thatcher and Reagan were not always of one mind. In 1981, on a visit to Washington, Thatcher told Reagan that people on both sides of the Atlantic had "total faith" in him to make the right decisions for "the liberty of common humanity." She quoted Wordsworth: "We must be free or die who speak the tongue that Shakespeare spake."[14] And Reagan hailed Thatcher with stirring words about shared "laws and literature, blood, and moral fiber."[15]

But when Reagan responded to the Polish workers' rebellion ("Solidarity") against Communist dictatorship in the same year, and the subsequent imposition of martial law, by ordering economic sanctions against the Soviet Union, Thatcher vigorously opposed him. Various European countries, including Britain, had signed contracts to supply equipment for a gas pipeline to Siberia. Breaking those agreements, in Thatcher's view, would hurt Europeans more than the Soviets. Despite all her devotion to the Special Relationship, and her hostility to Communism, she took the side of the Germans and the French against heavy-handed US efforts to bully NATO allies into harming their national interests.

Just over a year later, Argentinian troops landed on the beaches of the Falkland Islands. There was very little that a handful of Royal Marines could do to stop them from occupying this tiny speck of British territory off the coast of Argentina. The military junta in Buenos Aires was ecstatic. The Islas Malvinas, as Argentinians call the Falklands, claimed by Britain since the seventeenth century, were about to fall into Argentinian hands. Rex Hunt, the governor of the Falklands, said that he was "not surrendering to the bloody Argies, certainly not."[16] But surrender he very swiftly did. General Leopoldo Galtieri, the unpopular military strongman, could now bask in the tribute of vast crowds in Buenos Aires cheering for "the spirit of Argentina." Thatcher made a speech in Parliament about the need to defend the few hardy inhabitants of the cold and windy archipelago, whom she described as loyal subjects of the British Crown. This was a matter of principle to her. But there was also, perhaps, some of that same nagging anxiety that once drove Anthony Eden to his disastrous adventure in Suez, articulated this time by Alan Clark, raffish right-wing diarist, Tory member of Parliament, and devotee of the Iron Lady. On hearing the news of the invasion, he said to his wife, "It's all over. We're a Third World Country, no good for anything."[17]

And so, after considerable debate inside her cabinet, Thatcher, who had had no experience with war, dispatched a task force of the Royal Navy, with two aircraft carriers, to liberate the Falklands, eight thousand miles from Britain. Viewed from Washington, DC, the whole thing looked faintly ludicrous, something out of a Gilbert and Sullivan operetta. In Buenos Aires, the great Argentinian novelist Jorge Luis Borges called it "a fight between two bald men over a comb." Reagan himself did not really see why it was necessary to make such a fuss over a "little ice-cold bunch of land."[18] He remonstrated with General Galtieri to halt the invasion, but to no avail. Important figures in his government, including Al Haig, the secretary of state, wanted to stop the British from using force and to negotiate with the junta instead. "Pure Haigism," in Thatcher's disdainful words.[19]

Kinship and the language that Shakespeare spake did not count for much when American interests were at stake. Keeping Argentina onside was more important to many US policymakers than helping an old ally fight over a colonial relic. The worry that Cuba and the Soviet Union would gain influence in South America was reason enough to support military dictators who tortured their own people—a practice in which they were often instructed by expert American tutors. Jeane Kirkpatrick, US ambassador to the UN, had persuaded Reagan with her argument that authoritarians were worth defending against the common Communist foe. Richard V. Allen, Reagan's national security adviser, called Galtieri a "majestic general." Besides, Argentina felt closer to many Americans than foggy Britain.

But they all underestimated Margaret Thatcher's cussedness. She rejected with ill-disguised repugnance all American admonishments that she should compromise with Galtieri. She was not about to be robbed of her finest hour. Munich was invoked once again: "We in Britain had the experience of appeasing dictators."[20] She harangued Al Haig in London about being asked by the Americans to behave like Neville Chamberlain in 1938. To press her points home, she drew Haig's attention to portraits of the Duke of Wellington and Lord Nelson on the Downing Street walls. Thatcher's "war cabinet" discussed strategy at the prime ministerial country house. She wrote in her memoirs, "I am glad that Chequers played quite a part in the Falklands story. Winston had used it quite a lot during World War II and its atmosphere helped to get us all together."[21]

But Thatcher did have some important allies in her splendid little war, some of them rather unexpected. The French socialist president François Mitterrand gave her vital military assistance. The Democratic senator Joe Biden told the British ambassador, "We're

with you, because you're British."[22] George Shultz, secretary of
state after Al Haig resigned, admired Thatcher's demonstration that
a Western democracy would fight for its principles. The Anglo-
American intelligence agencies were cooperating closely as usual.
But Britain's most important supporter was Caspar Weinberger, the
US secretary of defense. He was a firm believer in the Atlantic alliance, an Episcopalian despite his partly Jewish origins, and a besot-
ted admirer of Churchill. There was no doubt in his mind that
Britain should prevail, and he did everything to make sure that it
did. British forces were offered a base on Ascension Island, leased
from Britain by the US, and supplied with ammunition, jet fuel,
antiaircraft systems, and missiles, without which the war could
never have been won.

On June 14, 1982, the Union Jack flew over the governor's house
once more. The conflict had lasted seventy-four days. Nine hundred seven people, including three civilians, were killed. Some
Americans still grumbled that US interests had been badly damaged by British folie de grandeur. But Thatcher's political fortunes
soared. Strikes and riots, resulting from her economic policies, were
temporarily forgotten in the hour of victory. And so was the fact that
the vast expense of maintaining a national nuclear deterrence had
forced Thatcher's government to radically cut the budget for conventional defense forces, including the Royal Navy, which had
tempted the Argentinians to make their move in the first place.

In Britain's long and often bloodstained history, the Falkland Islands War was little more than a skirmish. It was certainly a long
way from D-Day or El Alamein. But Thatcher's speech in July reveals perfectly the psychological condition of a once great power
that still felt its losses keenly: "We have ceased to be a nation in
retreat. We have instead a newfound confidence—born in the

economic battles at home and tested and found true eight thousand miles away. . . . We rejoice that Britain has rekindled that spirit which has fired her for generations past and which today has begun to burn as brightly as before. Britain has found herself again in the South Atlantic."[23]

Just days before the Argentinian surrender, Ronald Reagan, who had had such misgivings about Britain's military defiance, was in London to affirm the Special Relationship, liberally quoting Churchill, of course, and praising Thatcher's war. Yes, he said, there had been voices raised in Washington protesting that young men's lives should not be sacrificed for "lumps of rock and earth so far away." But the war had been fought for freedom and democracy: "If there had been firmer support for that principle some forty-five years ago, perhaps our generation wouldn't have suffered the bloodletting of World War Two."[24]

That same day at Windsor Castle, Reagan, dressed in a tweed jacket over a casually opened shirt, rather like a model in a Marlboro ad, every inch the rugged man from the West, went horse riding with the queen. The photograph of the president and the monarch went swiftly around the world. The Special Relationship could not have been illustrated more tenderly. Reagan's deputy chief of staff gloated, "Carter couldn't have done a thing like that!"

The tiny island of Grenada, in the eastern Caribbean, was no longer a British colony but an independent member of the Commonwealth. In 1979, a Marxist agitator named Maurice Bishop took power in a revolution. The Americans suspected him of serving the interests of Cuba and the Soviet Union. In 1983, a military faction in Bishop's party deposed the leader, shot him, and then cut his throat.

Several Caribbean nations asked the US to intervene. Without bothering to inform the British, Reagan ordered a military invasion, named Operation Urgent Fury. Securing this tiny tropical outpost was hailed by the US administration as a great victory. One of Reagan's men exulted. "Grenada showed that it could be done. It proved that boldness and determination could defeat Communists."[25]

One reason the US much needed a boost to its morale was a debacle in Beirut, where the US had stationed troops to bolster the Lebanese government under a Christian president during the brutal civil war. A week after Bishop was overthrown in Grenada, Islamist suicide bombers murdered 241 US servicemen, a humiliating blow to the Reagan administration. Then there was the so-called Vietnam Syndrome, the perception among American hawks—commonly known as "neoconservatives," who would do so much damage later on—that the US had gone soft after "losing" Vietnam and years of détente. It was time for the US to show "resolve." Grenada was an opportunity to do so.

But Operation Urgent Fury showed how illusory the Special Relationship, which Thatcher, for some reason, had renamed the "extraordinary relationship," often proved to be. Since the British had not been told about the invasion in advance, the foreign secretary, Geoffrey Howe, made a fool of himself by assuring Parliament that such an action was unlikely to take place. The prime minister was accused of letting the president treat her like a doormat or, in the words of Denis Healey, the shadow foreign secretary, "an obedient poodle."[26] She later expressed her dismay: "At best, the British Government had been made to look impotent; at worst we looked deceitful."[27]

In fact, Thatcher had not been in favor of any military action at all. This struck the Americans as ungrateful, even perverse, after all the help she had been given over the Falklands. But Thatcher argued, with some reason, that the Falklands conflict was a defensive war against an invasion, whereas Grenada was invaded to change a regime, and not a very important one at that. What made it all more awkward was that the queen was Grenada's head of state. Thatcher didn't really believe that Grenada was about to become another Cuba, or that Bishop's killers were any worse than Bishop had been. But in the end Thatcher was philosophical about the affair. She told her adviser George Urban that the US had done Britain a disservice in Grenada, but she "had learnt to think that this is how very large powers behave. Morality does not really come into the picture. The more the pity."[28]

(In fact, the regime change in Grenada turned out to be a success. Elections were held in December 1984, and the island has been a democracy ever since. It had the effect in some circles of making "regime change" look like a winning formula.)

Reagan then did what many US presidents have done when their junior partners' feathers are ruffled. He resorted to flattery. Thatcher received an award in Washington from the Winston Churchill Foundation of the United States. Reagan sent her a glowing tribute: "World affairs today demand the boldness and integrity of a Churchill. In his absence, I know he would want us to look at you as the legendary Britannia, a special lady, the greatest defender of the realm."[29]

Being oiled in this way may well have pleased Thatcher, but she understood the limits of British influence in Washington. The Grenada invasion shook her. And so did the next US intervention, in Libya this time. On December 27, 1985, Palestinian terrorists, trained in Lebanon, gunned down seventeen people at the airports of Vienna and Rome. Colonel Gaddafi of Libya publicly gloated.

Reagan chose to impose sanctions on Libya as a "terrorist state," and expected NATO allies to follow suit. Thatcher had not been consulted and had no intention of falling into line. She didn't believe in sanctions.

Then, on April 5, 1986, a bomb went off in a Berlin discothèque frequented by American soldiers. US intelligence found a Libyan connection. Reagan decided to bomb Libya to teach Gaddafi a lesson. Again, Thatcher disagreed, which irritated the Americans, especially, in her own rather curious telling, because of her "un-European habit of straight-talking."[30] (The chauvinistic trope of European deviousness versus John Bullish frankness was no less dubious for being rather stale by now.) Reagan wanted permission to fly US bombers from British bases. The French had refused to allow this from happening on their soil. Thatcher, despite her misgivings and her fears of an endless tit for tat, came to the conclusion that "the cost to Britain of not backing American action was unthinkable."[31]

"PM Thatcher as always was right behind us," Reagan wrote in his diary.[32] The French, in contrast, had even refused to let US bombers fly over their territory. Thatcher's policy, in her own recollection, was to give the US her full support, "both as regards use of bases and in justifying [America's] action against what I knew would be a storm of opposition in Britain and in Europe."[33] This undoubtedly kept the fires of the Special Relationship stoked. Whether it was wise to once again pick Washington's side against the French, whose views on bombing Libya Thatcher shared, is another matter.

Despite all the mutual back-scratching, however, the question of bombs, especially nuclear bombs, continued to cause frictions in the Anglo-American world. No sooner had Thatcher closed the deal, initiated by Callaghan and Carter, to buy the expensive

Lockheed Trident C4 nuclear missiles, than the Americans decided, without telling the British, to substitute them with a much more expensive missile system called D5, which Britain could ill afford. Another sore point was that the British had no final say on how the Americans would use their own nuclear weapons stationed in Britain. This, naturally, elicited a constant stream of comments from the opposition benches about doormats and poodles.

What worried Thatcher most, however, was Reagan's dream of giving up such weapons altogether. The usual role of British prime ministers since World War II, starting with Churchill, was to act as the counsel of caution, the wise veteran in the court of impetuous upstarts. British leaders had been hopping over to Washington every time they got a whiff of nuclear trigger-happiness. These roles, in the Reagan-Thatcher era, were reversed. Reagan had a moral loathing of nuclear weapons. The reason he was so enamored of the possibilities of Star Wars, or the Strategic Defense Initiative (SDI), was that he thought it might make nuclear weapons obsolete. He even promised to share the results of SDI research with the Soviets. If both the US and the Soviet Union had the means to shoot missiles down in space, neither would have any incentive to use a nuclear bomb.

Reagan's dream alarmed the Soviets, because they didn't believe for a second that the Americans would let them in on SDI secrets. And developing their own space-weapons research would be prohibitively expensive (which is one reason why the US pushed for it in the first place). The idea horrified Thatcher, because she was convinced that only nuclear deterrence kept the world safe—and, of course, Britain at the top table of major powers. In 1984, in Washington, she had reminded the members of Congress of Winston Churchill's warning to the Americans to be "careful above all things not to let go of the atomic weapon." Perhaps it was the mention of Churchill, or possibly it was due to the passion of her oratory, but Congress erupted in wild cheers of "Maggie! Maggie!" Reagan's team was mightily annoyed. But Thatcher was not to be appeased. The very idea that the US might bargain the British bomb away in a misguided and naive deal with the Soviets was abhorrent to her. And that is exactly what she thought Reagan had been close to doing in 1985, at a summit in Reykjavík with the Soviet leader, Mikhail Gorbachev.

The two men couldn't have been more different in temperament or style: the guileful, sophisticated Russian intellectual and the affable, horse-riding, showbiz-anecdote-telling American. But they got along somehow. And Gorbachev, presiding over a crumbling economy, was playing a weak hand. Huge cuts in nuclear arsenals were proposed, and to a large degree conceded. Reagan went so far as to suggest that in ten years strategic ballistic missiles should be eliminated entirely. Gorbachev agreed, but only on the condition that SDI would be confined to laboratory research. Reagan, to the intense relief of his advisers, refused to accept such a limitation on his dream project, and that is how the summit ended.

Thatcher was appalled: "My own reaction when I heard how far the Americans had been prepared to go was as if there had been an earthquake beneath my feet." She was convinced that the president had gone "wobbly," to anticipate a term she would later apply to Reagan's successor, George H. W. Bush. "Somehow I had to get the Americans back onto the firm ground of a credible policy of nuclear deterrence. I arranged to fly to the United States to see President Reagan."[34]

A history of the Special Relationship could be related quite nicely in a series of photographs of meetings between different

Anglo-American leaders: a pensive Churchill feeling left out in Teheran as the ailing Roosevelt leans toward Stalin; Kennedy grinning at one of Macmillan's sardonic witticisms in Bermuda; Lyndon Johnson towering over Wilson sucking on his pipe. And then there is the picture of Thatcher and Reagan at Camp David, sitting side by side in a golf cart driven by the president himself, Thatcher in a formal camel-hair coat and high-heeled shoes, Reagan in a leather bomber jacket and cowboy boots. Reagan liked these visits to be informal, leaving the boring details to others, but Thatcher wanted to cut the small talk and get straight to business. Like a dedicated accountant, she loved details. In this instance, she got what she had come for. SDI would go ahead, but the balance of nuclear and conventional power would be maintained. And what was most gratifying of all: the president "confirmed his full support for the arrangements made to modernize Britain's independent nuclear deterrent, with Trident. I had reason to be well pleased."[35]

One of the ironies of the Thatcher era is that Britain's prestige in Europe was actually quite high in the mid-1980s. Winning a war and standing up to Communism, as well as her blazing style, had given Thatcher an aura of glamour. She was extremely popular in Eastern Europe especially. And partly because Grenada had dented her trust in the US, she did what postwar British prime ministers had done before to show their country still mattered on the international stage; she reached out to Moscow. Thatcher had recognized Gorbachev as a man "to do business" with before the Americans did. Indeed, she appears to have enjoyed her debates with the Russian leader even more than her encounters with the charming but intellectually limited Reagan. She was in awe of the president's power, but never rated him as a serious thinker. Rides in golf carts were not really her style. She much preferred a serious discussion about policy with a worthy opponent. The fact that Gorbachev stopped over in Britain in 1987 on his way to his first summit with Reagan in Washington was a small sign that Britain could still at least pretend to play the role of the European broker between East and West.

However, Thatcher's most important contribution to European affairs had nothing to do with the US or the Soviet Union. She was responsible, together with Jacques Delors, president of the European Commission, for radically changing the European Community through the Single European Act. Delors, a typical French left-wing *dirigiste*, favored a single market with uniform rules and open borders because it would move the EEC closer to a federation. This was precisely not Thatcher's aim. She was a British Gaullist, who favored a loose economic community of sovereign nation-states. But she was so convinced that a free-trading single market would bring "Thatcherism" to Europe that she chose to forget that her economic goal had political implications. It was a marriage of convenience that would soon turn sulfurous. Beginning as an ally, Delors became the main foreign hate figure for British "Eurosceptics," including the prime minister herself. "Up Yours, Delors!" was the headline in *The Sun*, a dependably chauvinist tabloid paper, when the commissioner promoted a single European currency in 1990.

In any event, Thatcher had it in her gift to play the role at last that many Europeans, and quite a few Britons, as well as a large number of important Americans, had advocated for a long time. She could have made sure that Britain played a leading part in European affairs without alienating the Americans. Sufficient trust could have been built on both sides of the Atlantic to anchor the

Anglo-American order in an integrating Europe. The Germans wanted it. The small northern nations certainly wanted it. Even the French might have been brought along. But it was not to be. Thatcher blew her chance.

Personal relations had something to do with this. Thatcher had little patience with foreigners, aside from Americans. There was a certain mutual fascination between Thatcher and Mitterrand, it is true. He admired the dominatrix in her: "The eyes of Caligula and the lips of Marilyn Monroe." And she appreciated his intellectual agility. But she couldn't stand the German chancellor Helmut Kohl, whom she regarded as a verbose overweight Teuton with an unfortunate taste for sausages made from sow's stomach, a specialty of his native Rhineland. Thatcher called him the "gasbag." She also disapproved of the Italian prime minister Giulio Andreotti, who, in her opinion, had "a positive aversion to principle."[36] She disliked Mitterrand's successor, Giscard d'Estaing, whom she found insufferably haughty. The French, she opined, were selfish, bloody-minded, and obsessed with their virility. And what passed for European statesmanship, in her eyes, was corrupt and thoroughly "un-British."[37] Only the Dutch prime minister, Ruud Lubbers, was all right; he shared Thatcher's opposition to the French and Italian taste for Keynesian government expenditure, and, perhaps most important of all, they both distrusted the Germans.

Thatcher was not chiefly known for her literary bent, but she reached for her "old, battered collection of [her] favorite poet's verse" to express her deepest feelings about Britain's relations with the Gallic-flavored Continent. The favorite poet was Rudyard Kipling, and the poem was called "Norman and Saxon," about a Norman baron's advice to his son about the Anglo-Saxon race:

'The Saxon is not like us Normans. His manners are not so
   polite.
But he never means anything serious till he talks about justice
   and right.
When he stands like an ox in the furrow—with his sullen set
   eyes on your own,
And grumbles "This isn't fair dealing," my son, leave the
   Saxon alone.'[38]

In the late 1980s, even the most provincial British citizens finally
realized how far their country was lagging behind Germany in
wealth. Since the war, the British had been, on the whole, less vis-
cerally anti-German than the French or the Dutch. Spared the humiliation of Nazi occupation, they could afford a superior attitude
that was above raw hatred. Germans in British TV dramas about the
war were often figures of fun. The war was a rich source of British
comedy, in a way that was unthinkable in France, let alone in Russia
or Poland. But once the scale of German economic preeminence
had sunk in, a feeling emerged in Britain that this was somehow not
fair. After all, Britain had won the war. This was the age of the English soccer hooligans, who terrorized the Continent with boorish
reenactments of wartime hostilities. When playing against Germans, fans' arms would be spread in imitation of Lancaster bombers, the theme tune of *The Dam Busters*, a popular British war movie,
was given a raucous airing, and town centers were laid to waste.

Alan Clark, the Thatcher-worshipping diarist mentioned earlier,
once mused in my presence that the British hooligan spirit might be
"usefully tapped." Margaret Thatcher would not have gone that
far, but despite her pragmatic and sometimes even bold political
decisions (the single market), her views on the European continent

seem to have got stuck somewhere in 1940, when the Huns were loathsome, the Italians without principle, the French unreliable, and the poor Dutch at least plucky.

That Kohl tried his best to bury any incipient German nationalism in a grand vision of European unity only put Thatcher's back up even more. She suspected a devious German plot to dominate Europe by stealth. In 1990, I was working at *The Spectator*, a conservative journal highly sympathetic to Thatcher's politics. Our editor interviewed one of Thatcher's senior cabinet ministers, Nicholas Ridley, later made Baron Ridley of Liddesdale. Not generally known for his tact, the blue-blooded, chain-smoking Ridley didn't disappoint on this occasion. The EEC, he fumed through a curtain of smoke, was "a German racket designed to take over the whole of Europe." He wasn't against giving up national sovereignty in principle, he said, but "not to this lot. You might as well give it to Adolf Hitler, frankly."[39] On the cover of the magazine was a cartoon of Helmut Kohl daubed with a Hitler mustache.

The interviewer, Dominic Lawson, son of Nigel Lawson, Thatcher's former chancellor of the exchequer, knew what he was talking about when he wrote, "Mr. Ridley's confidence in expressing his views on the German threat must owe something to the knowledge that they are not significantly different from those of the prime minister." Quite true, no doubt. But Ridley had said out loud what was normally spoken only in private. He had to resign.

A toxic form of Euroscepticism was curdling inside the Conservative Party. Fear and loathing of Germany were mixed with a growing nostalgia for the mythical purity of 1940, when Britain faced its Continental enemies alone. Such emotions, not universally shared in Thatcher's cabinet but stoked by the right-wing tabloid press, began more and more to shape the prime minister's views on

Europe. Thatcher suspected that the Germans, helped by the sneaky French, were moving toward a kind of illiberal, undemocratic Europe, which first Napoleon and then Hitler had tried but failed to establish. She wrote in her memoirs that it was all very well for such nations as Italy or Belgium to take their orders from Brussels. But, she recalled, "the mood in Britain was different. I sensed it."[40]

And so, in 1988, Thatcher set out her own vision for Europe in a famous speech, delivered with great vehemence at the College of Europe in Bruges. An early draft, talking about European "waffling" and how Britain alone had once saved Europe from being united "under Prussian domination," horrified her own diplomats and Foreign Office officials.[41] But even the toned-down version was a not-very-subtle assault on the European Community. Thatcher's Europe, as she later put it, would "stretch to the Urals" and certainly "include that New Europe across the Atlantic."[42] Her most famous line was "We have not successfully rolled back the frontiers of the state in Britain, only to see them re-imposed at a European level with a European super-state exercising a new dominance from Brussels."

To the dismay of some of her colleagues, including the foreign secretary, Geoffrey Howe, this speech, still recalled with eyes turned up in humid reverence by Tory Eurosceptics, infuriated Britain's closest allies, and began Britain's shift to the margins of Europe. Thatcher's robust Atlanticism was applauded in some quarters of the Reagan administration, but if she expected universal American acclaim for her hostility to the European project, she would soon be disappointed. Her notion that the US should be regarded as an extension of Europe would have struck most Americans as quaint at best. Nor did they share her old-fashioned prejudices about the Germans. To see Europe as an extension of the US might have found a clearer echo in America, but that was not how most Europeans preferred to think of themselves.

But it was Thatcher's response to one of the greatest events of the twentieth century that isolated her even further. When Ronald Reagan, speaking behind a bulletproof shield in front of Berlin's Brandenburg Gate in July 1987, implored "Mr. Gorbachev" to "tear down this wall!" not even he would have expected it to happen just two years later. Some of his closest advisers had counseled against using such provocative language. Why annoy Gorbachev? The fall of the wall was almost unthinkable. When it did happen, on that glorious night of November 9, 1989, Reagan was no longer president. Helmut Kohl phoned up President George H. W. Bush in great excitement the following day. Without the US, he panted, "this day would not have been possible. Tell your people that."[43]

Kohl quickly decided that unifying Germany would be the only way to stabilize a volatile situation. East Germans demanded it in massive demonstrations. The earlier slogan "We are the people!" had morphed into "We are one people!" The most enterprising citizens of the former Communist state were already moving west in droves. People outside Germany were generally less thrilled about the idea of a reunited Germany. Bush was in fact the first Western leader to support Kohl in this dramatic move. As he later put it, "While Thatcher, Mitterrand, and others feared that Germany might cause more trouble and tragedy, I did not."[44] A united, democratic Germany, firmly lodged in the Western camp, had in any case always been the stated aim of NATO.

Thatcher never really warmed to Bush, and neither did he to Thatcher. Bush was too patrician, too averse to ideological zeal (that "vision thing"), too damned "wet" for her liking, a bit like those patronizing old Tories she had purged from her cabinet early on.

And Bush didn't like to be lectured. Thatcher wrote rather touchingly in her memoirs that she "later learned that President Bush was sometimes exasperated by my habit of talking nonstop about issues that fascinated me."[45] But it was her prejudices that caused the greatest damage.

Even as Bush, and after some hesitation all the other European leaders, as well as Gorbachev, in the end, perhaps faute de mieux, accepted the German wish to unify their nation, Thatcher was still seething on the sidelines. She told a group of distinguished American and British historians, summoned to Chequers to enlighten her on the question of whether "the Germans can be trusted," that she was convinced that they could not. It was the German "national character"—aggressive, angst-ridden, volatile, et cetera—that was the problem. The German beast, Thatcher argued, could only be contained by a permanent American military presence in Europe and a firm Franco-British alliance. But, alas, in Thatcher's words, Mitterrand "refused to follow his and French instincts and challenge German interests."[46] And neither did his successor, Giscard d'Estaing. On the contrary, Thatcher felt that he and Kohl were ganging up on her as a Franco-German axis, and what was even worse, with the backing of the US government.

Bush certainly had no time for Thatcher's German angst. This became obvious during his first visit to Europe as president in May 1989, less than six months before the fall of the Berlin Wall. The year before, Reagan traveled to Europe for the last time in his presidency to attend the NATO conference in Brussels. He appeared distracted and a little misty-eyed, leaving the difficult questions to George Shultz and gazing with delight as Thatcher rode her hobbyhorse hard on the need for a strong nuclear defense against the Russians. She recalled that it was "clear from the start that the West

Germans were likely to be the main source of difficulty." They were unsound on the nuclear question. The Germans did not want to commit to modernizing short-range nuclear forces, because this would be so unpopular with German voters that Kohl was sure to lose the election. Still, Thatcher left Brussels "reassured that the President and I were as one."[47]

The following year, when Bush was in power, Thatcher had hoped to organize the next NATO conference in London. This suggestion was turned down. It was to be Brussels again. But first, Bush spent two days in Germany, where he was taken on a cruise down the Rhine by Kohl, who hugged the president with delight on his arrival. This trip, in the words of Brent Scowcroft, the national security adviser, was part of Kohl's reelection campaign, to highlight US-German relations and "show off his great friend." Bush further made the chancellor's day by making a major speech at the Rhein-goldhalle in Mainz, where he referred to Germany and the US as "partners in leadership."[48]

To Thatcher, this remark "confirmed the way American thinking about Europe was going." She was sure that the US State Department, under James Baker III, was briefing against her and her policies. Bush was replacing the Special Relationship with a turn toward Germany. "I would be the first to argue," she wrote, "that if one chose to ignore history and the loyalties it engenders such an approach might appear quite rational."[49] But, of course, history is the one thing Thatcher was unable to shake from her mind.

No wonder Bush's one-day stopover in London, tacked onto his European jaunt, was not a success. There were no great speeches, no references to Shakespeare, Churchill, or kinship (even though the Bush family was said to have been distantly related to the queen). Asked for comments after dinner at 10 Downing Street, the president fumbled for an answer: "I tell you what, I'm awful busy. I have got to get home and go to bed real fast. No, I cannot do it."[50]

It looked as though Thatcher had managed to maneuver Britain into a position previous prime ministers had done their very best to avoid: isolated from Europe and not taken seriously by the US. She was rescued, in the end, by yet another little war, which offered the illusion that the old Anglo-American order might still be restored to its former greatness once more. In the summer of 1990, the Iraqi dictator Saddam Hussein invaded Kuwait. His aim was to control the oil wells, giving him a dominant position in the region. President Bush decided to wait before taking military action. He wanted support from other Arab leaders. UN resolutions were needed for economic sanctions. A coalition of allies had to be formed. Military options were carefully, and in some instances perhaps less carefully, weighed. US defense secretary Dick Cheney, visiting London, asked Thatcher what she thought of the idea of using nuclear weapons on Iraq.[51] She didn't think much of it. But she allegedly told Bush that this was "no time to go wobbly." Britain, she said, had experience with appeasing dictators. Bush did not need to be told. He had been reading Martin Gilbert's massive biography of Churchill. Preparing for a speech on television, Bush recalled, "I tightened up the language to strengthen the similarity I saw between the Persian Gulf and the situation in the Rhineland in the 1930s, when Hitler simply defied the Treaty of Versailles and marched in."[52]

Thatcher was now in her element. "The UN," she wrote, "might pass its resolutions; but there would soon be a full-scale war to fight. Suddenly a Britain with armed forces which had the skills, and a government which had the resolve, to fight alongside America, seemed to be the real European 'partner in leadership.'"[53]

For a few glorious months, it seemed like 1941 all over again:

Britain shoulder to shoulder with the US. The Germans were prevented by their constitution from taking part in combat. The French did join, but with fewer armed forces than the British. Other European countries did their bit. But all this confirmed in Thatcher's mind that Europeans could never be relied upon to defend freedom. The very idea, Thatcher thought, was "laughable." No, the West could be saved only through "the ties of blood, language, culture and values which bound Britain and America."[54]

Margaret Thatcher was a brave woman. And the past she invoked—Dunkirk, Churchill, fighting on the beaches, and so on—was indisputably heroic. But it was not an adequate basis for politics in a world that had changed so much since 1941. She was in the grip of a national myth that clouded her judgment. And in the end it brought her down. On November 1, 1990, before the Gulf War really got going, Thatcher's loyal foreign secretary, Geoffrey Howe, finally spoke out against his prime minister's damaging prejudices, which were undermining Britain's position in Europe, a continent, in his words, that she seemed to look upon as a place "positively teeming with ill-intentioned people, scheming, in her words, to 'extinguish democracy.'" He resigned. A few weeks later, so did she, tearfully, resentfully, and indulging in Churchillian conceits to the last.

After her downfall, Thatcher was not a popular figure in Britain, except among loyalists like Alan Clark, who described her resignation as an "assassination." But in the US, she could still bask in tributes far more lavish than anything in Britain. In 1991, Thatcher was the guest of honor at an award ceremony of the Heritage Foundation. As the distinguished guests all stood up, the US Navy Band in full dress played a stirring "Thatcher Freedom March," especially composed for the occasion by the Honorable J. William Middendorf II.

Two years later, Thatcher was in California to celebrate Reagan's eighty-second birthday at the newly opened presidential library in Simi Valley. This splendid gala was attended by show business luminaries like James Stewart and Merv Griffin. Betsy Bloomingdale and Rupert Murdoch were also among the five hundred guests who had spent a large amount of money to pay homage. Reagan was the one they had come to praise, but, as *The Los Angeles Times* reported, Thatcher "was clearly the most honored guest of the evening."[55]

She paid tribute to the president for bringing down "the Evil Empire" and liberating half of Europe. Then Reagan rose to his feet to praise Thatcher's heroic role. There was an awkward moment when the former president, already in the fog of dementia, repeated his tribute in precisely the same words. But the applause was no less effusive. Once more, the US and Britain had won a war for freedom, he said. To celebrate the occasion in proper historical fashion, a special exhibition had been mounted in the presidential library: *The Art and Treasures of Sir Winston Churchill.*

Nine

KINDER, GENTLER

George H. W. Bush was not an articulate man, nor did he share Ronald Reagan's fervor or talent for political salesmanship. His traditional brand of American patriotism was usually expressed in uninspiring boilerplate phrases. In his inaugural address in 1989, Bush stated that the US is "never wholly herself unless she is engaged in high moral principle. We as a people have such a purpose today. It is to make kinder the face of the Nation, and gentler the face of the world."

Even though Bush was not above letting others get rough on his behalf, he exuded civility and the discretion of a competent operator—a clubman, a team player. He was in fact much like his British counterpart, John Major. Major was elected to replace Margaret Thatcher as leader of the Conservative Party in 1990, precisely because he was not as outspoken, colorful, or contentious as his main rivals for the job. A thoroughly decent sort, easily caricatured in a popular satirical television program as a gray man spouting banalities, Major could be relied upon not to rock any boats. This is what his party wanted after the brawls over Europe and Thatcher's divisive leadership.

Perhaps that is why the two leaders got along so well. Neither Bush nor Major would seriously challenge the main tenets of the Reagan-Thatcher era—Major was indeed Thatcher's protégé—but they would calm things down, smooth ruffled feathers, especially in Europe, and remove from conservatism its recent radical sting. Bush also promised to usher in a new age of universal freedom; such a claim would have been absurd coming from a British prime minister. But Bush would do so diplomatically, cautiously, and, above all, without too much zeal.

According to Thatcher, and many others besides, Reagan had won the Cold War. The Soviet Empire had fallen. The end of history had been speculated on in a famous article that appeared between Bush's inauguration and Major's election.* No ideology would challenge the supremacy of liberal democracy again. No new system of government need ever be devised. In Bush's words, spoken at his inaugural ceremony: "We know what works: Freedom works. We know what's right: Freedom is right. We know how to secure a more just and prosperous life for man on Earth: through free markets, free speech, free elections, and the exercise of free will unhampered by any state."

Major did say that he wanted to build a "classless society by 2000," a country that would "provide a better quality of life for all our citizens."[1] But this would be achieved, he thought, by giving people "a hand-up, not a hand-out."[2] Markets would set us free. No doubt, Major's egalitarianism was genuine. But, like Bush, he saw little need in the brave new age of freedom unbound to challenge

---

* I refer of course to Francis Fukuyama's essay "The End of History?," in *The National Interest*, Summer 1989.

free market ideology. Socialism, after all, had lost. The limitations of this view were recognized by some people immediately. The left-leaning French philosopher Pierre Hassner, for example, warned that "humankind does not live by liberty or universality alone."[3] Community, identity, and a sense of solidarity were just as important. But these would be neglected in the first rush of post–Cold War triumph. Without a Communist enemy to combat, the need for a social democratic alternative had become a great deal less pressing.

The social backgrounds of the American president and the British prime minister could not have been more distinct. Bush was a Yankee grandee, a Yale graduate, and a decorated World War II hero who had served his country in some of the highest government jobs, including vice president, and had at least pretended to do so out of sheer noblesse oblige. Major, the son of a circus performer and supplier of garden ornaments, had barely completed his high school education.* He was born (in 1943) around the time when Bush was performing his wartime heroics as a navy pilot. But despite their differences, Bush much preferred Major's company to being browbeaten by Margaret Thatcher. And the president didn't patronize Major in the way Tory snobs often did. (I recall many an editorial meeting at *The Spectator* magazine, where Major's South London vowels were mocked with great hilarity—as were his notions about the classless society.) Bush said about Major, "I just like being with him. I love his humor. I love his honor, his sense of decency. And I love his wife."[4]

So there they were, in December 1990, sitting around the Christmas tree in front of a log fire at Camp David, Bush in cowboy boots and Major in a comfortable sweater, snug as could be, while a US

---

* Major's father had actually spent ten years in the US as a circus performer and minor league baseball player.

Army choir regaled the two men's families with Christmas carols. The image is serenely peaceful, like a Victorian Christmas print. In fact, Bush had already decided by then that he was going to war.

Saddam Hussein refused to end the Iraqi occupation of Kuwait and was unlikely to change his mind before a United Nations deadline set for January 15, 1991. The European Community considered sending a diplomatic mission to Baghdad. The Italians wanted to appeal to Yasīr 'Arafāt, the Palestinian leader, in the hope that he might find a way out. As for the French, Bush noted in his diary, "Mitterrand himself has been great. [Their foreign ministry] is off wanting to compromise and get their own [agenda]." And "the rest of the Europeans don't want to use force."[5] The Germans, constrained by their constitution, which wouldn't allow German troops to engage in combat outside the NATO area, offered money, but could do little else. Edward Heath, the former British PM, irritated the Foreign Office by traveling to Iraq to see if he could still persuade Saddam to back off. (The British tabloids accused him of being an "appeaser" or even a "traitor.") Some members of Congress, as well as leading figures in the Labour Party, warned about a possibly catastrophic war. Saddam's use of chemical or biological weapons was feared. Contingency plans had been made for fifty thousand British casualties.[6] But there was a great deal at stake, not least the flow of oil to the US and its allies. Bush also claimed that the conflict with Iraq was the "greatest moral issue since World War II."[7] He compared Saddam Hussein with Hitler.[8]

In the presidential limousine on the way to their Christmas party at Camp David, Bush told Major of his war plans. The attack would begin as soon as the UN deadline expired. "How about 0400 on the morning of the sixteenth?" asked Bush. "How does that grab you?" Bush would have understood if Major had needed to think it over or consult his cabinet. But the prime minister didn't hesitate. As Bush recalled, he "declared on the spot that the British would be with us all the way. I shall never forget that. He became the first foreign leader to know of our war plans and the first outside our inner circle—fittingly so, given his dependability and unwavering support and Margaret Thatcher's before him."[9]

Once more, the Special Relationship was rekindled in a war. The British contribution, though puny compared with the US, was not just symbolic: more than thirty thousand troops were dispatched, and the Royal Air Force was responsible for five percent of all combat missions. The French took part as well, but initially refused to put their troops under US command. The conservative German newspaper *Frankfurter Allgemeine Zeitung* sighed in frustration: "In the Gulf War, the old Europe was only the choir. The British and French were the resolute choir leaders, and Germany was a whining, weepy choirboy."[10] "No blood for oil" was one of the popular slogans displayed on banners near US bases in Germany.

Bush tried to strike the note of a principled war leader, indeed a leader with a vision. "What is at stake," he said on the day fighting commenced, "is more than one small country [Kuwait], it is a big idea—a new world order where diverse nations are drawn together in common cause to achieve the universal aspirations of mankind: peace and security, freedom and the rule of law."[11]

This big idea was of course not so new at all. It rehashed the old notion of the Anglo-Saxon mission to liberate the world from tyranny. For a resolute leader, Bush—like Major—was acutely sensitive to public opinion, always keeping a beady eye on his press. There had been much fearful discussion in the late Reagan years of German and Japanese economic success. Their "soft power" and industrial prowess threatened American preeminence. Many a bestselling book—*Japan as Number One* was just one typical title—had been written along these lines. The Gulf War, for a time, put a stop to all that. *The Wall Street Journal* crowed, "All the talk about Germany and Japan being the new number one has faded quickly. The Iraq crisis shows that the US is the only true superpower."[12] A Vietnam veteran quoted in *The New York Times* might have spoken for many: "VCRs may be made in Japan and Mercedes have their origin, but what's going on in the Middle East is undeniably made in the USA. I think that's a source of pride we've not had since World War Two."[13]

As it turned out, Operation Desert Storm was so successful that the war lasted just over a month. Iraq tried to provoke a wider conflict by lobbing Scud missiles at Tel Aviv. But the Israelis were persuaded to stay put. Kuwait was liberated on February 27. Iraqi soldiers scampering back to Baghdad along the "highway of death" were bombarded by US, British, and French forces in what was described by some giddy warriors as "a turkey shoot." Thousands of blackened corpses lay in the desert among the debris of burning vehicles and tanks. The following day, Bush declared a cease-fire. One hundred ten thousand sorties had been flown. Up to two thousand Kuwaiti civilians were killed by Iraqi forces. The US lost one hundred thirty-eight soldiers in action, Britain forty-seven, and France nine. There were some casualties from Senegal, Egypt, Saudi Arabia, and a few other allied nations. More than thirty thousand Iraqi troops were killed, in tank skirmishes, bombing, and the turkey shoot.

But Saddam Hussein was still ruling his country. He announced on the radio that the Americans had been forced to capitulate. Margaret Thatcher, along with other hawkish figures in Britain and the US, criticized Bush for allowing Saddam's troops to get away, and urged him to press on to Baghdad. Major was accused of lacking the stomach for a fight. One of Major's senior foreign policy advisers, the owlish Percy Cradock, observed, "The US forces had the Iraqis in the bag. I confidently expected that they would be destroyed in that bag."[14]

Bush, however, decided to stop once the Iraqi occupation of Kuwait was ended. That, after all, is what the UN resolution had demanded. He was afraid that an allied coalition of thirty-nine countries, including several in the Middle East, would not hold if Iraq were invaded. More bombing of fleeing troops might turn a war into a massacre, which would not look good. Veterans of the Korean and Vietnam Wars were afraid of being dragged into a conflict without a clear end. And Major later pointed out, correctly, that the war was fought to maintain the rule of law, not to break it. Bush may have been prudent, but dissatisfaction lingered in some circles, especially after Saddam murdered large numbers of Kurds, as well as Shiite rebels, who had been encouraged to revolt by Bush, even though the US did nothing to help them once they followed his advice. Major, to his credit, did manage to persuade Bush to create safe havens for the Kurds, but this was after much of the damage had been done.

The main thing was that Bush, with substantial British help, achieved his purpose. He didn't gloat. Bush was careful to pay tribute to all the allies who had helped his cause, including Gorbachev. And he acknowledged in his diary that the war had not had "a clear end." There had not been "a 'battleship *Missouri*' surrender," as happened in Tokyo Bay in 1945 when the Japanese capitulated to General Douglas MacArthur: "This is what's missing to make this akin to World War II."[15] And yet, as a result of his victory in the Gulf, Bush's poll ratings in the US shot up to 90 percent, and Major's ratings were the highest for any prime minister since Winston Churchill.[16]

What this showed, in Bush's eyes, was that "there is no substitute for American leadership." He said this in his address to a joint session of Congress. "In the face of tyranny," he continued, "let no one doubt American credibility and reliability. Let no one doubt our staying power." The moment of victory affirmed, as nothing else could, the order forged in World War II: "Once again, Americans have stepped forward to share a tearful goodbye with their families before leaving for a strange and distant shore."[17] It also confirmed the Special Relationship, for Britain had remained staunch while the Europeans dithered, and the Japanese and the Germans stayed at home. The hawkish Princeton scholar of Middle Eastern history, Bernard Lewis, remarked to *The Washington Post*, "This crisis really exposed the hollowness of European pretensions."[18] The foreign minister of Belgium seemed to concur. The Gulf War had shown that Europe was "an economic giant, a political pygmy, and a military larva."[19]

Victory in the Gulf War can be read in different ways, however. If Bush was to be believed, it was the pinnacle of postwar American success. The Anglo-American order had triumphed on all fronts: the Cold War had been won, and now a wide coalition of nations, led by the US, with Britain in tow, had defeated the Arab Hitler. In retrospect it might be seen more accurately as a moment of hubris that laid the ground for future nemeses. The fact that the superiority of the Anglo-American order, and thus of the Special Relationship, seemed to be proven once more in a military alliance, made it harder for both countries to move on from the assumptions that had emerged from the experience of World War II; the conviction of American hawks, liberal and conservative, that freedom and democracy could be imposed by military force, and the idea in Britain that its proper role was to stick by Washington's side, come what may. Both these assumptions would be severely tested in future wars, one of which erupted in a corner of Europe as soon as the Gulf War was over.

John Major was not anti-European. From the beginning of his premiership, he did his best to repair the damage done by Thatcher to Britain's relations with other European countries, and with Germany in particular. Major thought this is what his party needed to heal divisions over "Europe," and what his country needed too. Even though he had been Thatcher's foreign secretary for all of three months in 1989, Major was not an international figure with much experience in foreign affairs, or foreign anything. He prided himself on being a very English everyman, who enjoyed his game of cricket with a pint of lukewarm beer close at hand. But he had no memories of World War II and didn't share Thatcher's prejudices about the European continent. Major deliberately chose Germany to make his first speech abroad. His most famous lines spoken at the Konrad-Adenauer-Stiftung in Bonn were "My aims for Britain in the Community can be simply stated: I want us to be where we belong. At the very heart of Europe. Working with our partners at building the future."[20]

Helmut Kohl was delighted by this change of tone. In France, *Le Monde* rejoiced: "Interventions, tirades, arguments and foot stamping are a thing of the past. In its place there arrives the smiling, softly spoken, amiable new British Premier." Nothing, however, could have been designed to annoy Thatcher and her supporters more. She had personally campaigned for Major to succeed her, and here he was utterly contradicting the message of her Bruges speech. In the heart of Europe is precisely where she did not wish her country to be. Much to Major's chagrin, Thatcher had already announced that she was not planning to retire gracefully. Resentful over her loss of power, she promised to be "a good backseat driver." The comment was meant for President Bush, whose potential wobbliness in war continued to worry her. But Major took it personally and it made him even more defensive. The first thing Thatcher did, while Major was trying to mend fences in Europe, was to make bellicose speeches warning about German domination. She did this on American television.

Thatcher was backed by a motley group of nationalists, many of them on the fringes of the Conservative Party, called the Bruges Group. Referred to by Major at an unguarded moment as "the bastards," a hard core of these Eurosceptics, as well as Thatcher herself, would make life hell for him. But he helped to egg them on by doing what other Tory prime ministers have done since; he tried to make them go away by playing to their gallery.

One of the dirtiest phrases in the British Eurosceptic lexicon is "Maastricht Treaty." This is the treaty, signed in February 1992, that turned the European Economic Community into the European Union. Before signing the treaty that would bind member countries closer together, economically and politically, Major had already made it clear that he would not commit Britain to plans for an Economic and Monetary Union (EMU) or for a Social Chapter to improve the condition of workers, as this would supposedly undermine "the ability of Britain to compete."[21]

The Europeans did everything to accommodate the amiable prime minister, especially after he threatened to sabotage the treaty if Britain didn't get its way. In the end the EU signed on both to

EMU and the Social Chapter, while allowing Britain to opt out of both. Major was proud of his achievement. His press spokesman declared "game, set, and match," affirming the common view in Britain that the nation was engaged in a constant battle with the rest of Europe. Major was initially applauded in the press for going to bat so effectively for his country. Even Thatcher called his performance brilliant.

But "the bastards," led by the former prime minister, soon turned on Major. The Maastricht Treaty began to be seen as an outrage. Thatcher repeated the formula she once used in a parliamentary debate on Europe: "No, no, and no!" The treaty paved the way toward a federal Europe, she said. The opt-outs were meaningless. Major had been a negotiator who lacked real conviction. Irate Eurosceptics demanded that the British people should be allowed to vote in a referendum before any decision on a single currency was made. Major refused to say yes or no. For this he was accused of being arrogant, ignoring the wishes of "the British people," a line of argument that would resurface again and again.

A catastrophic event in the British economy would give a huge boost to the Eurosceptics. Rather against her inclination, Thatcher had been persuaded in 1990 (by John Major, then chancellor of the exchequer) to enter the pound sterling into the exchange rate mechanism (ERM), which fixed rates of European currencies within narrow bands. Pegging the pound to the deutsche mark was seen as a sound way to fight inflation. The Germans would impose the necessary discipline—too much so, as it turned out.

The trouble was that Britain had refused to join the ERM when it was established in 1979, and the pound was weaker. A more serious problem was that Britain was going through a severe recession in the early 1990s. The ERM prevented the government from lowering interest rates to stimulate the economy, for the pound would then have lost parity with the deutsche mark. And devaluation was seen as an intolerable loss of face. If the Germans had agreed to cut their interests rates, it might have been possible to save the situation. But the Germans, still haunted by memories of hyperinflation in the 1920s, and having to spend huge sums on absorbing the impoverished eastern half of Germany, refused. On September 10, Major made a quixotic speech saying he would do everything to defend the pound inside the ERM. There was a run on the currency. Interest rates rose as fast as 5 percent in one day. Speculators were poised to make a killing. And on September 16, known henceforth as Black Wednesday, the British government had to announce its withdrawal of the pound sterling from the ERM.

Major's fortunes never really recovered from this humiliation. That disaster came from pegging the currency to a European mechanism, driven by German interests, confirmed everything the Eurosceptics had been saying all along. Savoring their moment of ascendency and smelling the blood of the man who had had the temerity of replacing their beloved Thatcher, they chose to call the debacle White Wednesday. Norman Lamont, Major's chancellor of the exchequer, who had been a keen supporter of the ERM, now became one of the leading bastards, and declared that he was "singing in the bath" when the pound's exit was concluded.[22]

Major himself began to rethink Britain's relations with Europe. A year later he wrote an article in *The Economist* sounding almost like Thatcher, arguing that "it is for the nations to build Europe, not for Europe to attempt to supersede nations." As for European plans for a single currency, that would have "all the quaintness of a rain dance and all the potency."[23] He was right of course to foresee problems with a currency union not backed by political union. But to dismiss the very idea that it would happen was foolish (six years later, eleven European countries signed on to it). It certainly didn't put Britain in the heart of Europe.

As was true of many British leaders, however, Major was never quite sure where Britain should be placed. The choice between closer ties with Europe or the Special Relationship was not always straightforward, to be sure, and Major hoped that he would never have to make it. Leaving the EU was not an option for him. At the same time, he didn't think there was a European alternative to the existing Atlantic alliance. The US remained the guarantor of European security through NATO, and "we are the second nation of NATO."[24] So, he said, it would be mad to make a choice between Europe and the US.

And yet, Major *would* make a choice, and it was to be a highly ironic one. His most serious rift with Washington would concern a hideous war that brought back mass killing and concentration camps to the heart of Europe for the first time since World War II. Not only did the Anglo-American alliance do nothing to stop it, but when the US believed that concerted and probably forceful intervention would be needed to prevent an even greater bloodbath, the British led Europe in trying to block such a move.

One of the unforeseen consequences of the collapse of Communism in the West was the violent dismemberment of Yugoslavia, a federation of several nations. Josip Broz Tito, the strongman who had held the nations of Yugoslavia together, died in 1980. In June 1989, the Serbian leader Slobodan Miloševic, a Communist apparatchik turned nationalist demagogue, made an inflammatory speech at the Field of the Blackbirds, site of an ancient battlefield in Kosovo, where, according to legend, the Serbian prince Lazar had been defeated by an Ottoman army in 1389 because of disunity in

Serbian ranks. The Muslim enemy had humiliated the Christian Orthodox Serbs. This problem would now be remedied, Miloševic promised. The Serbs, wherever they lived, would recover their dignity and unite in memory of the tragic heroes of the Battle of Kosovo. The basis for a greater Serbia had been laid.

Fearful of a Serbian *reconquista*, Slovenia and Croatia seceded from the Socialist Federal Republic of Yugoslavia in 1991. Afraid for their future, and egged on by Miloševic, the Serb minority in Croatia decided to claim its own chunks of the country. Bloody fights broke out between the Serbs and Croatian forces. The Serb-led Yugoslav National Army came to the rescue of the Croatian Serbs. Bloody battles and massacres followed. In the end, the Croats held on to most of their territory, apart from a Serb enclave carved out under UN supervision. The first step toward that terrible Balkan coinage, "ethnic cleansing," had been taken.

A year later, Bosnia and Herzegovina, a multiethnic state with 44 percent Muslims, 32 percent Serbs, and 17 percent Croats, decided to secede after a referendum that was boycotted by Bosnian Serbs. Miloševic responded with extreme brutality. Serb militias with names like Yellow Wasps and Tigers, led by vicious ex-convicts, crossed the Serbian border together with well-trained Yugoslav National Army troops and attacked Zvornik, a town in Bosnia. Mosques were destroyed. Homes were looted. Muslim and other non-Serb civilians were murdered en masse. Survivors were driven out of town to prisons and concentration camps, where many were tortured, raped, and killed. This was just the beginning of the Bosnian War. When the fighting ceased in 1995, more than one hundred thousand people, almost half of them civilians, had been killed.

The initial response in Washington could be summed up in the words of James Baker, Bush's secretary of state: "We have no dog in this fight." Baker explained in his memoirs that there were no vital US interests at stake. The smooth-talking Milošević disclaimed any responsibility for atrocities carried out by Serbs in Bosnia, led by a deranged psychiatrist and minor poet named Radovan Karadzic, even though he armed, financed, and controlled them. Still, Milošević, to many Western leaders, was a less plausible incarnation of Hitler than the thuggish Saddam Hussein. So the Americans were happy to let the Europeans sort this out for themselves. If they succeeded, that would be a weight off America's back, and if they didn't, well, that would prove once more that the US was the only indispensable nation. If there ever was a chance for Europe to show it could take action independently from the US, this was it. In the rather absurd words of Jacques Poos, foreign minister of Luxembourg: "This is the hour of Europe, not of America."

All sides in the war were no doubt guilty of heinous acts, but the moral case for some kind of intervention was clear: this was not about the control of oil wells in a tiny sheikhdom; a small, multi-ethnic state was in danger of being wiped out by a regime bent on ethnic cleansing. Barbarism of this kind hadn't happened in Europe since 1945. But when Baker tried to rally European leaders, all he got was hand-wringing and fine words. The British blamed the Germans for having recognized the secession of Croatia too swiftly; the Portuguese, who held the EEC presidency, said the French were an obstacle. The Germans had no desire to intervene and were in any case constrained by their constitution. Western Europeans, accustomed to half a century of comfort, peace, and US protection, appeared to be paralyzed in the face of mass violence.

The interesting question is why the British were so reluctant to act. All the talk of standing up to tyranny, of staunch Anglo-Saxon love of liberty and of exorcising Chamberlain's ghost, now suddenly seemed to belong to another age. Was it that British memories of their finest hours could be rekindled only if the Americans led? Were people right to claim that the end of the Cold War also spelled the end of the Special Relationship, for which there would no longer be any need? The official indifference to a slaughter taking place just a few hours away by plane from London was remarkable in any case.

Baker believed that the Europeans were hampered by bureaucratic inertia—every decision had to be unanimous—but also by historical prejudices. When he asked John Major whether the British could help stop the atrocities in Bosnia, or at least to make sure that victims received aid, the prime minister replied: "In theory, yes" but "in practice, no."[25] Major said he had to consult the other European leaders first. This was often an excuse for doing nothing. Baker was convinced that the British and French sided with the Serbs, their old allies against Nazi Germany, while the Germans "consistently gave the Croats the benefit of doubt"—the Croatian fascists had been Nazi Germany's wartime allies, albeit so brutal in their methods that even the SS was shocked.[26]

Baker's judgment may not have been entirely wrong. Serb officers in their crisp uniforms were sometimes seen as gentlemen one could do business with, whereas the Bosnian Muslims, although often highly sophisticated, secular, and not ethnically distinct at all, were seen as rabble. The Serbs called them "Turks." But the main reason the British and the French backed the Serbs probably had more to do with a hard-nosed form of realpolitik. Many people were persuaded that the war had erupted because of "ancient hatreds." This was supposedly a messy civil war, not a clear-cut invasion of a sovereign country. To intervene would only make things worse.

Since the Serbs were the strongest power in the former Yugoslavia, it was best to let them restore order, however harshly.

That is why the British were against protecting terrified civilians from bombardment by imposing a no-fly zone; why they were against armed intervention to allow humanitarian aid to get through; against lifting an arms embargo that deprived the Bosnians of weapons to defend themselves; and why Britain abstained from a UN resolution comparing "ethnic cleansing" to genocide. No matter how much John Major and his foreign secretary Douglas Hurd blamed other Europeans for inaction, it was the British who most often stood in the way. This was certainly the view of some other European leaders. Poland's prime minister Tadeusz Mazowiecki said in May 1993, "Any time there was a likelihood of effective action, a particular western statesman [Hurd] intervened to prevent it."[27]

Margaret Thatcher, still driving hard from her back seat, was not wrong to call this policy a "disgrace." She strongly opposed the claim that lifting the arms embargo, which favored the very well-equipped Serbs, would create "a level killing field," as Hurd liked to put it. The "killing field" was in Europe, she said. It was "in Europe's sphere of influence. It should be in Europe's sphere of conscience.... We are little more than an accomplice to massacre."[28]

But this is not how the British foreign secretary saw things. He recalled the debacle of Suez, the quagmire of Vietnam, and the endless Troubles in Northern Ireland. His brand of realism had a precedent in British history. Benjamin Disraeli refused to intervene on behalf of the Bulgarians in the 1870s, when they were being slaughtered by the Ottoman Turks. He regarded the Turks as a solid bulwark against the Russians. National interest trumped moral outrage.

Gladstone, on the other hand, then in opposition, believed in standing up to mass murder as a matter of principle. Disraeli and Queen Victoria dismissed him as a fanatic. Just so, Major and Hurd dismissed critics of their policies as "windbags" and grandstanders being "heroic with other people's lives."[29]

In a way, the behavior of Major and Hurd was to be expected. And the same probably goes for President Bush, who shied away from the European conflict, despite his high-flown rhetoric about a new world order during the Gulf War. Their realism was a reaction to the ideological fervor of the Reagan and Thatcher era. Both Bush and Major argued, without much proof, that domestic opinion would surely be dead set against embarking on another war. Hurd even challenged Bush's notion of a new world order. No such thing existed, he said: "We have a traditional set of world disorders and we are trying, case by case, and institution by institution, to equip ourselves to deal more adequately with those disorders."[30] This statement was not exactly wrong, but it did nothing to help the people in Bosnia who were being driven out of their homes to be killed, raped, and deported to horrific camps. Sarajevo, the cosmopolitan capital of Bosnia, was under siege. The airport was closed. And the local population was being bombarded daily by Serb guns and mortars nestled in the surrounding hills. The Serbian general Ratko Mladić boasted about his snipers: "Whenever I come to Sarajevo, I kill someone in passing. . . . I go kick the hell out of the Turks. . . . I f--- them."[31]

After a while, however, newspaper and television reports about the carnage became hard to ignore in Western capitals. A photograph of a cadaverous, hollow-eyed young man, staring through the barbed wire of a Serbian concentration camp, was on the cover of *Time* magazine, bearing the headline "Must It Go On?"[32] Thatcher remarked, "I never thought I'd see another holocaust in my life."[33] More than a million refugees were trying to find shelter.

Bush still refused to commit American troops. Canada, Britain, France, and others did contribute soldiers as blue-helmeted UN peacekeepers. But even though a UN resolution of December 1992 asked member states to use "all necessary means" to restore the sovereignty of Bosnia and Herzegovina, UN peacekeepers were not given the authority to engage in combat, except in self-defense. They were there to protect humanitarian aid, not to defend the Bosnian Muslims. And their vulnerable presence "on the ground" would be used as a reason not to allow NATO air strikes on Serbian positions. Bosnian Serbs later felt cocky enough to seize peacekeepers as hostages.

A bad-tempered conference was held in London in 1992, and a "statement of principles" was issued, making it clear that human rights should be protected, borders observed, and ethnic cleansing condemned. The Serbs were promised trade deals and economic aid only if they would agree to stop their violence. The UN would supervise heavy weapons in Bosnia and impose a no-fly zone. Meanwhile, a lasting diplomatic solution would be sought. The British and the French, who had wanted the old Yugoslavia to hold together, now looked for ways to slice up Bosnia into ethnic enclaves, and so in effect formalizing the results of ethnic cleansing.

But none of this made any difference. Promises were broken. Peace was not enforced. The killing went on. James Baker recalls with a certain smugness how he managed to open the Sarajevo airport for humanitarian supplies. A "game plan" was devised in Washington to threaten the Serbs with economic sanctions, a halt to their oil supplies, diplomatic isolation, and even, if necessary, multilateral air strikes. The EEC endorsed the plan. The UN issued an ultimatum. The Serbs agreed to open the airport. The French president François Mitterrand immediately flew in on a helicopter, to show off the tricolor. A French transport plane arrived with supplies. The blue UN flag was raised in front of the airport terminal. And yet, even as Mitterrand looked on helplessly, Serb guns kept blasting away at apartment buildings filled with civilians, whose water and electricity supplies had been cut off.

Baker, in his memoirs, said he didn't believe the "humanitarian nightmare" could have been prevented by "any combination of political, diplomatic, and economic measures." Only the use early on of military force could have done that. But, he concluded, "Bush's decision that our national interests did not require the United States of America to fight its fourth war in Europe in this century, with the loss of America's sons and daughters that would have ensued, was absolutely the right one."[34]

Even if it was, the Bosnian War exposed the fickleness of Anglo-American pretensions to spread freedom and keep the peace. The British prime minister and the US president were not yet at loggerheads over Bosnia. That would come later, when a new president was in power. The year 1992 was a campaign year. Bush's campaign manager was James Baker. Bill Clinton criticized Bush for his passivity in the face of a genocidal war. His campaign language was robust. What was needed, Clinton said, was "lift and strike"—lift the arms embargo, get US weapons to the beleaguered Bosnian Muslims, and strike hard if the Serbs stood in the way. The British wanted nothing to do with "lift and strike," and neither did the French.

Even though Americans were suffering through an economic recession, the mood in the Bush campaign was confident. He, after all, was the world leader who won the Gulf War, which had made his poll ratings soar. It was no secret whose side the Major government was on. Tory campaign operatives, who had successfully got Major elected in 1992 by smearing the Labour leader Neil Kinnock as a shifty, socialist tax and spender, were sent over to Washington to advise the Bush campaign. The Tories thought they had to do this, since they were afraid that a Republican defeat would threaten the Special Relationship. A trawl was even done through Home Office files to see if anything damaging might be found on Bill Clinton when he was a Rhodes scholar at Oxford. On the morning of the election, Douglas Hurd sent a private cable to Baker, his former counterpart. "You will be very much in my thoughts today," it read. "May you bring down every duck in the last flight of the shoot."[35]

But Clinton was not Kinnock. The Bush campaign never really caught fire. The shoot was a disaster. Stunned by his loss, Bush quoted Winston Churchill, who said after his electoral defeat in 1945 that he had been given the "order of the boot." And that, said the Gulf War hero, "is the exact same position in which I find myself today."[36]

Ten

TOO MUCH CONVICTION

Bill Clinton was born in 1946. He was the first US president with no memories at all of World War II. He was also the first to study in Britain, at Oxford University, between 1968 and 1970, as a bearded Rhodes scholar who, curiously, claimed never to have inhaled when smoking a joint. John F. Kennedy had applied in 1935 to be a student at the London School of Economics, but he had to bow out because of illness. While at Oxford, Clinton took part in demonstrations against the Vietnam War, hence—to help George H. W. Bush's campaign—the Tory interest in Home Office files, which might have shown that he applied for British citizenship. Nothing of the kind was ever found.

Despite his time spent in Britain, Clinton was not an Anglophile, and was obviously immune to any lingering wartime nostalgia. Unlike the smooth East Coast upper-class men who appreciated the cut of a fine English suit, Clinton grew up in provincial Arkansas as the stepson of an alcoholic car salesman. A Conservative prime minister, members of whose staff had worked hard to stop Clinton's election, certainly held no claim to his affection. Clinton didn't even make time to meet John Major in the winter of 1992.

Aside from bruised feelings about Tory meddling in the presidential campaign, there were other reasons why Britain didn't loom large in Clinton's thoughts about the world, which it was now his turn to help shape. His campaign revolved around promises to improve the American economy and boost jobs. In this respect at least, he was an America Firster. Even though Britain was the biggest investor in the US, countries like Germany and Japan had more economic clout. Clinton had also struck a tougher tone on Bosnia. Distancing himself from Bush, at least in words, he had decided that the US had a dog in that fight after all: standing aside in the face of mass murder was immoral, and it would damage Western standing in the world. Force would be used, Clinton warned, if "the will of the international community" were defied. The US would call for air strikes against anyone who stood in the way of humanitarian aid.[1] British opposition was viewed in Washington with contempt. There was also talk, without consulting the British, about adding more nations to the UN Security Council, diminishing Britain's influence. Clinton, under pressure from influential Irish Americans, such as Senator Edward Kennedy, upset the British even further by promising to get directly involved in the Irish Troubles by sending a "special US peace envoy" to Northern Ireland. (The designated envoy, Tom Foley, actually thought this was a "cocka-mamie" idea; it was swiftly dropped, only to be revived in 1995.)[2]

President Clinton appeared to confirm, more than any of his predecessors had done, that Britain really didn't matter much. John Major, understandably in this light, was desperate to make sure he would be the first foreign leader to meet the new occupant in the White House. The atmosphere there was nicely described by

Raymond Seitz, the US ambassador in London, who was one of the people assigned to soothe hurt feelings on both sides of the Atlantic and make the British feel a little special after all. Waiting for the prime minister to arrive, Clinton was chatting with his staff in the Oval Office. One of his aides joked, "Don't forget to say 'special relationship' when the press comes in." Whereupon Clinton said: "Oh, yes, how could I forget? The 'special relationship.'" And he "threw back his head and laughed."[3]

In fact, Clinton did turn on his charm for the PM. The Irish problem was tactfully left aside until Clinton was asked in a press conference about British human rights abuses in Northern Ireland. Major jumped in at once to remind people of IRA bombs killing innocent civilians in Britain. Clinton apparently rather admired him on this occasion for being so quick on his feet. Major had no success persuading the Americans to send troops to Bosnia to implement the "Vance-Owen plan," initiated by the UN, to carve up the former Yugoslavia into ethnic cantons. But he politely called Clinton's intention to drop food and medical supplies over Bosnia "imaginative," even though his foreign and defense secretaries were vehemently against it.[4] In any case, there was enough superficial bonhomie between the two leaders to prompt a headline in *The Guardian* that read "Clinton and Major Pull Old Alliance Together."[5]

This was too optimistic. Clinton and Major didn't actively dislike each other, but there wasn't much warmth either. The Irish question and Bosnia drove the two countries further and further apart. Not that Clinton, in spite of his tough campaign talk, could be described as especially gung ho on Bosnia. The disastrous US intervention in Somalia in October 1993, when eighteen American soldiers were killed by local militiamen and two were dragged through the streets by gleeful mobs, dampened any enthusiasm for further military adventures. The president, who managed to avoid military service during the Vietnam War, was ill at ease with soldiers anyway. Somalia wasn't Bosnia, of course. First Bush and then Clinton had gotten the US involved there for honorable reasons (the population was starving). But Somalia was a lawless place ruled by warlords fighting one another in vicious gang wars. The consequences for Somalians were awful, but the political stakes in Bosnia were higher. Richard Holbrooke, who would later play a major diplomatic role in the Bosnian war, wrote a memo to Clinton saying that Bosnia would be "the key test of American policy in Europe. . . . Continued inaction carries long-term risks which could be disruptive to US-European relations."[6]

Important voices, Republican and Democrat, were urging Clinton to at least threaten the Serbs with air strikes and lift the arms embargo. Even the cautious general Colin Powell, a prime exponent of the Vietnam Syndrome, was persuaded that this would be the right move. But when "lift and strike" was put to the British at the foreign secretary's country house in Kent, Major, Hurd, and the defense secretary Malcolm Rifkind were appalled. It was unworkable, they said; it would anger the Serbs, hinder humanitarian aid, put British blue helmets in danger, and prolong the war.

Warren Christopher, Clinton's secretary of state, found little more enthusiasm in other European capitals, but the British were the most passionate in their disapproval. The most common British riposte was that the Americans had no right to threaten the Serbs without putting their own troops on the ground. Rifkind, who had no military experience himself, countered the Republican senator Bob Dole's demand for lift and strike with the words "you Americans don't know the horrors of war"—an unfortunate statement to make to Dole, who had almost died in 1945—a year before Rifkind was even born—fighting the Germans in Italy.[7]

Things got so bad that Christopher declared the Special Relationship over. In 1994, the US granted a visa to Gerry Adams, the Sinn Féin leader who was regarded in London, for sound reasons, as a terrorist. This was before Adams had agreed to a cease-fire in Northern Ireland. No doubt the Irish American lobby was getting to Clinton, but the invitation was also a useful way to punish the British for their obstructionism in Bosnia.

Anglo-American relations reached their worst point in the winter of 1994, when Serb forces were advancing on Bihać, an ancient and once prosperous town on the Bosnian side of the Croatian border, designated by the UN as a "safe haven." Under siege from Serb armies, bombed and shelled constantly, Bihać had become a vast squalid refugee camp deprived of food and medical supplies. UN security was so inadequate that Serbs managed to loot a UN aid convoy carrying tons of food, which they proceeded to hand out to Serbs in Croatia. Serb fighters took off from the Udbina air base, just inside Croatia, to drop napalm and cluster bombs on buildings full of refugees in Bihać. Under pressure from Washington, US, British, French, and Dutch NATO fighters bombed the runway of Udbina, but they were careful to leave Serb planes unscathed. It was a symbolic act, a mere pinprick, but that was the point. A symbolic action is all UN officials, and the European governments, would stand for lest the Serbs retaliate.

Clinton called the raid the right thing to do. A number of Americans wanted to go much further. That is why Bob Dole received his lecture on the horrors of war from Malcolm Rifkind. Dole wanted to get the UN out of the way so NATO could crack down on the Serbs. The US decided no longer to enforce the arms embargo. The

British were outraged by the American temerity to effectively pick sides. NATO was now divided between the Americans and the Europeans. Americans, and several British newspapers, too, hinted at Chamberlain's ghost haunting Major and his Foreign Office. The French saw a chance to exploit the rift in NATO by inviting the British to weaken US leadership and strengthen the role of a purely European defense force—something that was still more theoretical than real. Major and Hurd were open to the idea. This was, in the opinion of more than one official, the worst cross-Atlantic crisis since Suez. But in 1956, it was Americans who stopped Europeans from continuing on a rash military intervention. Now the French and British had banded together to prevent the US from using force in the bloodiest European conflict since World War II. This particular Franco-British alliance was as misconceived as the one before.

The Serb leaders, however, high on their own brutality and encouraged by the timid UN and European response, overplayed their hand. Twice they shelled the central marketplace in Sarajevo, killing more than a hundred civilians. Two hundred eleven UN soldiers, including British, were kidnapped at gunpoint and chained to potential NATO targets as human shields. Even then British and French politicians were cautioning against military action. In April 1992, Srebrenica, another "safe haven," was overrun by Bosnian Serb troops led by General Ratko Mladić. The UN, backed by Britain and France, refused to help the outnumbered Dutch blue helmets with air strikes. Bosnian men were separated from the women and small children. More than seven thousand males, some as young as eleven years old, were shot in the head and dumped into a mass grave.

Still, the British, as well as UN officials, were against retaliation. But the French president Jacques Chirac had a change of heart. On

Bastille Day, he compared the West's failure to stop the Srebrenica massacre—and by the West he meant mainly Britain, not his own General Janvier, who had blocked efforts to support the Dutch battalion—to the deal made with Hitler in 1938. This was rich coming from the president of a country that had sat on its hands almost as much as Britain. But Chirac did help to persuade Clinton to "save the West" by blasting Milošević with the full force of US military power. The effect was swift. A deal was worked out in Dayton, Ohio. The chief US negotiator, Richard Holbrooke, pressed the Serbs to accept a large chunk of a former multiethnic, multifaith republic that was now pockmarked and sliced up by a war of savage ethnic cleansing.

If the West was saved, this also showed how European security was still wholly dependent on the US. John Major once said, "Every time the Europeans have tried to do something without the Americans on defense, they have made a bog of it."[8] But now the British were mostly to blame. On this rare occasion that they had chosen to be on the European side of an Atlantic rift, the consequences were dire. The Atlantic alliance was really an American order. It had been for a long time, of course, but British behavior in the Bosnian War had taken away the last illusion of a special Anglo-American bond. At least for the time being. Illusions often die hard: another wave of hubris would not be far off, one that would do so much damage that it almost erased the memory of slaughter in the Balkans.

In 1997, John Major lost the general election by a landslide. This had nothing to do with his policies on the Bosnian War. Once again, Europe was the main reason for a British prime minister to be driven out of Downing Street. Britain's relationship with the

European continent was still tearing the country, and particularly the Tory Party, apart. Major had decided not to decide about joining a common European currency. "Wait and see" was the way he sought to play for time, while other Europeans proceeded with their monetary union quite quickly. Wait and see was the official Conservative policy, which "the bastards" and other Tory Eurosceptics immediately did everything to undermine. When Margaret Thatcher was asked whether she supported a single European currency, she said, "Good heavens, no! I was the one who invented the answer. No. No. No."[9]

But instead of fighting back against such sentiments, Major gave in to them. He even struck a more Eurosceptic tone himself, saying on television that he regretted ever having said that Britain should be "at the heart of Europe." And so, he managed to alienate his most loyal pro-European supporters, while failing to appease the bastards, thus widening rifts in his party even further. Tony Blair, his Labour opponent, was quite right to say, "There are two Conservative parties fighting this election. John Major is in charge of neither of them."[10]

Europe was not the only reason Major lost, however. After eighteen years of Thatcher's leadership cult and Major's lukewarm conservatism, people were tired of the Tories. Major was a pleasant fellow who genuinely wished to give people the chance to better themselves, as he had done himself, scrambling up from his humble beginnings in shabby South London. But he seemed out of touch and hopelessly old-fashioned, as in his much mocked vision of Britain, put to the Conservative Group for Europe in 1993. Britain, he rhapsodized, "will still be the country of long shadows on county [cricket] grounds, warm beer, invincible green suburbs, dog lovers, and—as George Orwell said—old maids bicycling to Holy Communion through the morning mist."

Holy Communion would also prove to be to Tony Blair's taste, but otherwise his idea of Britain could not have been more different. Blair's New Labour promised youth, modernity, excitement, progress, new challenges, new opportunities, new everything. Blair's actual policies were vague and, in many respects, not so different from Major's. He even stole Major's own campaign slogan, promising not to give people handouts, but hand-ups—a phrase he trotted out at least twice in his autobiography. But he was a master of the narrative, of the hard sell, of spin, often expressed in strange staccato phrases: "Our party: New Labour. Our mission: New Britain. New Labour. New Britain. New Britain."[11]

This would be the foundation for a new Anglo-American relationship. Blair and Clinton understood one another perfectly. Clinton had won two presidential elections, but he felt rather lonely in his efforts to promote his so-called Third Way, neither socialist nor laissez-faire, liberal but capitalist, hand-ups but no handouts. Tony and Bill had a cozy dinner in London with their wives, Cherie and Hillary. Bill recalled they felt like old friends from the start.

Blair's master of spin, his "director of communications and strategy" Alastair Campbell, described Blair's first meeting with Clinton when Blair was still in opposition in November 1995. They talked politics. But what really animated the discussion was marketing. Here is Campbell: "Clinton had an interesting line about how achievement was less important than definition in the information age. . . . Like TB, he talked a fair bit about the polls and media. . . . He said it was important to have mainstream values and mainstream economic policies."[12]

What the Third Way was selling, apart from the candidates themselves, was a meritocracy that would do away with class privileges. Major had offered the same thing, but the aspirations of Clinton and Blair, personally and politically, were less restrained and more in tune with Margaret Thatcher's "meritocratic" notion that greed is good. As Peter Mandelson, one of Blair's closest advisers, nicely put it: "New Labour is intensely relaxed about people getting filthy rich."[13] The pursuit, even worship of money, celebrity, and success would replace the advantages of birth. That Blair and his wife, Cherie, should cultivate the friendship of rock stars and spend their holidays as guests of the louche Italian parvenu, Prime Minister Silvio Berlusconi, should not have surprised anyone. The same was true of Clinton's decision, in the last days of his presidency, to pardon a distinctly dodgy group of wealthy international fraudsters who had done him financial favors. This was not just a matter of greed, but of strategy. Gone were the days that the Left would be associated with worthy austerity, beards and sandals, and hostility toward the rich. That people on the left could make lots of money was a sign that the Third Way was working. This is one reason why Blair has been called the most American of British prime ministers.

There was another reason too. Blair was an intensely religious man. As a student at Oxford, he was more interested in theology than in politics. Bill Clinton was serious about his Southern Baptist faith, but Blair's Anglicanism, later to be converted to his wife's Roman Catholicism, veered toward the messianic. It has often been pointed out that British socialism was always more Methodist than Marxist. And there had been other pious British prime ministers. But not since Gladstone had Britain had a prime minister whose politics were driven by a missionary zeal to fight the forces of evil.

Blair called Gladstone "one of my political heroes."[14] He would be Gladstone to John Major's and Douglas Hurd's Disraeli. But he was even more zealous than the great Victorian.

One of Blair's mentors in his student days was an Australian priest named Peter Thomson. Blair wrote about him: "Politically, Pete was on the left, but religion came first. Therefore, so, in a sense, it did for me. Not that the two were separated by him, or me, but the frame within which you see the world is different if religion comes first."[15] This frame puts the believer firmly on the side of the good, at least in his own mind. In the US, Blair's statement would not have made him stand out. In Britain, it did.

Being good is by no means incompatible with the pursuit of money and worldly success. It is in fact an old Protestant conceit that such accomplishments prove a person's favor in the eyes of God. This attitude has deep roots in northern European but especially in American culture: the pursuit of wealth combined with a degree of moral smugness.

Bill Clinton once described the Third Way as "putting a human face on the global economy."[16] But this was too modest. His adviser and tireless defender, the writer Sidney Blumenthal, hit the giddy tone of the Clinton-Blair relationship more accurately. The two leaders met in 1997 at Chequers, the prime ministerial country residence, where they laid out Third Way strategies. "The Anglo-American special relationship," Blumenthal writes, "had never before been politically parallel. This parallel gave Clinton's presidency a new sense of coherence and depth, and ratified his course. . . . The Prime Minister was an ally like no other. . . . With Blair's election in 1997, Clinton felt that he himself was leading an international movement."[17]

Blair echoed this sentiment on a visit to Washington a year later, when he declared that his aim was to put New Labour at the head of a "worldwide movement of ideas."[18] These ideas on globalism and meritocracy were not quite as new as the Anglo-American leaders pretended, but they were injected, certainly on Blair's part, with a passion that seemed to go straight back to nineteenth-century notions of a joint mission to morally improve the world with Anglo-Saxon values and liberal ideals. One thing missing, of course, was the British Empire. And this new "transatlantic" project would soon tangle Blair into the same kind of European knots that plagued his predecessors.

Like John Major, Blair didn't suffer from any wartime hang-ups. He declared himself to be "passionately" European. And he spoke reasonably good French. Again like Major, he said he wanted Britain to be "at the center of Europe." Blair even expressed his desire to replace the pound sterling with the common European currency, the euro. Some of his rhetoric, however, sounded more like a throwback to a time when Britain could see itself only as primus inter pares. Although firmly ensconced in Europe, Britain still had a "historical role in the world" to play as a "major global player" that would be totally new, totally modern.[19]

The specialness of the British prime minister, compared to his European confreres, is described in Blair's memoirs as follows. The British, he explains, "prefer their prime ministers to stand tall internationally. Most foreign leaders wouldn't have turned a head if they wandered down Guildford High Street. The US president, yes. . . . However, Brits would want to know that in a French city people would recognize me."[20]

Soon after his resounding election victory, Blair set off to lecture his fellow Europeans on the superiority of the Third Way, which smacked to them as another claim to Anglo-American superiority. He told European socialists that the "social Europe" should become the "people's Europe": young, vigorous, creative, competitive. Old-fashioned welfare-state social democracy was passé. What was needed was a dose of decent Anglo-Saxon liberalism, with "a human face," of course.

This did not go down so well in France, where more statist politics were still favored. Germany's Social Democrat leader Gerhard Schröder saw some merit in the Third Way, but most members of his Social Democratic Party were highly skeptical. The more conservative chancellor Helmut Kohl, still haunted by chilly memories of Margaret Thatcher, was prepared to warm to Blair. But Blair's own attachment to the European project soon wavered. After having appeared to commit Britain to the monetary union, he quickly withdrew to the wait-and-see position that caused John Major so much grief. He even held out the promise of a referendum. The ostensible reason was economic disparity between Britain and the Continent. But Blair always paid close attention to the right-wing tabloid press, whose hostility to "Europe" was unrelenting.

Despite Blair's "passionate" feelings about Europe, his view on Britain's role as a bridge between Europe and the US was entirely traditional. Speaking to businessmen in New York, he said that it would be "absurd to imagine that, for Britain, there is a choice between the relationship with Europe and that with America."[21] But if a choice had to be made, Blair, like almost all his predecessors, veered toward the latter. One of his cabinet ministers once said, "Supporting the Americans is part of Tony's DNA."[22] Blair himself stated, with typical bravado, "When Britain and America work together on the international scene there is little we cannot achieve."[23]

As had so often been the case before, it was in military conflict that British zigzags between Europe and the US were most sharply visible. After Clinton managed in the late summer of 1995 to bomb Slobodan Miloševic into submission, or at least into willingness to negotiate, he began to feel more comfortable about using military force, especially if it could be dished out from a great height. French, British, and even German fighters had taken part in the NATO intervention against the Serbs, too, but it was initiated and led by the US, which Clinton now liked to call "the indispensable nation." There are times, he said a year later, "when America, and only America, can make a difference between war and peace, between freedom and repression, between hope and fear."[24]

In 1998, the US president ordered missile strikes on targets in Afghanistan and Sudan, marked as strongholds of al-Qaeda terrorists. In the latter country, Operation Infinite Reach hit a harmless pharmaceutical plant on the mistaken assumption that it was producing chemical weapons. Clinton was about to be impeached for lying under oath. Some said the bombing was done to distract public attention. But the US had some reason for lashing out against al-Qaeda, which had, after all, attacked American embassies in two African countries and murdered 221 people. In any case, when Clinton decided to send bombers to the Middle East, even as he prepared to testify before a grand jury about his sexual misbehavior, Blair was just about the only European leader to stand by him.

The next military action in the Middle East was a truly Anglo-American affair. When Saddam Hussein was obstructing UN inspectors' efforts to check that he wasn't developing "weapons of mass destruction" (WMD), Clinton wanted to punish the Iraqi strongman. Neoconservatives in Washington were arguing that it was America's duty to liberate the world from dictators. Clinton was not a neoconservative. They were, on the whole, more sympathetic to the Republicans. But their views were close to those of so-called liberal hawks in the Democratic camp. In London, Blair had had Saddam in his sights as a major force of evil for some time. All his instincts told him to back the Americans. Standing next to the president in Washington in February 1998, he declared, "We have stood together before in the face of tyranny. It's important, not out of machismo or a test of international virility, but in the interests of long-term world peace that Saddam Hussein is made to back down."[25]

At that point, Britain held the presidency of the European Council, which rotated every six months. The council is where government leaders set European policies. There was no policy in the EU on what to do about Saddam. The French were very much opposed to military action. Blair had gotten himself into hot water by agreeing, without consulting the US, to work with France on a common European defense force. This irritated the Americans. But immediately after that, Blair annoyed the French even more by deciding to join the US in Operation Desert Fox without telling his fellow Europeans. "Bill decided we had to act," writes Blair in his memoirs. So British Tornados and US B-1 bombers pounded Iraqi military installations for four days, and victory was declared. "It was a nerve-racking time," Blair recalls, "and the operation was a limited success."[26] Saddam was still there, even though his military force had been somewhat "degraded." And the UN inspectors were no longer in Iraq. But once more, the British had chosen to stick with America as the lone European brother-in-arms.

Compared to the next battle, however, Operation Desert Fox was just a kind of finger exercise. Tony Blair's true "awakening on foreign policy," as he put it, "happened over Kosovo."[27] This conflict showed Blair in his full pomp as a warrior for good against evil, and it put—again in Blair's own words—"a colossal strain on my personal relationship with Bill Clinton."[28]

It all began when Milošević, beaten back by the Dayton Accords, decided to crack down on anti-Serb agitation in Kosovo, a part of the former Yugoslavia with a majority population of Albanian Muslims. Relations between Serbs and Albanians in Kosovo had always been troubled. The Albanians decided to free themselves from Serbian oppression by forming the Kosovo Liberation Army. Serious fighting broke out. Milošević sent in police battalions and troops. This led to massacres, and large numbers of refugees were stuck in the mountains with nowhere to go. With the icy winter approaching, about two hundred thousand Albanians were forced to sleep in the open air. Diplomatic moves were made. Milošević made promises to rein in his troops and then broke them. The killing continued. Blair decided that what happened in Bosnia should not be allowed to happen again. The traditional option of ignoring atrocities in faraway countries was abhorrent to him. The kind of "realism" associated with John Major's government was out of date. Blair: "I happen to think as Gladstone did that it is also immoral."[29]

In one of the most fascinating passages in his memoirs, Blair describes how around this time he came across Chamberlain's diaries in the library at Chequers. He read his account of meeting Hitler in 1938, when the British leader decided to buy peace for our time at the expense of Czechoslovakia. Blair "tried to imagine being him, thinking like him." He concluded that Chamberlain "was a good man, driven by good motives," but that he made a fundamental error. He failed to see that fascism represented a force that was so strong and rooted that it had to be "uprooted and destroyed." Churchill, on the other hand, understood this perfectly. And there Churchill "had sat at the same table in Chequers"[30] where Blair was now musing about the great questions of history and sound leadership. "Why was I so keen to act [on Kosovo]? I saw it essentially as a moral issue. And that, in a sense, came to define my view on foreign and military intervention."[31]

In May 1999, Blair visited an Albanian refugee camp. As he emerged from a Black Hawk helicopter, people cheered with shouts of "Tony! Tony!" He listened to stories of horrifying violence and compared the deportations of Kosovar Muslims to what happened to the Jews. "This is no longer just a military conflict," he said. "It is a battle between good and evil, between civilization and barbarity."[32]

Clinton had hoped to stay out of another military conflict in the Balkans. In Washington, Kosovo was seen as a European problem. The Russians, as well as the French, were leery of any NATO intervention. Miloševic doubted whether the West had the stomach for a fight, and despite more diplomatic promises to withdraw his troops, Serb forces continued to murder Muslims in Kosovo. In the end, Clinton, pressed by Blair, was persuaded to act. NATO bombers would be let loose on Kosovo. Clinton's adviser Sidney Blumenthal gives an almost rapturous account of what followed: "The natural alignment of the United States was cemented in shared objectives as never before—closer than Franklin Roosevelt and Winston Churchill had been. . . . Already, the Clinton-Blair relationship had been tested during the bombing of Iraq. Across Europe, leaders of entrenched social democratic parties looked to Clinton as a political trailblazer."

Blumenthal saw the Balkan conflict in terms of the Third Way, not surprisingly, since he was the ideological point man between London and Washington. Kosovo, in Blumenthal's telling, was a crisis for all social democrats: "If they succeeded in Kosovo, they would gain a strengthened platform for the Third Way and for their new ideas about globalization and interdependence. Clinton himself well understood the stakes."[33]

Perhaps he did. But there was also a lingering shame over the lack of any Western action when more than a million people were slaughtered in the Rwandan civil war between 1990 and 1994. In Blair's case, Gladstonian moralism and superficial, though no less heartfelt, references to World War II were probably more important than promotion of the Third Way. In speeches arguing for armed force against the Serbs, both leaders stressed that this war was fought, in Blair's words, "in defense of our values, rather than our interests."[34] He said this in Chicago, to a group of businessmen, in April 1999. In this speech, which took his own diplomats by surprise, Blair argued that forceful intervention was not only justified, but essential, when large numbers of people were being killed, even by their own leaders.

Consequently, NATO fighters bombed and bombed and bombed, first just Serb positions in Kosovo, then targets in Serbia itself, at one point hitting the Chinese embassy by mistake because the CIA had forgotten to update its maps of Belgrade. As a result, hundreds of thousands of refugees now tried to get out of hellish Kosovo. And soon NATO began to run out of targets. Blair put the dilemma well: "The question then arises: now what? The targets get more interspersed with civilian areas. 'Collateral damage'—a ghastly phrase that I tried to ban—grows, and the wrong targets get hit."[35] As is almost always the case, bombing alone does not win a war. Milošević could take it. Which is why Blair, in his speech in Chicago, went further. He said, "We will not have succeeded until an international force has entered Kosovo and allowed the refugees a return to their homes."[36]

But this was precisely what neither Clinton nor the European NATO allies wanted to do. Blair called Clinton every day to try to convince him. The traditional roles in the Special Relationship had been neatly reversed once again: no longer was the wise old Greek trying to rein in the impetuous Roman; it was other way around. Indeed, Blair behaved much like Margaret Thatcher when she thought Reagan was going wobbly on nuclear weapons. Clinton's people began to get annoyed with Blair's cajoling. Some were calling him "Winston" behind his back. And Clinton himself resented being upstaged by a British prime minister, especially when neo-conservatives and liberal hawks started sporting "Blair for President" stickers on their car bumpers. One former left-wing American journalist called Blair "the leader of the free world."[37]

Blair kept pressing Clinton, who claimed American public opinion wouldn't stand for a ground war; they barely knew where Yugoslavia was. When the British defense secretary, George Robertson, visited his US counterpart, William Cohen, in Washington, Cohen said the British were pushing a hard line because it would be American boys who would get killed. Whereupon Robertson said that fifty thousand British troops were ready to go.

Stung by the implication that he was a weak leader, and perhaps beaten down by Blair's persistence, Clinton finally made a statement that all options were open, even the dispatch of ground troops to Kosovo. Milošević would presumably still have held out, if he could have counted on the continued support of the Russians. When Boris Yeltsin, in an increasingly rare moment of lucidity, told him that this would no longer be the case, the Serb leader gave up and agreed to withdraw from Kosovo.

It was a moment of triumph for Blair. He was in Germany when he got the news on Thursday, June 3. The BBC correspondent John Simpson said to Alastair Campbell, Blair's strategist, "Congratulations. It looks like game, set and match."[38] The German chancellor Schröder was glad it was all over. The first postwar leader to have sent Germans into active combat (fighter pilots), he had been adamantly against an invasion. Jacques Chirac made a speech saying the Americans could have ended the violence sooner, if only they had talked to the Russians. Campbell concluded, "Within NATO, the truth was we really were more like the Americans and we were not like the Europeans in the final analysis." And Blair told him, "That is exactly what Thatcher said when I saw her on Tuesday."[39]

Blair's conviction that military intervention should become the norm when human rights were seriously violated anywhere on the globe got a further boost in 2000, when roughly one thousand British marines and paratroopers ousted a brutal rebel junta from the capital of Sierra Leone. No great national interest had been involved. Britain, the old colonial power, had saved a civilian population from being raped and murdered by fighters of the Revolutionary United Front, many of whom were teenagers in combat gear, hopped up on heroin and cocaine. This was Blair's "ethical foreign policy" in action. It had been a relatively easy victory.

Clinton's term as president came to an end in the same year. He was still quite popular in the US, but his tainted reputation as a reckless philanderer meant that the new Democratic candidate, his vice president, Al Gore, decided to keep his distance, perhaps to his cost. The Third Way would soon be over in the US. Its accomplishments were patchy. The economy had boomed under Clinton. But he failed to reform the iniquities of American health care. Like Blair, Clinton put more money into public education. The crime rate declined, but the number of mostly black men in federal prisons doubled. One undoubted achievement was the Good Friday Agreement that restored peace to Northern Ireland. Active American help had much to do with this. Blair's summing up of the changed face of Northern Ireland is not inaccurate: "People who had wanted to kill each other were now wanting to work together. Remarkable, moving and satisfying."[40]

There are other, more disturbing legacies left by the Blair-Clinton years. One was the greater importance than ever before of "spinning the narrative," of politics as a form of marketing, of "definition" being more highly prized than "achievement." That, and the fact that the Third Way leaders had become rather too relaxed about "people getting filthy rich." Those people very much included themselves. But the most important legacy did not stem from greed but from more noble sentiments. Blair, especially, more than Clinton, in fact, had become convinced that the West, and Anglo-America in particular, should be on a mission to civilize the world, with armed force if necessary.

Before leaving the political scene, Clinton had a last word of advice to Blair: "Don't let your friendship with America wane, just because I've gone."[41] Blair, Clinton said, "should get as close to George Bush as you have been to me."[42] Blair's chief of staff, Jonathan Powell, had already given similar advice to the British ambassador in Washington, Christopher Meyer, a few years before: "We want you to get up the arse of the White House and stay there."[43]

Neither Meyer nor the prime minister himself really needed to be told. They would remain ensconced in that increasingly dark place, not because they were forced to, or because they were sentimental about the Special Relationship, or even just because they thought sticking with the US was the only way for Britain to punch above its weight, but chiefly because of Blair's deep conviction that it was the right place to be.

Eleven

THE FINEST MOMENT

Our leaders should stand out, and if not cut a dash, at least make an impact. . . .
Again, I stress: It's not the reason for acting in Afghanistan and Iraq, or anything else, but our alliance with the US gave Britain a huge position.

· TONY BLAIR[1]

Like most US presidents, George W. Bush was a great admirer of Churchill. The British wished to ingratiate themselves with the new president, whose politics were hardly in tune with Blair's Third Way, let alone with the views of Blair's cabinet ministers far to his left. Hence the loan to him of Winston Churchill's bust. Hence, also, the gift of a copy of the Atlantic Charter, with Churchill's scribbles in the margins. Christopher Meyer, the British ambassador, had already observed these particular American enthusiasms in Washington. He had "sensed the goodwill" in the Special Relationship "whenever Margaret Thatcher was in the presence of Americans; or when the memory of Winston Churchill was invoked, which was often, including in the White House."[2]

Despite Bush's love of Churchilliana, Blair's people were quite nervous about how the two leaders were going to hit it off. There were mutual suspicions to be overcome. Blair's earlier agreement with France to strengthen European defense capabilities had raised hackles in Washington. There was a common view among the Republicans that "the Europeans" were a bunch of spoiled untrustworthy "socialists" who were taking America for a ride. And quite a few people in London saw Bush as a crass Texan know-nothing, whose first move was to show his contempt for international efforts to cope with climate change by withdrawing from the Kyoto treaty on global warming.

This much was made clear by Bush's people early on: American interests would come first. International alliances could be formed on an ad hoc basis to serve those national interests. The result would be a further break from the postwar international order set up at the end of World War II and cemented in the Cold War. Western solidarity between Europe and America, faced with a common Communist enemy, could no longer be counted on. This put Britain in an awkward spot, since the choice to cling to the Special Relationship would pose a bigger risk of isolation in Europe.

To the long series of photographs that illustrate official Anglo-American encounters, one might usefully add the one of Blair and Bush meeting for the first time at Camp David in the winter of 2001. There they are walking Bush's dog in the woods, Bush in the presidential leather bomber jacket and cowboy boots, his long arms splayed in a rather simian pose, and Blair, grinning self-consciously, trying to look just as tough and informal with his fingers squeezed into the pockets of what the British ambassador called "ball-crushingly tight" blue corduroy trousers. They discussed politics, family, and God. And they apparently got along fine.

Blair continued to see Britain's role as a bridge between Europe and the US. This role was turned into a mission after September 11, 2001, when three catastrophic acts of terrorism killed more than three thousand people. Two passenger planes, hijacked by al-Qaeda operatives, crashed into the Twin Towers in New York; a third blasted a hole in the Pentagon in Washington, DC; and a fourth exploded in a Pennsylvania field after passengers overwhelmed the terrorists, in time to avoid hitting a target but too late to stop the crash.

Blair immediately declared that "9/11" constituted a war against "the free and democratic world," that Britain would stand "shoulder to shoulder with our American friends," and would "not rest until this evil is driven from the world."[3] To show solidarity, Blair's foreign policy adviser, David Manning, immediately flew to Washington in a private jet with the top British intelligence chiefs to have dinner at the CIA headquarters. George Tenet, the CIA director, called this "an affirmation of the special relationship between our two nations and as touching an event as I experienced during my seven years as DCI [director of Central Intelligence]."[4]

Bush, like many Americans, saw al-Qaeda terrorism as an attack on "our way of life, our very freedom." He also invoked memories of World War II: "The Pearl Harbor of the twenty-first century took place today."[5] Blair did the same, from a more British perspective, recalling in New York how his father had lived through the German bombings. Blair said that while the Blitz was raging over London in 1940, "there was one country and one people that stood side by side with us then. That country was America, and the people were the American people."[6] This was quite wrong, of course. There was indeed a strong constituency in the US that was hostile to Nazi Germany. But most Americans were still very much opposed to helping

Britain, an attitude that changed only when the Japanese forced America's hand in December 1941, and Hitler declared war on the US.

But Blair's sentiments made him enormously popular in the US. He was invited to hear Bush address a joint session of Congress. "America has no greater friend than Great Britain," the president said, glancing up at Blair, sitting in the VIP gallery. "Once again we are joined together in a great cause. So honored the British prime minister has crossed an ocean to show his unity of purpose with America. Thank you for coming, friend." This was greeted with moist eyes and prolonged applause. A banner was waved at a baseball game in Yankee Stadium that read GOD BLESS GEORGE BUSH AND TONY BLAIR. Civilization itself, Bush claimed, "our shared civilization," was at stake.

It is easy to forget that all this rhetoric followed three criminal acts, not the declaration of a world war. But it might have gone to anyone's head. It certainly brought out the messianic streak in Blair. He shared this with the born-again Christian president. Both used the word "evil" a great deal. Three days after 9/11, Bush chose the Episcopal national cathedral in Washington, DC, as the right spot to declare that "our responsibility to history is already clear: to answer these attacks and rid the world of evil." If anything, Blair, in his speech to the Labour Party conference in October, sounded even more unhinged. He spoke of the "fight for freedom." Here was "a moment to seize." The "kaleidoscope has been shaken. The pieces are in flux. Before they do, let us reorder the world around us."[7] Quite who "they" were was left vague. But there was no doubt about who was going to do the reordering. Blair's foreign secretary, Jack Straw, sounded almost as grandiose. Britain, he intoned, was "a very powerful force for good."[8] Britain, he said, would lead Europe in the war against terrorism.

Following Churchill's example, Blair began sending the US president short missives with advice. Afghanistan was where the al-Qaeda leader, Osama bin Laden, scion of a wealthy Saudi Arabian business family, should be hit. He still had the protection of the Taliban theocratic regime. Bush had already promised Blair that Afghanistan would be targeted by the "full force of the US military . . . bombers coming from all directions."[9]

As was his wont, Blair had been browsing through the history books at Chequers for inspiration and came across the diaries of Field Marshal Roberts, the man who helped to crush the Indian uprising against British colonial rule in 1857. In his memoirs, Blair has little to say about the reasons for the Indian rebellion, but he is impressed with "the remarkable spirit of the British soldier." In one hopeless assault on an Indian redoubt, Scottish Highlanders had ridden to their certain deaths: "But how the pride of their regiment swelled in the endeavor."[10]

This is very odd language indeed for the New Labour leader who had promised a new, modern "Cool Britannia." It was more like something out of a colonial adventure story by John Buchan. But at least Blair realized how difficult a war in Afghanistan would be. Afghans had always been a thorn in the flesh of the British imperialists. Which is why, in Blair's view, it would be essential that "we" should not simply embark upon a war to punish. "It had to liberate."[11] Blair's "humanitarian interventionism" overlapped with American neoconservatism. He didn't simply go along with the old idea that it was America's destiny to spread freedom and democracy across the world; he believed it was *his* mission too. The trouble was that some of the most powerful figures in Washington, such as Vice President Dick Cheney and defense secretary Donald Rumsfeld, had less sentimental reasons for projecting American force.

That the "war against terror" would not stop in Afghanistan was already in the cards immediately after the brutal killings in New York and Washington. On the day itself, Donald Rumsfeld, in a National Security Council meeting, wondered why the US shouldn't go for Iraq as well as al-Qaeda. The next day, Bush asked for proof that Saddam Hussein had masterminded the attacks. The idea that Saddam was behind al-Qaeda had been promoted for some time by academic cranks and neocon think-tankers. Cheney, Rumsfeld, his deputy Paul Wolfowitz, and Bush's national security adviser Condoleezza Rice, appeared to believe in the conspiracy. Or perhaps it just offered a convenient excuse for violent action. Told by their intelligence agencies that there was no proof, they asked them to dig deeper until they could find some.

There is no reason to assume that Blair thought Saddam was responsible for 9/11. His intelligence chiefs certainly didn't. But he had warned about the dangers of Saddam Hussein early on. What if a brutal dictator like Saddam would get his hands on biological, nuclear, or other "weapons of mass destruction"? UN sanctions had been imposed on Iraq to enable inspectors to make sure this didn't happen, but they continued to be obstructed by Saddam. There was an element of hypocrisy in these Western worries about Saddam, since the British government had helped him build a chemical plant in 1985 that produced the mustard and nerve gas put to murderous use in the war against Iran. And the Reagan administration actively backed Saddam in that terrible conflict. A troubleshooter was sent over to Baghdad in 1983 to see how the US could help the dictator.

This US envoy was Donald Rumsfeld. Western hypocrisy, however, did not mean that Saddam was now harmless.

In 1998, Bill Clinton signed the Iraq Liberation Act: "It should be the policy of the United States to support efforts to remove the regime headed by Saddam Hussein from power in Iraq and to promote the emergence of a democratic government to replace that regime." This was not exactly a declaration of war, but 9/11 precipitated it, even though there was no evidence that Saddam had had anything to do with the atrocities in the US. Taking out Saddam would be part of "reordering the world."

Blair's worries about the damage Saddam could do were not absurd. Paul Wolfowitz and other neocons may also truly have believed that it was America's mission to use military force to promote the emergence of democratic governments, in the Middle East and elsewhere. Comparisons were made with the aftermath of World War II, when the US guided Germany and Japan back to democracy, as though invading Iraq would amount to the same thing. But the hysterical core of the Bush administration found its truest expression in a memo sent in September 2002 by Douglas Feith, undersecretary of defense for policy, to John McLaughlin, deputy director of the CIA. War, Feith argued, was "not optional." The survival of the US as a free society was at stake. Proving a connection between al-Qaeda and Saddam was "not (repeat not) of the essence."[12]

In short, it was so important to topple Saddam that any plausible reason would do. Ways were even suggested to provoke him, for example by flying a reconnaissance aircraft in UN colors over Iraq in the hope he would provide a casus belli by shooting it down. There were signs that Bush was ambivalent early on about going to war with Iraq. His secretary of state, Colin Powell, was advising him not to do anything so rash. But for Bush, mindful perhaps of his father's failure to bring Saddam down after the Gulf War, the issue had become personal. Early in 2002, his press secretary, Ari Fleischer, had been pressed by a reporter on the likelihood of an invasion. Told about this later that day, Bush responded to Fleischer in words that Blair is unlikely to have used, even in private: "Did you tell her I don't like motherfuckers who gas their own people? . . . Did you tell her I don't like assholes who lie to the world? . . . Did you tell her I'm going to kick his sorry motherfucking ass all over the Mideast?"[13]

American intentions could hardly be misunderstood when Blair visited Bush at his ranch in Crawford, Texas, on April 6, 2002. Alastair Campbell's diary entry for that day is oddly banal, as though he were downplaying the importance of the occasion. He mentions a discussion with Bush about alcoholism (they bonded over overcoming that affliction). He talks about Blair being compelled to go on an exhausting run with the president, and about Bush's wonderful sense of humor. He doesn't mention that Bush told the press on the day before that "I made up my mind that Saddam needs to go." Nor does he say that Blair agreed with him and promised to support the US. Blair had already told his aides, "We're not going to be with the other Europeans. Our policy on Iraq has always been different to them. We've always been with the Americans on this one."[14]

The question was how it could be finessed, defined, presented, and, most important of all to Blair, sold to members of his Labour Party, the British public, and other European leaders, who were sure to oppose a preemptive war to change a foreign government. Blair impressed on Bush the importance of international support. The Security Council of the UN had to endorse any attack on Saddam. The US also needed to actively engage with the conflict between

Palestinians and Israelis, which had erupted once again in violence. And the war aim should be focused on weapons of mass destruction, not regime change. Bush nodded politely when Blair spoke, and said he understood the prime minister's position.

At a joint press conference after their get-together, Bush told reporters that he had "explained to the prime minister that the policy of my government is the removal of Saddam and that all options are on the table." Blair was a little more nuanced and said that Iraq would be a better place without Saddam Hussein, to be sure. But what was truly intolerable was that Saddam wouldn't allow inspectors to make sure he had no weapons of mass destruction. Saddam had to follow the UN resolutions.

There was no single reason, besides his personal animosity, for Bush's belligerence. After 9/11, the Americans wanted to lash out and show they still were the greatest power on earth. Donald Rumsfeld pointed out that it would be easier to tackle a relatively minor state than a nebulous band of terrorists who could be holed up in Afghan caves or in the backstreets of Hamburg. There was money to be made in a post-Saddam Iraq. Oil interests were involved. Victory in Iraq would also allow the US to withdraw troops from Saudi Arabia; pious Muslims didn't welcome American soldiers so near the holy sites. And quite a few people on the liberal left in America were just as convinced as the neocons that toppling a dictator would be a noble enterprise, and that it might lead to a democratic spring all over the Middle East. Cheney, no liberal himself, reassured doubters that American and British troops would be greeted as liberators, just as they once were when they defeated the Nazis in Europe.

Blair's motives for going along with George W. Bush so early on, aware of the political risks he was taking in Britain, and the rest of

Europe, should not be simplified either. He was genuinely worried about weapons of mass destruction. But even though he couldn't say so in public, this was not actually his main concern. A few days before going to meet Bush in Texas, Blair held a strategy meeting at Chequers with British military and intelligence officials. The idea was to furnish the prime minister with arguments to influence Bush. When the question was raised whether regime change or WMD should be the main war aim, one of the generals remarked that it had to be the former. But Campbell records in his diary that Blair "felt it was regime change in part because of WMD but more broadly because of the threat to the region and the world."[15] This is something Blair could not say in public. He knew that other European leaders, especially Jacques Chirac, would disagree, and so would most people who voted for him in Britain.

Ever since Winston Churchill began to see (and resent) Britain's waning and America's waxing power during World War II, the British have been obsessed with the notion of influence. There are many reasons for this obsession: the weary concern of the older and supposedly wiser nation that the young upstarts would run wild; the desire to cling to the last vestiges of quickly fading power; and perhaps a less conscious wish, driven by atavistic ideas of a common culture but also by a form of power worship, to identify with America. Blair was no different. He decided to support Bush because he wanted influence. He didn't want the US to go it alone. And although, unlike Churchill or Harold Macmillan, Blair could not claim American ancestry, he was seen as the most American prime minister in history. He was even compared by one American enthusiast to Abraham Lincoln.

British influence on American leaders was never as great as was hoped in London. Blair, too, was destined to be disappointed. The

Bush administration had no interest in pressing Ariel Sharon, the Israeli prime minister, to resolve the Palestinian conflict; on the contrary, Sharon was given a free hand to crack down on Palestinians. And there was little interest in the Bush camp in involving the UN. Vice President Cheney, among others, was actively hostile to the idea. But there was a meeting of minds on a deeper level, where Blair's messianic streak and Bush's evangelical view of American destiny dovetailed in a joint desire to topple dictators and reorder the world. As Blair said: "I had reached the same conclusion from a progressive standpoint as George had from a conservative one."[16]

In Campbell's odd list of banalities that took place on that historic day in April 2002 when Blair and Bush met in Crawford, Texas, there is one telling anecdote from his diary worth repeating. Campbell was working out on a treadmill in the gym of his hotel. Next to him, padding along slowly, was a large woman who asked him whether he was English, and when she heard that he was, whether he knew Tony Blair. Yes, he replied, he did. She then expressed her great joy that "the world was run by two God-fearing young men." She prayed for Tony every day. Was Campbell a religious man? No, he was not. She felt sad, but kindly offered him a spot on her "George W. Bush email prayer group."[17]

The publicly stated aim of the war was chosen for reasons of expediency, and not just because it suited Blair. Paul Wolfowitz made this clear in an interview in July 2003: "For bureaucratic reasons we settled on one issue, weapons of mass destruction, because it was the one reason everyone could agree on."[18] But there was no proof that Saddam had any. This created a problem of public relations, if nothing else. When efforts to find evidence failed, speculations, suppositions, and in some cases outright fantasies had to be presented as proof, in press conferences, intelligence dossiers, front-page news articles, and slideshows.

Condoleezza Rice told viewers on CNN that Saddam was known to have biological weapons, and that aluminum tubes had been found that were "really only suitable for nuclear weapon programs."[19] Her assessment was not shared by everyone in the intelligence community, American or British. But Rice warned that we "don't want the smoking gun to be a mushroom cloud." A story was pushed by the Bush administration that meetings took place in Prague between al-Qaeda operatives and Saddam's agents. Iraq was alleged to be training al-Qaeda terrorists in biological warfare. Intelligence was produced to show that Saddam's people had been trying to acquire yellowcake uranium in Africa to make nuclear bombs. This factoid emerged in a dossier coaxed out of British intelligence to show that Saddam's regime presented a huge and immediate danger, a message that showed the handiwork of Alastair Campbell. Blair provided a foreword to the dossier that claimed Saddam needed only forty-five minutes to launch his WMD. Most of the above was patently false.

Colin Powell, the hapless secretary of state, had been more skeptical about the need to go to war than most of his colleagues. This is why he was asked to present the case against Saddam at the UN. He had more credibility than they did. But he was simply repeating allegations that were unproven at best. Much of the "intelligence" provided by the British and the Americans was based on dubious single sources or cribbed from unreliable published accounts. Blair wrote the following astonishing sentence in his memoirs: "The intelligence on Saddam and WMD turned out to be incorrect. It is said—even I have said—that how this came about to be so remains a mystery."[20]

It is not really a mystery at all. Blair may not have been consciously lying. He believed what he wished to believe. Saddam was often bluffing. Despite the vain efforts of UN inspectors, led by Hans Blix, to find any WMD in Iraq in late 2002 and early 2003, it was hard to prove beyond any doubt that Saddam didn't have them. There is also reason to believe that inconvenient facts were ignored. In September 2002, a report from the US Joint Chiefs of Staff, commissioned by Donald Rumsfeld, stated clearly that much about Iraqi WMD remained unknown: "We range from 0% to about 75% knowledge on various aspects of their program," and "our knowledge of the Iraqi (nuclear) weapons program is based largely—perhaps 90%—on analysis of imprecise intelligence."[21] The document was not circulated outside the Pentagon. This was the same month that Condoleezza Rice warned about a "mushroom cloud," and Blair claimed that Iraq could attack Britain with WMD in forty-five minutes.

In any case, Hans Blix's inspectors were not allowed enough time by the Americans to finish their job. The troops were ready to go in. The invasion could not be postponed to the summer; fighting in the desert heat would be unendurable. Besides that, if there were plausible reasons to believe that Saddam lacked the means for mass destruction, or if he were seen to be cooperating fully with the inspectors, the casus belli would be lost. Blix, who had reason to be very angry about the way he was treated by the US and Britain, remained the perfect diplomat. He never accused Bush and Blair of acting in bad faith, but he ascribed the narrowing of their minds to a lack of "critical thinking." Blix compared them to "witch hunters of the past."[22] Once you have concluded that a person is guilty, the charges become self-evident.

George W. Bush is often described as a man who bears grudges but is loyal to his friends. He understood Blair's political difficulties at home, and he made at least one concession to the prime minister against the wishes of some of the president's closest associates. The UN Security Council would be asked to vote on a resolution that threatened "serious consequences" if Saddam refused to comply with unrestricted UN inspections in Iraq. The resolution, drafted by the US and Britain, was passed. But there were important disagreements about the consequences. If Saddam didn't fully cooperate with the inspections, the US would go to war without further ado. The French, among others, were against the use of any military force without another UN resolution.

Saddam did cooperate to some extent, but not enough to satisfy the Americans, who wanted him gone in any case. Blair asked Bush to give the Security Council one more chance. He promised Bush that he would persuade Jacques Chirac, Gerhard Schröder, and Vladimir Putin to come around to the Anglo-American point of view. He was, after all, the solid bridge between the Old and New Worlds, and indeed in his own mind the leading European politician. But Blair overestimated his own powers of persuasion. The German voters, upon whom Schröder depended for reelection, were vehemently opposed to a war. So was Chirac, who thought a military intervention would cause untold suffering, and the world would be worse off. He no doubt saw a chance to demonstrate his Gaullist defiance of the "Anglo-Saxons." But he also happened to be right. Schröder joined the French in opposition. Donald

Rumsfeld contrasted the "New Europe" of former Communist countries, such as Poland, who supported the American cause, favorably with the decadent, cowardly, unreliable "Old Europe" of Germany and France. Javier Solana, the Spanish EU chief on foreign policy, was surprised how deeply thinking in the White House was influenced by religion: "It is a kind of binary model," he said. "It is all or nothing. For us Europeans it is difficult to deal with because we are secular. We do not see the world in such black-and-white terms."[23]

Blair was one European who was not in the secular camp. Up to a million people marched through the streets of London to protest against the looming war (and many more in Rome and Madrid), but Blair remained convinced that he was doing the right thing to deliver the world from evil. He could have joined Chirac and drawn back on the brink of war. Donald Rumsfeld offered him an escape when he said that the US could find a "workaround" in case the British weren't able to participate in military operations. In other words, British support would be of political use, but wasn't really necessary on the ground. Blair chose to view Rumsfeld's tactless but accurate assessment as "just a cock-up." His army was raring to go and "took amiss any sense that we might be in the second rank."[24]

Despite Solana's view of American zeal, the Spanish prime minister José María Aznar decided to be on the Anglo-American side. On his way to see him in Madrid, Blair gave a reflective interview on the plane, once more reviving the great ghost hovering over Anglo-American military enterprises. History would be his judge, he said. "A majority of decent and well-meaning people said there was no need to confront Hitler and that those who did were warmongers. . . . I'm proud of what we've done on regime change in

Kosovo and Afghanistan, and, in a different way, by supporting the regime in Sierra Leone."[25]

When Chirac declared that he would vote against any resolution for war, Blair knew that there would not be enough votes in the UN Security Council to support an invasion. But he still needed backing at home. So he gave a rousing speech in Parliament recounting the undoubted horrors of Saddam's regime, "the torture camps, the barbaric prisons for political opponents. . . . That is how the Iraqi people live. Leave Saddam in place, and the blunt truth is that that is how they will continue to be forced to live." With the help of many Conservatives, he received the support he needed for his "war of liberation."

On March 19, 2003, as soon as the deadline had passed for Saddam to leave his country voluntarily, US bombers launched their first raids on Baghdad. Blair had not been told beforehand, let alone consulted. He watched "Operation Shock and Awe" on TV. British troops entered Iraq on the following day. They stayed there until 2009. More than four thousand US soldiers died in the conflict. One hundred thirty-six British soldiers were killed in action. Exactly how many Iraqis died from the violence is unknown. Estimates vary from half a million to many more. Two million Iraqis lost their homes and fled abroad, often to face more violence, forced prostitution, and unspeakably squalid conditions. One point seven million Iraqis were displaced inside their own country. Countless people are still missing.

On May 1, 2003, George W. Bush landed on the deck of the aircraft carrier USS *Abraham Lincoln*. He posed with members of the crew in his flight suit. Behind him was a banner that read MISSION ACCOMPLISHED. He said, "Major combat operations have ended. In the battle of Iraq, the United States and its allies have prevailed."

Blair had always worried, with excellent reason, that the Americans had given insufficient thought to rebuilding the country after Saddam was gone. The influence he craved proved to be an illusion. The peace process in Israel was neglected. The UN had been bypassed. The WMD were never found. The administration of the wrecked country was botched. Even the juicy contracts for reconstruction in the ruins of Iraq mostly went to companies close to the Bush administration, such as Bechtel and Dick Cheney's old firm, Halliburton. And far from leading Europe, or bridging the gap between Europe and the US, Blair ended up more isolated than ever. When Europeans met in April 2003 to discuss a future defense and security union, admittedly with scarce results, the British were not even invited.

To claim, as many have done, that Blair was nothing more than America's poodle, or that his lack of influence was simply a case of American imperial arrogance crushing the junior leader's naive but nonetheless noble intentions, is to miss an important point. Blair was a true believer. This was never more evident than in 2006, after Israel retaliated against Hezbollah rocket attacks by bombing and invading Lebanon. The latest eruption of Middle Eastern violence was discussed at a meeting of the G8 in Saint Petersburg, where Bush cried out, "Yo, Blair!" when he spotted the British prime minister. This unorthodox greeting was widely regarded in Britain as a humiliating sign of the true state of Anglo-American relations. Blair sportingly chose to see it as "a great 'George' moment."[26]

Hezbollah is a militant Islamist party, backed by Iran. Guerilla warfare and acts of terrorism by Hezbollah have caused a great deal of trouble in the Middle East, but Israel's response was regarded almost everywhere as disproportionate. What sparked it was little more than a local incident. The Israeli invasion, as well as massive bombing and shelling, killed more than a thousand Lebanese and displaced more than a million people, many of them civilians who had nothing to do with Hezbollah. The French called for a UN-sponsored cease-fire. The US blocked efforts to stop the fighting. Blair, almost uniquely in Europe, backed the US and stood with Israel, not as America's poodle, but because he "defined the problem" in religious terms, as "the wider struggle between the strain of religious extremism in Islam and the rest of us."[27]

In the case of Iraq, however, it was hard to make this convincing. Saddam may have been a brute, and possibly may have backed religious zealots when it suited him, just as the US did when Islamist guerillas fought the Soviet Union in Afghanistan, but he was a secular dictator. The invasion of his country cannot be defined as a war against religious extremism. In fact, religious extremism was one of the main consequences of the invasion.

Less than a month after war in Iraq was launched, pictures went around the world of a spectacular event that took place in the center of Baghdad. People saw on their TV and computer screens how a crowd of delirious Iraqi men cheered as a man pounded away with a sledgehammer at the plinth of Saddam Hussein's statue in Firdos Square. A thick rope from a US Army armored truck is attached to the dictator's bronze neck, a US flag is wrapped around his face, the rope is pulled, and Saddam, his right hand pointing to a glorious future, tumbles like a man dying in slow motion, whereupon a number of young Iraqis stamp and dance on the prone figure. Images of this "spontaneous" event were shown as proof of Iraqi joy at their liberation. It seemed to confirm all the happy predictions emanating from Washington and Downing Street. Tony Blair recalled, "When people look back on this time, I honestly believe they will see this as one of the finest moments of our century."[28]

In fact, the toppling of the statue was not spontaneous at all. Camera angles can deceive. The square was almost empty. Larger mobs were busy looting public buildings nearby, including museums and hospitals. The sparse crowd arrived dancing behind US Army vehicles. The sledgehammer had been handed to the mob by a GI. And the Stars and Stripes was folded across Saddam's face by another GI, only to be quickly replaced by an Iraqi flag when the Americans realized that such a heavy-handed sign of triumph might not play so well on TV. The "iconic" images of Firdos Square on April 9, 2003, were just another example of the art of spin, which had already contributed so much to the war that George W. Bush and Tony Blair began with such fervor, so little foresight, such disregard for international laws, and so much extraordinary incompetence.

Twelve

AFTER THE CRASH

▬▬▬

*In the depths of the Depression, when Franklin Roosevelt did
battle with fear itself, it was not simply by the power of his
words, his personality and his example that he triumphed.*

*. . . What mattered more was this enduring truth: that you, the
American people, at your core, were, as you remain, every bit as
optimistic as your Roosevelts, your Reagans, and your Obamas.*

· GORDON BROWN, BRITISH PRIME MINISTER, 2007–2010

nother photograph, this one taken on July 29, 2007, at Camp
David, two men in a golf cart: George W. Bush and Gordon
Brown, the new British prime minister. They attempt to look jolly,
Bush a bit dutifully, Brown with a rictus look of hilarity that sug-
gests an uncomfortable man trying too hard to join in the fun. Gone
were the leather bomber jacket and the tight jeans. Both men
wore suits and ties, at Brown's request. Bush called the prime minister "Gordon," and Brown replied with "Mr. President." (A gift of a
fur-trimmed American bomber jacket was discreetly handed to
Brown in a gold-colored box on his way back to England; it was
never worn.)[1]

The buildup to this meeting was not propitious. Condoleezza

Rice already told Bush about Brown's awkward manners; the PM had harangued her about Africa, a pet subject of his. Two of Brown's ministers had just made speeches that would have irritated the Americans to no end. Douglas Alexander, the international development secretary, criticized "unilateralism" and talked about "new alliances based on common values,"[2] suggesting that such values were not necessarily shared with the Bush administration. The Foreign Office minister, Mark Malloch Brown, went even further. Coalitions, he said, should go beyond "the bilateral blinkers of the normal partners," and Britain and the US would not be "joined at the hip, like the Blair-Bush relationship was."[3] Considering the usual pious rhetoric trotted out when Anglo-American leaders first meet, these statements almost amounted to blasphemy.

Gordon Brown wanted to avoid being caricatured as America's poodle, an image so often applied to Blair. He refrained from Blairish braggadocio about going to war for freedom and democracy, but he reassured Bush that Britain would not withdraw its troops from Iraq too soon. And he did his best to stick to the usual pieties. Brown didn't actually use the words "Special Relationship" but spoke of "a partnership founded and driven forward by our shared values—what Winston Churchill, who was the first British prime minister to visit Camp David, called the joint inheritance of liberty, a belief in opportunity for all, a belief in the dignity of every human being."

Brown didn't need to grit his teeth over such phrases. He was a great admirer of the US, where he sometimes spent his holidays on Cape Cod. Brown was effusive about the brilliance of American thinkers, such as Alan Greenspan, chair of the Federal Reserve, and could recall the thrill of seeing the Stars and Stripes planted on the surface of the moon. While in the US, Brown even spoke about religion, a subject he tended to keep to himself in Britain. His father was a minister of the Church of Scotland, and Brown felt bound to the faith of his childhood, but he lacked the messianic fervor of Blair or the born-again devotions of Bush.

When Tony Blair finally resigned his premiership in 2007, he founded the Tony Blair Faith Foundation. At a prayer breakfast in the US, he said he wished to restore faith "to its rightful place, as the guide to our world and its future."[4]

Brown, as Blair's chancellor of the exchequer, had been churning with frustration for years, since he felt that it should have been him in 10 Downing Street rather than his much savvier and more media-friendly comrade. Even though Brown's behavior barely stopped short of outright sabotage, Blair could never bring himself to fire him. Like Anthony Eden, who had been made to wait his turn by Churchill for too long, Brown finally slipped into the coveted job only to see it end in failure soon after. For once, it wasn't the European question that brought down a prime minister. Brown's fall came in the wake of the great global recession, which began in America. But neither Blair nor Brown was blameless for what happened.

Brown's image as a stiff, blue-suited technocrat would seem ill matched with prayer breakfasts, and during his premiership from 2007 to 2010 he didn't talk much about his religious faith. In his autobiography, however, he warms to the theme.

He regretted that "despite my strong personal religious beliefs," he was seen as "a technocrat lacking solid convictions." He blamed himself for being "in denial of who I really am."[5] This is perhaps a little harsh, for Brown talked more about "values" than most British politicians normally do. This, too, was influenced as much by American rhetoric as by the Church of Scotland. Brown was often mocked for his attempt to define "Britishness." Unlike John Major's vision of village cricket matches on late summer afternoons, Brown was not nostalgic. He took account of the increasingly multiethnic, multicultural, multireligious makeup of modern Britain. His country, in fact, had become ever more like the US. Just as Americans celebrate their nationhood on July 4, Brown wanted the British to have a national day. Britishness, in his view, had to "bring into the public square" the "beliefs and values that are common to all religions." By this he meant something that reached back to old self-admiring Anglo-American assumptions: "Our commitment to liberty and tolerance, to civic duty and strong communities, and to fairness, or, as Churchill put it, 'fair play'—in other words, a civic humanism that had originated from religious beliefs but was justified on ethical and rational grounds."[6]

However, the economic crash of 2008, which hit Brown's government with full force, exposed a great deal of unfairness in both Britain and the US. The "neoliberal" ideology, promoted in the Thatcher-Reagan years as a prime example of the Anglo-Saxon love of liberty, had ended up wreaking havoc by encouraging loosely regulated financial institutions in the City of London and Wall Street to behave recklessly, and often unethically, in pursuit of ever bigger profits. Brown reflects on this with considerable bitterness in his memoirs. He mentions the "unsupervised and shadow banking system" that allowed risky, speculative, and dubious financial transactions. He had no doubt "right from the start" that "the financial crisis was also a moral crisis. . . . Put in more biblical language, the world had worshipped at the altar of wealth and greed."[7]

A year later, the new US president, Barack Obama, spoke in very similar terms: "We will not go back to the days of reckless behavior and unchecked excess that was at the heart of this crisis, where too many were motivated only by the appetite for quick kills and bloated bonuses."[8] And yet, this behavior cannot be laid only at the feet of Thatcher and Reagan. President Clinton, champion of the Third Way, repealed the Glass-Steagall act of 1933 that banned financial institutions from combining commercial and investment banking. Dispensing with such regulations encouraged precisely the kind of recklessness that Brown and Obama deplored after the crash.

Just a few years before that calamity, Brown, as chancellor of the exchequer, had actually been a great booster of deregulation, globalization, and the "greedy" players in the City of London. In a speech to bankers and businessmen in London in 2007, Brown congratulated the City for entering "a new golden age." He praised the "dynamism allied to the City's openness" that led London to create "the most modern instruments of finance." Thus, he continued, "Out of the greatest restructuring of the global economy, perhaps even greater than the industrial revolution, a new world order was created."[9]

Was Brown being a hypocrite, when he expressed such moral indignation a year later? Not necessarily. The fascinating thing about Brown's speeches to bankers is how closely they matched his ideas about Britishness and British values, some of them remarkably hoary, and not usually associated with the politics of the left. In a speech in 2006, Brown hailed Adam Smith as an ancestral inspiration for Anglo-Saxon get-up-and-go—Smith as the original pro-globalist. Smith's ideas on competition were "founded on our fundamental beliefs in freedom, liberty and internationalism." These beliefs put down "the foundations for an open not closed international monetary system." Churchill wasn't mentioned, for once, but Brown did refer to that other old trope of Anglo-Saxonism, also mentioned by Churchill more than once: "Whenever the choice has been between protectionism and the open seas, Britain has chosen the open seas."[10]

Brown, like his prime minister, was a proud promoter of the Third Way, but his belief in British values was remarkably old-fashioned and closely allied with American values. He was never anti-European, in the manner of Thatcher-worshipping Tory Eurosceptics, or indeed people on the far left who regard the EU as a capitalist cabal. But he was convinced that Britain should lead Europe, that supposedly inefficient, inward-looking, protectionist continent, into the new golden age of deregulated global markets, led by the titans of London and Wall Street. One of those men, Lloyd Blankfein, chief executive of Goldman Sachs, once said that banks perform of great social purpose; they do "God's work."[11] Before 2008, Brown would surely have agreed. After 2008, he felt that God's high priests had let him down. But he never really renounced their faith.

Brown and Obama have received much credit for preventing the Great Recession from sinking into a global depression. Even though none of the Wall Street titans who created the disaster were held accountable, and the Obama administration still included powerful figures from the Clinton era who had done so much to deregulate the banking system, Obama's economic stimulus staved off an even more catastrophic outcome. Most of the banks were bailed out by the government, and borrowing was made easy by keeping interest rates low. Brown, too, was a great advocate for using government money to pump life back into the global economy. He saw this form of Keynesianism as an international duty. Protectionism had to be avoided at all costs. At the same time, the international banking system had to be reformed to stop a similar or worse crisis from happening again. This Anglo-American approach was not wrong. But there was a sense of grandiosity in its presentation, especially by Brown, that had distinct echoes of the 1940s.

Brown portrayed himself as the savior of Europe, even the world. He wanted "the post-2008 period to be as energetic a time for rebuilding and reform as the post-1945 period, which had produced the IMF, the World Bank, the Marshall Plan and the United Nations." The corrupted financial system would be replaced by "what I sometimes called a new London consensus." The "mindset of deregulation, privatization and liberalization" would be abandoned.[12] The French and Germans didn't necessarily disagree, but one can see why they didn't enjoy being lectured to by a British leader, or indeed by Americans, who had, in their view, landed them in the mess.

Of course, Britain couldn't lead the world alone. Brown was adamant to be the first leader to congratulate Obama on the phone after he won the presidential election, and in March 2009, even as the stock markets were crashing, Brown rushed to Washington to meet the new president. He got a mixed reception. The British tabloid press taunted Brown about what many regarded as "snubs." The White House decided that the prime minister's visit merited a photo op, but no formal press conference in the Rose Garden. Brown promised the world "a global new deal"; Obama failed to respond in similar terms. Downing Street had put much thought into a gift that would please Obama: a penholder carved from the wood of a nineteenth-century British ship sent out to suppress the slave trade. In return, Brown was given a box set of old American movies. Alas, because of their North American codes, the DVDs couldn't even be viewed on a British player.

The British should not have been surprised. In his thoughtful campaign book, *The Audacity of Hope*, Obama lays out his view of the US and the world. There is not one reference to Britain in the index (Galesburg, Illinois, merits six mentions). In his chapter on US foreign policy, there are many pages about Indonesia, where Obama partly grew up, but none on Britain. History is not neglected. References to World War I, US isolationism in the 1930s, and Franklin D. Roosevelt are there. Obama also discusses NATO, China, the Middle East, and the Vietnam War. But Britain's role is hardly considered at all. Most unusual of all, the name Winston Churchill is entirely absent.

I actually did find one comment about Britain in the book, which tells us all we need to know about Obama's view of the Special Relationship. He makes a strong argument for multilateralism. The US, he says, needs strong allies to support American ventures abroad. Not that he wants the UN Security Council to have a veto over US actions. "Nor do I mean that we *round up the United Kingdom and Togo* and then do what we please."[13] The italics are mine. The sentiment couldn't be clearer. Not for nothing did Obama, as presidential candidate in 2008, give his first European speech on freedom, democracy, and America's place in the world in Berlin. London was no longer the natural first place of call.

This doesn't mean that Obama had "ancestral" prejudices against the British Empire, as was suggested by Boris Johnson. He just didn't care about Britain enough to be an Anglophile, or indeed an Anglophobe. Obama was a modern patriotic American. Anglo-Saxonism, Milton, Churchill, the Atlantic Charter, D-Day, English tailors, and gentlemen's clubs meant little or nothing to him. And he wasn't enamored of British spies or James Bond. These things had sentimental value for an older elite, mostly on the Eastern Seaboard. When Gordon Brown addressed Americans, it often seemed that he was still talking to the likes of them, and not to a man born in Hawaii in 1961, the year when Kennedy became president and the Freedom Riders were bused to the Deep South to fight against racial segregation.

During that same trip to the US in March, Gordon Brown addressed both houses of Congress. He spoke of "forefathers" fighting side by side "in the sands of Tunisia, on the beaches of Normandy, and then on the bridges over the Rhine." He recalled that "cemetery after cemetery across Europe honors the memory of American soldiers, resting row upon row—often alongside comrades-in-arms from Britain." He cited "the battlefields of liberty" and paid tribute to American "courage and sacrifice." All this might still have brought tears to the eyes of Eisenhower, Kennedy, Nixon, Reagan, or the elder George Bush, but there had been a change of generations. Obama was part of a very different elite: multiethnic, less rooted in Europe, more interested in Asia.

Still, Obama was nothing if not courteous. When he realized that the British, egged on by their sneering press, felt a little bruised by their perfunctory reception at the White House, Obama called Brown in his airplane by satellite phone. He assured "Gordon" that the wooden penholder was now standing proudly on the presidential desk, and that he wanted him to know how much he was looking forward to meeting again in London for the G20 conference. Brown was so relieved by the president's kind words that he walked down the aisle with a freshly opened bottle of champagne.

The G20 meeting was Brown's chance to impress the world with his leadership, side by side with the president of the US. He had already announced this new partnership in his speech to the houses of Congress: "Past British prime ministers have traveled to this Capitol building in times of war to talk of war. I come now to talk of new and different battles we must fight together; to speak of a global economy in crisis and a planet imperiled." The goal in London was to convince the eighteen other members of the G20 to rev up the world economy with another boost of fiscal stimulus. The "London consensus" would also provide new banking regulations and other measures to keep the world safe from future catastrophes.

At last, Obama found the right words to flatter the British. The two countries, he said, would always be linked by a "kinship of ideals."[14] Over breakfast in Downing Street, the president expressed his sympathy with his host. He purred, "Just Roosevelt and Churchill sitting in a room with a brandy, that's an easy negotiation." But to get all the world's leaders to agree "must be like herding cats."[15]

Brown was by all accounts a brilliant chairman of his conference, even though he failed to convert the world to the London consensus. The Chinese and the Russians worried that international regulations would step on their sovereignty. The Chinese wanted the French to apologize for having entertained the Dalai Lama. The French and the Germans balked at massive stimulus plans and wanted to discuss tightening up regulations on tax havens instead. At one point the French president Nicolas Sarkozy, never one to cede the spotlight to another leader, especially a Brit, threatened to walk out on the proceedings. Michelle Obama was told off by the British tabloids for touching the queen's back at a banquet. Silvio Berlusconi wanted pictures taken with Obama and asked for the supermodel Naomi Campbell's telephone number. In the end, however, everyone got something, largely thanks to Brown's energy and Obama's tactful diplomacy. Measures would be taken to deal with tax havens, allowing Sarkozy to claim that "a page has been turned" on "Anglo-Saxon" capitalism. And more resources would be transferred to the IMF to bail out troubled economies, as Brown had

wished. This was not exactly a new Anglo-American order. But at
least a modicum of international cooperation had stopped the crisis
from spinning out of control.

Brown wrote rather poignantly in his memoirs that he had wanted
to do so much more. But this would have meant "overcoming more
obstacles than I had time left in government to surmount."[16]

Brown's government came down out of sheer exhaustion. The
recession dragged on. People weren't confident that Brown had lost
his infatuation with big bankers. He still thought Alan Greenspan,
under whose watch the Great Recession began, was a genius. And
the corruptions that creep into most parties when they have held
power for too long enveloped Brown's government in an air of
sleaziness. This may not have been any worse than under a Tory
government, but the Left had always prided itself on its moral pro-
bity. Brown himself remained a figure of dour Scottish rectitude.
But access and political favors had been traded for money by some
of his close associates. A publisher of skin magazines was enabled to
buy a major newspaper after he paid a substantial donation to the
Labour Party. A former minister of trade called himself a "cab for
hire"—£5,000 a day would buy whatever the client required. A
transport secretary boasted to an undercover reporter that he would
turn his Rolodex into "something that, frankly, makes money."[17]
The famous utterance by Peter Mandelson, Tony Blair's strategist, that New Labour would be intensely relaxed about people
getting filthy rich now came back to haunt the last Third Way
government.

Compared to David Cameron, the suave and bouncy young
Conservative leader who rushed about the country claiming it was
"time for a change," Brown, a nail-biting insomniac who never over-
came his stiffness in public, looked to be at the end of his tether.

Brown believed that no political leader could "survive for long if people think of him or her as false, as a PR creation, as an invention of a focus group."[18] Cameron was once a PR man for a media company. Public presentation was so important to him that he once changed clothes four times in a few hours during a Tory Party conference. He beat Brown handily in the general elections of 2010.

Hillary Clinton recalls that Obama and Cameron "took to each other right off, starting with a private meeting before Cameron's electoral victory."[19] There was no talk of snubs when Cameron visited Washington in the summer of that same year. A photograph taken on the South Lawn of the White House shows both men in lively conversation, dressed in ties and white shirts, jackets flung casually across their right shoulders, informal yet all business. Obama duly repeated for Cameron's benefit the kind of clichés his predecessors had used over and over: "Mr. Prime Minister, we can never say it enough. The United States and the United Kingdom enjoy a truly Special Relationship." "Common values" were invoked, as well as "common heritage," "sacrifices," "brave men," "bled together," and so on. "When the United States and the United Kingdom stand together, our people—and people around the world—are more secure and they are more prosperous."

It was as though the fresh-faced former PR man had managed to bring out the sentiments, authentic or not, that had gone missing on the US side when Brown made his pilgrimage to the White House. There was something slightly incongruous about this "bromance," as the British press called it. Cameron was a Tory. He had been selected as leader of his party to match Tony Blair's sex appeal. The new prime minister admired Blair and sought to emulate him. He declared to a group of sympathetic journalists, "I am the heir to Blair."[20] He had approved of Blair's support of George W. Bush during the Iraq War, which Obama had opposed.

Cameron also aired his views on Britishness, like Brown. His own place in British society was secure, as a wealthy upper-class Old Etonian. Hoping to widen his appeal, he sometimes reached for the common touch ("Dave") without really convincing anyone. In any case, he chose to hold forth on Britishness to children in a secondary school in Birmingham. Cameron's concept of nationhood would have fit easily into speeches made by Brown, or any other politician who wasn't an archconservative: "a country of many faiths," "bound by the love of liberty," et cetera. Indeed, Cameron was more progressive than many of his Tory Party colleagues. Like Blair, he tried to polish his party's rough edges and aim for the soggy middle. One of his achievements was to make it possible for gay people to get married. Blair had effectively purged the Left from his party; Cameron promised to get rid of the Tory image as "the nasty party," the one obsessed with traditional social order and always on the side of the rich. Obama even said to Cameron that if he had been an American politician, Cameron "would be on the soft right of the Democratic Party."[21]

But once his ecumenical, freedom-loving principles had been established, Cameron dedicated the rest of his speech at the Birmingham school to what he saw as the greatest threat to British values, namely Islamist extremism. "Cultural practices" that threaten British values would be crushed. Sharia courts would be reviewed. School regulations would be tightened. The speech ended in a rousing crescendo: "Our Great British resolve faced down Hitler; it defeated Communism. . . . We have refused to compromise on our values or to give up our way of life. And we shall do so again."[22]

It is possible to imagine Blair using those words, but not Brown, let alone Obama. Cameron had eloquence and public charm in common with the US president. But Obama was more like Brown in other respects. Both were intensely clever men who read more widely and reflected more deeply than most politicians. But these intellectual qualities hampered them from reaching decisions with the speed of more instinctual leaders. They were worriers, fretters, who saw two or more sides to every argument. This prevented Brown from calling an election when he was still popular. And it proved to be a problem in Obama's foreign policy, one instance of which involved the British in a major way.

From the beginning, there was a schizophrenic quality to the way the Obama administration faced crises abroad. The split seems to have been partly a matter of age. Some influential younger members of the administration, such as Samantha Power, on the National Security Council, and Susan Rice, the UN ambassador, were liberal hawks who believed in "humanitarian intervention" to topple dictators and stop mass murder. Older figures, such as defense secretary Robert Gates, stressed order and counseled against abandoning even unsavory foreign rulers as long as they supported the US and kept their regions stable. Hillary Clinton, as secretary of state, wavered between the two. Obama's instincts were against military action that wasn't strictly defensive. He said he had had enough of the US blundering into foreign wars like a lumbering giant, and he promised to get the US troops out of Afghanistan and Iraq. Obama admired George H. W. Bush and his cautious, lawyerly national security adviser Brent Scowcroft. David Cameron, the man who modeled himself after Blair, albeit without his hero's religious zeal, saw himself more as a man of action, and so was closer to the young hawks in the Obama administration.

Obama was a realist, but not a cynical realist. "Don't do stupid shit" was his far from reprehensible motto. But he, too, was susceptible to the ideals of the younger members of his administration. After all, he was closer to them in age. "That is not who we are," was a common Obama criticism of practices, such as torture, that he disapproved of (quite rightly, of course, even though he declined to hold those who had been responsible for torturing to account). But, like Hamlet, Obama sometimes had difficulty making up his mind about quite who he was.

The great test in foreign affairs for the Obama administration began with the Arab Spring of 2011. First the Tunisians, then the Egyptians, the Yemenites, the people of Bahrain, the Libyans, the Syrians, and others took to the streets to protest against their corrupt rulers. It was a time of great hope, especially after the Tunisians managed to oust their president and his thieving wife after months of street demonstrations. Liberal idealists saw a chance for the US to play an active role in support of freedom against the Arab tyrannies. Some years before, in his famous speech in Berlin, Obama had already stated clearly, "This is the moment we must help answer the call for a new dawn in the Middle East."

Matters became more complicated when huge crowds in the center of Cairo demanded the ouster of Hosni Mubarak, the military strongman who had been supported over the years by Democratic as much as Republican administrations. Hillary Clinton knew him well. The Israelis and the Saudis trusted him. He may have been a thug, but he was seen as a rock of stability in the Middle East. Nevertheless, the Egyptians had had enough of Mubarak's corrupt autocracy, which threatened to become a dynasty with his son's planned succession. The street protesters, a combustible mix of Islamists, liberals, rowdy soccer supporters, and ordinary angry citizens, were not about to give up.

The older members in Obama's team urged the president to stick to their man. Egypt, like other Arab countries, lacked a democratic tradition. Revolution would just end in further oppression and violence. Better the devil we know . . . The young ones appealed to Obama's idealism. He chose, after some deliberation, to side with them, and told Mubarak by phone to step down immediately. But these were just words—important words of course, but they didn't compel any US action. Even as Obama decided that the US would no longer support its Egyptian ally, an American envoy to Egypt told an audience in Germany that Mubarak should stay until a new government was formed. Cameron called Obama to voice his concern. He wanted a more aggressive approach. The schizophrenia in the White House was starting to create confusion.

The skeptics turned out to be right. Mubarak was brought down to huge cheering crowds, delirious at their first glimpse of political freedom. But only a year later the democratically elected Islamist government was ousted by a military coup. Again, there was soul-searching in Washington. What to do? Obama refused to call it a coup. The new military strongman, General Abdel Fattah al-Sisi, would be a more brutal dictator than the man who had been pushed out of power in the Arab Spring. The US, blamed by the Islamists for having backed dictators and by the Egyptian military for supporting the revolution, quickly reverted to its traditional support of an autocratic regime in Cairo.

The next crisis had even more lethal consequences. For more than four decades, the Libyan despot, Colonel Muammar Gaddafi, had tormented his people and ruined his country in a whimsical dictatorship, whose brutality was justified by a personal ideology that was a mishmash of Maoism, fascism, Islamism, and new age mumbo jumbo. Gaddafi, given to clownish uniforms, pretty female bodyguards, and outlandish behavior, was responsible for blowing up a Pan Am Boeing 747 airplane over Scotland in 1988, killing 270 people. But he was open to business with the West once more after agreeing to give up his nuclear weapons program in 2003. Inspired by the revolt against Mubarak in Egypt, Libyans decided they had had enough of Gaddafi and his murderous antics. But Gaddafi was defiant in the face of mass demonstrations. He vowed to "purify Libya, inch by inch, house by house."[23]

Tanks and heavy weapons were deployed. Soldiers who refused to shoot civilians were executed. The protests turned into an armed rebellion. A civil war broke out, with tribal militias and rebel forces fighting government troops, strengthened by foreign mercenaries. The city of Benghazi was under siege. A fairly decent transitional governing council was formed. Gaddafi called the rebels "rats" and threatened to track down every last person and "show no mercy and no pity."

Once again, President Obama demanded that a foreign leader had to "step down from power and leave immediately."[24] Once again, the president had to make up his mind how best to bring this about. And again, the older people split from the younger ones. Vice President Biden thought US intervention would be madness. Robert Gates saw no US national interest at stake. Samantha Power warned that a mass atrocity was about to take place under Obama's watch. Susan Rice compared the threat to Benghazi to the genocide in Rwanda in 1994. Obama dithered.

This was one of those rare occasions when the British and the French found a common cause. Now, they believed, was the moment to act and show the world that Europeans still counted for something. Nicolas Sarkozy had been rather too close to the ousted Tunisian dictator, and he had also hosted Gaddafi in France, where he did good business with the Libyan leader, who stayed in a Bedouin tent pitched in the center of Paris. There were also rumors of Libyan money transferred to Sarkozy's election campaign. The French president clearly had something to prove. Like David Cameron, he was a fierce advocate for military intervention. Cameron believed that the rebel council in Benghazi had "political legitimacy." Sarkozy agreed. Both leaders wanted the UN to impose a No-fly zone, to stop Gaddafi from bombing people. But they knew that only the US could help to make this a success, so they urged Obama to join them.

Obama was prepared to go as far as freezing Gaddafi's assets abroad and imposing travel bans as well as an arms embargo by working through the UN. But he was wary of going any further, partly because a No-fly zone would not protect Benghazi, which was threatened by tanks, not bombers. And he didn't trust the display of Franco-British zeal. Obama felt that wealthy Western European countries had been taking the US for a ride for too long. He once warned Cameron that if Britain didn't spend at least 2 percent of its GDP on defense, the Special Relationship would be over. Too often, in his view, Europeans had been happy to improve the world by spilling American blood.

But Angela Merkel, too, agreed that Gaddafi had to go. And so did other Arab leaders, who couldn't stand him. The UN Security Council voted to "use all available measures" to protect Libyan civilians. The French were about to go in with fighter aircraft to bomb Libya. Cameron was ready to unleash the RAF. But they still needed US military support. Convinced by some of his own advisers, as well as the European leaders, that a genocide was at hand in Benghazi, Obama finally decided that doing nothing was "not who we are." He dispatched American bombers to destroy Libyan air defenses and ground forces. After that, it would be up to the NATO allies, mainly the British and the French, to finish the job.

The result was bloody and swift. Tripoli, the Libyan capital, fell to the transitional governing council rebels. Gaddafi fled into the desert in a convoy that was bombed by NATO forces without him being hit. Sarkozy and Cameron made a quick visit to Libya, where they basked as "liberators" in the adulation of crowds in Tripoli and Benghazi. Cameron remembers fondly how "people chanted 'Cam-er-on' and 'Sar-ko-zy.'" And that someone "had even named their baby Sarkozy."[25]

Soon after that, Gaddafi was dragged by rebel fighters from his hiding place in a drainage pipe, sodomized with a bayonet, and shot. His mutilated corpse was preserved in a freezer and displayed to the public for several days. After that, it didn't take long for Libya to disintegrate into what Obama described in private as a "shit show."[26] No government has managed to assert its authority over the country, which is now a semi-anarchic patchwork of rival parliaments, tribal militias, and Islamist terror groups, causing large numbers of refugees to risk and often lose their lives to reach squalid camps in southern Europe.

In an interview given during his last year in office, Obama pointed out that Sarkozy was able to wash his hands of Libya, since he was no longer in office a year after his intervention. And Cameron, in Obama's extremely polite wording, became "distracted by a range of other things."[27] Whatever bonhomie might have existed between the two leaders before was now under great strain. Obama had himself to blame for taking part in the military action. But he was right to be angry about the way his allies had botched things. A British parliamentary inquiry into Cameron's Libya policy revealed that he had based his decisions on very shaky intelligence. The case for military intervention had been much thinner than was commonly assumed. But the worst thing Cameron and Sarkozy had done was to casually allow an action meant to protect civilians from being killed to evolve into a war of regime change, without having a plan for how to rebuild the country after Gaddafi was gone. Cameron refused to take part in the parliamentary inquiry and blamed the Libyans for failing to grasp their chance to build a democracy.[28] He comforts himself with the thought that Libya "never would have had that chance if I had listened to official advice . . . and decided not to take action, leaving Gaddafi in power."[29]

Obama, who dearly wished to be rid of problems in the Middle East so he could "pivot" to Asia, was yet to face the toughest test to emerge from the rapidly collapsing Arab Spring. Bashar al-Assad, a dull ophthalmologist who had succeeded his brutally effective father, Hafez al-Assad, as president of Syria, was the latest Arab strongman told by Obama to relinquish power. After many civilians, whose protest against the Syrian regime began peacefully, were killed, Obama said in August 2011, "For the sake of the Syrian people, the time has come for President Assad to step aside."[30] The usual forms of pressure were applied: assets frozen, travel banned. The Russians refused to endorse a UN resolution to demand a peaceful transition to democracy. More and more people were being tortured and killed, with Assad, backed by Iran and Russia, on one side, and various rebel groups, some of them more extremist than others, on the other.

Obama, as usual, spoke fine words. As the number of victims

in the Syrian civil war mounted, he gave a speech at the National Defense University in Washington, DC: "To brush aside America's responsibility as a leader and—more profoundly—our responsibilities to our fellow human beings under such circumstances would have been a betrayal of who we are. Some nations may be able to turn a blind eye to atrocities in other countries. The United States of America is different. And as president, I refused to wait for the images of slaughter and mass graves before taking action."[31]

But despite pressure from the usual hawkish advisers, including Hillary Clinton, as well as David Cameron and the new French president François Hollande, the president resisted military intervention. Remembering what happened in Iraq and Libya, he felt that the consequences of toppling a regime with force had not been thought through. Who among the rebel groups would take over? And he was wary of confronting the Iranians in Syria, even as he was pushing for an international treaty to stop them from developing nuclear weapons. Arming "moderates" was considered. But who were the moderates?

Then Assad was accused (rightly, as it later turned out) of using chemical weapons to gas his own civilians. Obama decided that this was a "red line" that should not be crossed. Allowing that kind of atrocity was not "who we are." His secretary of state, John Kerry, called it a "moral obscenity." Obama said, "If we fail to act, the Assad regime will see no reason to stop using chemical weapons."[32] In a joint press conference with Obama, David Cameron tried to goad the president into quick action. He said, "Syria's history is being written in the blood of her people, and it is happening on our watch." And he told Parliament, "We must not let the specter of previous mistakes paralyze us."[33] The problem, however, as

Cameron chose to see it, was that he, the British PM, was haunted by the failure of the West to stop the genocide in Rwanda, while Obama was haunted by the disastrous invasion of Iraq.

Still, it looked as if Obama was finally going to act, not by launching an invasion but by bombing various targets in Syria as a sharp warning to Assad. Angela Merkel told him to be careful. He dithered once more. Then, a sheepish Cameron called him to report that Parliament had voted against his plans to join any military attack. He lamented in his memoirs that "Britain, the world's fourth-biggest military power, time-honored defender of liberty, decades-long partner of America, would be hanging in the shadows."[34]

Obama decided to ask Congress to vote on the use of force. Since many Democrats were wary of interventions, and many Republicans, having first accused Obama of weakness, were now inclined to sabotage any Obama venture, Congress refused to endorse the attack. Obama called it off.

Obama believes he did the right thing. And he may be right to think that a US military intervention would not have done much to help the Syrians out of their misery, and it might even have made things worse. Still, his refusal to act on his words did considerable harm to his reputation. But perhaps not as much as Cameron's bluster did to his. The response in Britain to his humiliating defeat in the House of Commons was ferocious. Paddy Ashdown, leader of the Liberal Democrats, tweeted that "in 50 years of trying to serve my country I have never felt so depressed/ashamed."[35] The BBC political editor thought that Cameron had lost control of foreign policy. Cameron's chancellor of the exchequer, George Osborne, called for a bout of "national soul-searching" about "our role in the world." The defense secretary, Philip Hammond, worried that the Special Relationship would be harmed.[36]

Hammond's concern would have been more valid if Obama had taken the Special Relationship more seriously in the first place. But there never was all that much there to be harmed. When Obama declared before his last trip to Europe as US president that he would "visit with Chancellor Merkel, who has probably been my closest international partner these last eight years," this was probably less a deliberate snub to Cameron than a simple statement of fact.[37]

I t was not failure in Libya and Syria, or indeed any damage done to the Special Relationship that ended Cameron's time in office. It was "Europe" once again. Cameron was the latest prime minister to fall because of Britain's fraught relationship with the European continent. And it was largely his own fault.

While still in opposition in 2006, Cameron made a speech to his party conference, wishing that the European question would just go away: "While parents worried about childcare, getting the kids to school, balancing work and family life—we were banging on about Europe." But this did nothing to stop Eurosceptic politicians, and the viciously anti-European tabloid press, from banging on regardless. They were joined in their demands for a referendum on Britain's continued membership of the EU by the newly formed United Kingdom Independence Party, led by Nigel Farage, a privately educated former commodities broker in the London City, who became a demagogue running for the "people" against "the establishment."

Cameron did what previous prime ministers had done so often with a conspicuous lack of success; he tried to appease the anti-Europeans, and to undercut Farage, by giving in piecemeal to their demands. In 2011, Cameron isolated Britain in Europe by vetoing the European Fiscal Compact, a treaty to stabilize the euro, forcing the Europeans to come to an agreement without Britain. For this, he was greeted back home as a hero. The following year, Cameron promised the referendum on Europe that "the bastards" and others had been clamoring for. But first he would go cap in hand to other European leaders to renegotiate Britain's membership of the EU. After his obstruction of the Fiscal Compact, Cameron's goodwill in Europe was a trifle limited. Still, since most European leaders wanted Britain to remain in the union, he got some of what he asked for, mostly ways to restrict benefits to EU migrants in Britain, and British exemption from the aim to promote greater European integration. But this was never going to be enough for the "Brexiteers," who wanted a divorce from Europe.

Cameron now had to make the argument that Britain was better off inside than outside the EU. He no doubt sincerely believed this, but like most British politicians he had never made a positive case for Britain's membership. As was true for most Tories, "bastards" or not, the lure of British sovereignty, myths about wartime heroism and Britain's love of the open seas, as well as the Special Relationship, had far greater emotional appeal. But these were the arguments harnessed by the other side, in a leave campaign that often degenerated into sentimentalism about Spitfires, Churchill, and the "Dunkirk spirit" at best, and xenophobic demagoguery at worst. Boris Johnson raised a false alarm about Britain being swamped by Turks (Turkey was not an EU member). Nigel Farage posed in front of a billboard pointing at a picture of large numbers of young Middle Eastern men (actually refugees in Slovenia). "We must break free of the EU and take back control" was the slogan on the poster.

All Cameron could do was to warn British voters of the negative consequences of breaking away from Europe: damage to the City of

London, British exports, Britain's status in the world, and so on. He even asked Obama to visit Britain and help his cause. Despite their past differences, Obama complied. He wrote an article for the pro-Brexit paper *The Daily Telegraph*, pointing out that the US would not swiftly negotiate a trade deal with Britain after Brexit. On the contrary, he said, repeating a phrase suggested by Downing Street operators, Britain would be "at the back of the queue."[38] In a joint press conference, he even spoke of his love of Winston Churchill—a sentiment he had never expressed before, or since.

All this achieved was to confirm the idea, lodged in many British minds already, that the "remainers" stood for the corrupt liberal establishment, big business, and the City plutocrats. This was the world that Cameron knew best. A child of privilege, he was sure that people would opt for safety and vote for the status quo. He had not had many setbacks in his political life. Why should this situation be any different?

Hillary Clinton, Obama's anointed successor, had earned her privileges in a harder way than Cameron. But she was no less sure that her education, expertise, and liberal credentials would make her the natural choice to be the next president of the United States. She felt entitled to it, as the wife of a former president, as a senator from New York, and secretary of state under Obama. Who could be better qualified? Donald Trump, who hailed Brexit as a wonderful thing and praised Nigel Farage as a great leader, was simply too vulgar, ignorant, and bizarre to become the most powerful leader in the Western world.

Ben Rhodes, Obama's speechwriter and foreign policy adviser, was in London with the president in April 2016, a few months before the Brexit vote. He was asked by some of Cameron's people whether he thought Trump stood a chance. The occasion was relaxed, almost like an intimate family gathering. Well, said Rhodes, if Trump had been a more skilled politician, he might have exploited the message of taking back control to his advantage. Rhodes continued: "I took a sip of red wine, enjoying the easy chatter of voices from a Saturday night crowd at a comfortable London restaurant. 'But you know,' I said, 'like you, we need people to break for the safer choice.'"[39]

Thirteen

GRAND ILLUSIONS

Fascism arose as a religion of disappointment, a spreading nausea at the hypocrisy of the owners of the twentieth century. It is important to see that Fascism is a disease, as catching as influenza.

· CYRIL CONNOLLY

They will soon be calling me MR. BREXIT!

· DONALD TRUMP

The first foreign leader to congratulate Donald Trump on becoming the forty-fifth president of the United States was the Egyptian military dictator Abdel Fattah al-Sisi. The second was the Australian prime minister Malcolm Turnbull, who had managed to get hold of Trump's cell phone number from Greg Norman, the famous golfer. I'm not sure where the British prime minister Theresa May was in the telephonic pecking order, but when she did call, Trump wished her to know that if ever she had any plans to travel to the US, she should get in touch.

The first foreign politician to actually meet Trump after his victory was a British rabble-rouser who had never managed to hold any government post in his own country, the man who basked in the yells and whoops of Trump's supporters in the summer of 2016, on a campaign stop in Jackson, Mississippi, when he promised that "the little people," "the ordinary decent people," would crush the "political class," the "establishment," the "experts," the elites of "modern global corporatism," and of course, "Washington."

There they stood, the two of them, a few months later, on November 12, in the reflected glow of Trump's gilded elevator doors at Trump Tower in New York, grinning and pointing and sticking their thumbs up: the newly elected president and Nigel Farage, chairman of the UK Independence Party, identified by Trump to his adoring fans as "Mr. Brexit." "We were both roaring with laughter," Farage recalled. "Suddenly, you know, we'd won."[1]

One way of describing this Anglo-American duo is as gross examples of particular national stereotypes: Trump as the carnival huckster, the swaggering loudmouth, the bottom-pinching used car salesman, the "ugly American" of the 1950s; and Farage as the beery chancer, the man in the loud tweed jacket and velvet-collared coat, dispenser of dodgy racing tips and crude jokes, the pub bore with hard-right opinions and a hearty contempt for foreigners. Trump would have liked his English friend to be prime minister of the UK. Lacking that possibility for the time being, he publicly urged the British government to appoint Farage as ambassador to the US, an odd piece of unsolicited advice from a president-elect.

Both men drew parallels between their respective campaigns to take back their countries from the immigrants, the international bankers, the liberal media, Washington insiders, London city slickers, "Europe" and other enemies of the ordinary, decent people. Both admired the Russian strongman Vladimir Putin, whose secret agencies had a hand in manipulating public opinion in Britain and the US in favor of Trump and Brexit. And both had a particular loathing for the financier and philanthropist George Soros, who spent a fortune on liberal causes around the world. The subtext of Soros hatred, all too common among populist agitators in Europe and the US, was articulated most succinctly by a shady British businessman named Arron Banks, who provided Farage's Brexit campaign with much of its financial backing, accumulated from Banks's diamond mines in South Africa: "I suppose there are good Jews and bad Jews, then George Soros."[2]

The Trump-Farage alliance, tapping into the anger and resentment of people who felt "left behind" and were seeking mostly foreign scapegoats to blame this on, gave the Special Relationship a whole new twist, albeit with echoes of older prejudices about Anglo-Saxon "kith and kin." That Trump has German and Farage French family roots was perhaps less important to their "base" than their barely disguised contempt for people who were not white, or indeed not male.

Nigel Farage held no official position of power, however. The prime minister in 2016 was Theresa May. But without Farage and his UK Independence Party, the effort to get enough people to vote for Brexit would not have succeeded. He was the dark face of the Brexit campaign. Pro-Brexit politicians in the Conservative Party were happy to leave the dirty work to him and other shady operators on the rancid fringe of right-wing politics. The Tories could keep a fastidious distance from overt bigotry and xenophobia as long as UKIP did the job of stoking those fires. But there is no doubt that the "bastards," who had tormented so many Tory leaders over the years, had won. The longed-for break with "Europe" had finally come, but at the same price that Americans paid for Trump's takeover of the Republican Party. Brexit radicalized British politics and divided the normally pragmatic British public into mutually antagonistic tribes egged on by strident ideologues and the tabloid press; the middle of the road began to disintegrate. And Theresa May, by trying to appease the Brexit hard-liners, soon became their helpless foil, whose efforts to come to some kind of sensible arrangement with the EU would end in abject failure. This made her hopes to restore a more conventional alliance with the US all the more urgent, indeed desperate.

Almost immediately after Trump's inauguration, she flew to Washington for a meeting. The usual pleasantries ensued. Both leaders posed in front of Churchill's bust in the Oval Office. Trump said Brexit would be wonderful for Britain. May, who had voted against Brexit, remarked that her visit showed the importance of "the special relationship that exists between our two countries, a relationship based on the bonds of history, of family, kinship and common interests."[3] She invited Trump for a state visit to Britain, a gesture that could easily have been left until later. The only awkward moment came during a joint press conference when the BBC political correspondent had the temerity to ask the president about his decision to ban Muslims from entering the US, and his apparently favorable views on torture. Trump observed to May, jokingly one hopes, "This was your choice of a question. There goes that relationship."[4]

Despite her best efforts, May never managed to establish anything like the rapport with Trump that Farage enjoyed. Trump's chest-beating machismo didn't sit well with the stern, slightly gauche Anglican vicar's daughter. His brand of demagogic populism was a long way from her old-fashioned English conservatism. Farage had praised Trump for "dominating" Hillary Clinton like a "silverback gorilla." This was not May's style at all. She could be steely, even ruthless, and her views on the non-English-speaking peoples were almost as provincial as Trump's. But she was neither a gorilla nor an admirer of dominating men.

When Trump finally went on his state visit to Britain in the summer of 2019, after the event was postponed several times for fear that protesters would hurt his feelings, the president insulted Theresa May by criticizing her negotiations with the EU and stating once again what a fine fellow Nigel Farage was. He added that Boris Johnson, leader of the Brexit hard-liners, would make a great prime minister. And while he was at it, Trump also managed to disparage the mayor of London, a Muslim and the son of Pakistani immigrants, as "a stone-cold loser," and the queen's daughter-in-law, the African American Meghan Markle, as "nasty." But he liked the queen, he said: "We just had a great time." She gave him a first edition of Churchill's *Second World War.*

Right-wing populism and the politics of resentment are hardly limited to Britain and the US. Quite the contrary. Such trends have a dark history in countries like Italy or France, and they have been inflamed in Eastern European countries by post-Soviet corruption. But in Britain and America it all seems more shocking. For the era of Trump and Brexit marks a radical break with the postwar order shaped by Churchill and Roosevelt. British prime ministers, with the exception of Edward Heath, and more sporadically Macmillan and Blair, were all uneasy about fitting Britain into any kind of European union. Some felt superior to other Europeans. Some were sentimental about the Commonwealth. Almost all were sentimental about the Special Relationship. But none of them, since

Britain joined the European Economic Community in 1973, dreamed of a divorce. Certainly, no president of the US would have endorsed it, let alone cheered it on.

Trump, Farage, and the more rabid Tory Brexiteers spoke obsessively about taking back their countries and making them great again. This talk was either grandiose—Britain as a great global power—or reflected a narrow, chauvinistic view of the world that Roosevelt and Churchill would have found abhorrent. Trump's "America First" slogan, borrowed from the isolationists of the 1930s, some of whom felt warmly toward the Nazis, advanced an idea of America that Roosevelt actively resisted. The restoration of "greatness" in the era of Brexit and Trump meant the planned destruction of the very ideals—open, internationalist, liberal—that many people once admired most about the Anglo-American order. That neither Britain nor the US always lived up to their own ideals does not make their demolition any less alarming.

It was left to the chancellor of Germany, Angela Merkel, to stand up for the liberal standards articulated by Britain and the US in the Atlantic Charter of 1941. Her formal congratulations to Trump included the following words: "Germany and America are connected by values of democracy, freedom, and respect for the law and the dignity of man, independent of origin, skin color, religion, gender, sexual orientation, or political views. I offer the next president of the United States close cooperation on the basis of these values." She said this in December 2016. The following year, after Trump had demonstrated his scorn for postwar institutions, such as NATO, set up by the US to defend those values, Merkel said that Western democracies could no longer rely on their Anglo-American allies. The EU had to be prepared "to take its fate into its own hands."

There are many reasons why the world had taken such a

dramatic turn, reasons that reach far beyond the borders of Britain and the US. Trust in political elites was dented by the financial crash of 2008, when politicians of all major parties were blamed for shielding the bankers from the consequences of their malfeasance. The European Union, originally established as a driver of peace, democracy, and prosperity, comes across to many people in a period of economic stress as a remote cabal of cold-eyed technocrats looking after their own interests and out of touch with the common people. With the rise of the internet, the moderating filters of mainstream news media are increasingly regarded as obsolete and dismissed by demagogues as elitist purveyors of "fake news." Immigrants from poor countries, initially welcomed as sources of cheap labor, came to be seen as threats to the livelihoods of native populations. Acts of terror by Islamist fanatics sharpened old prejudices against Muslims into outright hostility. Fears stalked the West about demographic upheavals and ethnic "replacement," of Europe turning into "Eurabia," and white America "swamped" by Mexicans and other "undesirable aliens." These were the perfect conditions for charismatic demagogues who promise to "drain the swamp" of liberal democracies, carry out "the people's will," and "take back" their countries.

In the 1930s, Britain and the US, despite the America Firsters and Oswald Mosley's British Union of Fascists, resisted similar tendencies and saved Europe from Nazi tyranny. Many refugees from European totalitarianism found a safe haven in Anglo-America. Now, far from being beacons of hope and freedom, both countries are moving in the direction of increased isolation, driven by the existential fear of immigrants and the temptation of illiberal leadership.

Underlying most varieties of modern populism is resentment

about being overtaken, dismissed, ignored, outpaced, the sense, that is, of power and privilege slipping away. This feeling can be based on economic deprivation, ethnicity, or national decline. The Germans no longer dream of "greatness"; they tried that before and learned their lessons from failure. French *gloire* is not a plausible idea anymore either. The Chinese do dream of restoring greatness. And while they feel their power growing, Americans feel theirs sliding. Expensive wars in the Middle East that seem to have no end, and certainly no victory, in sight, added to that feeling. Trump's isolationism feels like a fit of pique, not unprecedented in US history, a deliberate turning away from the outside world that is supposedly taking Americans for a ride.

But that is not the only reason for Trumpian bitterness. The politics of resentment in America go deeper than wounded nationalism. Popular anger in America often has a racial basis, the sense of certain white people that their ethnic privileges have been slipping ever since Lyndon Johnson signed those bills in the 1960s that gave civil rights to all Americans. This explains the rage in some circles, often though by no means always rural and not highly educated, against President Obama: he was not only better educated than most people, at the best universities, but he was partly African too. A highly educated black president provoked the social and racial anxieties that helped to propel Donald Trump to power.

The social divisions over Brexit in Britain were much like those in the US over the election of Trump: urban against rural, educated against less educated, old against young. What gave the Brexit campaign its peculiar sting was the combination of nativism and wartime rhetoric. Britain's Finest Hour was not only frequently invoked, but those who were in favor of staying in the EU, or who had doubts about some of the Brexiteers' tactics, were regarded as traitors.

Three High Court judges who ruled that Parliament should give its consent to a Brexit notice were denounced on the front page of a right-wing tabloid as "Enemies of the People."[5] A well-known columnist wrote, "For Brexit to work, we need Dunkirk spirit not 'Naysaying Nellies.'"[6]

Some of the language was not only inflammatory but also delusional. The problem for Theresa May was that no possible deal with the EU could satisfy enough members of Parliament to vote for it. Britain would either have to abide by EU rules without any authority to influence them or be shut out of the single market, harming British business. When Theresa May eked out an arrangement that obliged Britain to follow EU rules for a transitional period, the editor of a major newspaper intoned, "Britain cannot accept this horrific, humiliating surrender to the EU."[7] A columnist in the same paper shouted, "No Surrender, Mrs May: The EU Is Weak, and Britain Is Strong."

Clearly, then, Britain was at war, or so it seemed from the point of view of many Brexiteers. Theresa May was Neville Chamberlain, an abject appeaser who failed to hold firm and let the country down. She didn't help her own cause by pandering to the nativists by using some of their pet phrases. It was she who hinted that cosmopolitan people, who "behave as though they have more in common with international elites than with the people down the road," were "citizens from nowhere."[8] And so she became the latest prime minister to fall in the endless British civil war over "Europe" and in finding the nation's role after losing an empire.

Her successor, Boris Johnson, was as much a self-created caricature as Trump and Farage. Although not born to a grand old family, Johnson deliberately exaggerated the upper-class mannerisms he acquired at Eton and Oxford: the stammering drawl, the self-deprecating jocularity that can come only from a deep reservoir of assumed superiority, the cultivated amateurishness, the Latin quotations, the carefully studied slovenly dress. Unlike David Cameron, his contemporary at Eton and Oxford, who was much grander by birth but who affected a common touch without convincing anyone, Johnson realized that playing down his upper-class education would only make him look shifty, and so he played it up. His model was Winston Churchill, whose traits he appeared to be mimicking down to the old man's stooping posture.

Johnson's Churchillian rhetoric about the Brexit negotiations—"I'd rather be dead in a ditch" than delay Brexit—played into a mood of nostalgia for greater days, of reliving the Dunkirk moment. Class played a part in this, just as race did in Trump's America. Johnson's mimicry of wartime defiance didn't convince many young people in large cities, nor did he do very well with most highly educated citizens. But he was popular with the older generation in the more provincial parts of the country, and with angry white working-class people. Johnson also appealed to the soccer hooligan spirit, which Alan Clark, the right-wing Tory politician, told me was there "to be tapped." A more charitable way of putting this would be to say that Johnson's upper-class bellicosity merged with working-class patriotism.

It was indeed a curious aspect of the Brexit campaign that it was led by expensively educated members of the traditional British elite who pretended to be representing the "people" against the "establishment." In fact, of course, they *were* the establishment: Johnson, or his fellow MP Jacob Rees-Mogg, Old Etonian, son of the former editor of *The Times*, and, because of his weirdly old-fashioned appearance, known as "the Honorable Member for the eighteenth century."

To claim, as some have done, that the British are nostalgic for their lost empire is certainly too general, and probably much exaggerated. Most people don't much care. But it might help to explain the particular animus against "Europe" among certain members of the elite, such as Johnson and Rees-Mogg. When Johnson visited Myanmar as foreign secretary, his reaction to seeing the famous golden pagoda in Yangon was to start reciting Kipling's poem "Mandalay": "Come you back, you British soldier." This tactless reminder of empire upset his hosts and alarmed the British ambassador, who had to advise Johnson that it really was "not appropriate." This doesn't mean that Johnson yearns for the restoration of colonial rule. But the sense that joining Europe has meant a loss of British sovereignty, which must now be regained, has many layers. One is a concern that the authority to make laws cannot be delegated to pan-national institutions without diluting the authority of a national parliament. This may be an inevitable and necessary consequence of an arrangement that offers greater benefits in exchange. But the concern is legitimate.

There is, however, another reason for resentment. A hundred years ago, when the empire was still fully intact, men like Johnson or Rees-Mogg could have expected to be ruling much of the world from London, or at least running big chunks of India. The European Union is not the reason why this is no longer feasible. But for some people it does stand as a symbol of Britain's diminished status and power. That is why Britain's soccer hooligans abroad startled the natives by chanting, "Can't wait to get out of the EU!" and why Johnson offers grandiose visions about the British lion roaring once more. It was he, after all, who wrote in *The Spectator*, in 2002, about empire, "The problem is not that we were once in charge, but that we are not in charge any more."

Churchill in his pomp would have concurred with this sentiment. And, like Johnson, he was an upper-class toff with a deft
common touch, which appealed to the patriotic workingman. But
Churchill was also devoted to parliamentary democracy. He loved
the Houses of Parliament. When World War I was raging, Churchill
remarked, while gazing at the empty chamber of the House of
Commons at dusk, "This little place is what makes the difference
between us and Germany." The citation is in Johnson's biography of
his hero.

But to win the Brexit war in Britain, Johnson has promoted himself as the people's tribune against Parliament. Like other Brexiteers, Johnson made a fetish of "the people's will," expressed in a
referendum (a form of voting dismissed by both Clement Attlee and
Margaret Thatcher as profoundly un-British). To stop politicians
from standing in the people's way, Johnson decided in September
2019 to cut off any further debate on the matter by suspending Parliament. When twenty-one members of his own party, including
Churchill's grandson, argued for a bill to give Parliament the right to
stop Britain from crashing out of the EU without a deal, they were
brutally purged from the party. They were EU "collaborators," in
Johnson's words, proposing "a surrender bill." They were "hoisting
the white flag." And so the war went on, with Churchill's self-
appointed heir trampling on the unwritten norms of Britain's liberal
democracy, all in the name of the people.

Trump had the greatest admiration for Johnson's moves. Johnson, in the president's tweeted phrase, was "exactly what the UK is
looking for." Better still, the prime minister was, in Trump's curious
expression, "Britain Trump." This was the highest praise he could
have bestowed on his British counterpart. Britain and the US are
very different in many ways, and parallels between Trump's erratic

policies and Brexit should not be carried too far. But the two leaders have more in common than many presidents and prime ministers had had before them. They were both men with boundless ambition and few fixed ideas who grabbed their chances at coming to power by stirring up popular rage. Their stated goal was to restore greatness. But by breaking so many norms, they did their best to destroy the very basis of what once made Britain and America great in the eyes of so many people around the world.

On one of his fruitless trips to the European continent, hoping to press the EU into offering terms of divorce that would suit Britain but do great damage to the rest of Europe, Johnson came up with an extraordinary image. If the EU failed to accede to Johnson's demands, he said, Britain would "break out of its 'manacles' like the Incredible Hulk." And if Parliament stopped him from breaking those manacles, he warned, "The madder Hulk gets, the stronger Hulk gets."[9]

It is a bizarre and pitiful image: Britain as the furious green-skinned humanoid in an American cartoon, inspired according to his creator, Stan Lee, by Frankenstein's monster. In the age of Trump and Brexit, the vision of Anglo-America offered by its leaders has become a grotesque caricature: hulking, muscle-bound, angry, preening, exulting in brute force. In one comic book version of the Hulk, the monster suffers from multiple personality disorder.[10]

Like most things, this, too, will pass. Today's scary headlines are tomorrow's old news. Perhaps enough "enemies of the people" will manage to claw something back from the ravages of Brexit, and Trump will one day be seen as a temporary phase of insanity in America's proud democratic history, a figure along the lines of Senator Joe McCarthy who will stand as a warning for future generations of a route not to take. But the Anglo-American world I grew up admiring, naively, perhaps, but not without some basis in historical truth, has been severely damaged.

Weeping at the sight of American and British soldiers in a creaky Hollywood movie crawling onto the beaches of Normandy to liberate my continent is sentimental, no doubt. But the ideals expressed in the Atlantic Charter by Roosevelt and Churchill, and the institutions they built, did represent something noble, despite the foolish and destructive wars undertaken by their successors, who were too eager to be seen as Churchill's heirs. The order that emerged from World War II is coming to an end. The reasons why that war was fought are rapidly being forgotten. For me this is a reason for sadness. The political freedom and openness of Britain and the United States gave many people hope. That the ideals were often betrayed is no reason not to celebrate them.

Acknowledgments

I owe a great debt to many people who have encouraged me in one way or another while writing this book. Sean Wilentz and Andrew Delbanco gave me their expert advice as distinguished historians and loyal friends. So did Geoffrey Wheatcroft, Richard Aldous, and David Woolner, who were kind enough to read all or parts of the manuscript. Their comments were invaluable. I would also like to thank John Kerr and Sidney Blumenthal for sharing their memories as "insiders" in the story I wanted to tell.

True friendship often reveals itself in less than easy times. The moral support of a number of people meant more to me than they know. They are, in alphabetical order: Gini Alhadeff, Lisa Appignanesi, Carol Archer, Noga Arikha, Roger Berkowitz, Leon Botstein, Joan Buck, Simon Callow, Kent Carrol, Jim Conte, Julie Corman, Robert Cottrell, Robyn Creswell, Prudence Crowther, Mark Danner, Dawn Delbanco, James Fenton, Gabriella Ferrari, Hamilton Fish, Arnon Grunberg, Stephen Holmes, Andrew Horvat, Michael Ignatieff, Julie Just, Tom Keenan, Nina Khrushcheva, Michael Kimmelman, Laura Kipnis, Robert Kirschenbaum, Rem Koolhaas,

Enrique Krauze, John Lloyd, John MacArthur, Janet Malcolm, Avishai Margalit, Beatrice Monti, Marie D'Origny, Darryl Pinckney, Sabine Rewald, David Rieff, Gwen Robinson, John Ryle, David Salle, Margaret Scott, Matt Seaton, Adam Shatz, Fred Sherry, Josh Siegel, Elisabeth Sifton, Graham Snow, Michael Specter, Lorin Stein, Jean Strouse, Gay Talese, Judith Thurman, Marina Warner, Lawrence Weschler, Edmund White, Simon Winchester, Zsuzsannna Zsohar, Marina van Zuylen.

Andrew Wylie and Jin Auh of the Wylie Agency gave me the kind of backing over the years that went well beyond professional obligation.

In an age when good literary editors are becoming an increasingly rare commodity, I cannot praise Scott Moyers and Will Atkinson highly enough. Many thanks also to Mia Council for her meticulous editing.

Finally, I owe the greatest debt of all to Eri Hotta, who shares my life.

Notes

CHAPTER ONE: UNDER THE SIGN OF VICTORY

1. Christopher Hitchens, *Blood, Class, and Nostalgia: Anglo-American Ironies* (New York: Farrar, Straus and Giroux, 1990), p. 214.
2. Boris Johnson, quoted in *The Guardian* (UK edition), January 21, 2017.

CHAPTER TWO: BLOOD AND HISTORY

1. Trent A. Watts, *One Homogeneous People: Narratives of White Southern Identity, 1890–1920* (Knoxville: University of Tennessee Press, 2010), p. 116.
2. Hitchens, *Blood, Class, and Nostalgia*, p. 135.
3. Robin Renwick, *Fighting with Allies: America and Britain in Peace and War* (New York: Times Books, 1996), p. 52.
4. Max Hastings, *Winston's War: Churchill, 1940–1945* (New York: Vintage, 2011), p. 149.
5. Renwick, *Fighting with Allies*, p. 11.
6. Andrew Roberts, "When Churchill Dissed America," *Smithsonian Magazine*, November 2018.
7. Marc Wortman, *1941: Fighting the Shadow War: A Divided America in a World at War* (New York: Grove Atlantic, 2017), p. 37.
8. Renwick, *Fighting with Allies*, p. 74.
9. Peter Clarke, *Mr. Churchill's Profession: The Statesman as Author and the Book That Defined the "Special Relationship"* (New York: Bloomsbury Press, 2012), p. 101.
10. Thomas F. Gossett, *Race: The History of an Idea in America* (New York: Oxford University Press, 1997), p. 100.
11. Derek Leebaert, *Grand Improvisation: America Confronts the British Superpower, 1945–1957* (New York: Farrar, Straus and Giroux, 2018), p. 219.
12. Clarke, *Mr. Churchill's Profession*, p. 60.
13. Arthur Schlesinger, Jr., "The Supreme Partnership," *Atlantic*, October 1984.
14. Alfred Thayer Mahan, *The Influence of Sea Power Upon History, 1660–1783* (Boston: Little, Brown, 1918), p. 52.
15. Mahan, *The Influence of Sea Power*, p. 55.
16. Hitchens, *Blood, Class, and Nostalgia*, p. 110.
17. Renwick, *Fighting with Allies*, p. 32.
18. Clarke, *Mr. Churchill's Profession*, p. 255.
19. Clarke, *Mr. Churchill's Profession*, p. 101.

20. Jon Meacham, *Franklin and Winston: An Intimate Portrait of an Epic Friendship* (New York: Random House, 2003), p. 124.
21. Speech to Mansion House, November 10, 1941. Transcript at http://www.ibiblio.org/pha/policy/1941/1941-11-10a.html.
22. Clarke, *Mr. Churchill's Profession*, p. 88.
23. Erik Larson, *The Splendid and the Vile: A Saga of Churchill, Family, and Defiance During the Blitz* (New York: Crown, 2020), p. 352.
24. Winston S. Churchill, *The Second World War*, vol. 3, *The Grand Alliance* (Boston: Houghton Mifflin, 1950), p. 381.
25. Bosley Crowther, "'That Hamilton Woman,' the Story of a Historic Love Affair, at the Music Hall—Other New Films at the Roxy, Capitol and Palace," *New York Times*, April 4, 1941.
26. Wortman, *1941*, p. 274.
27. Wortman, *1941*, p. 386.
28. Warren F. Kimball, ed., *Churchill and Roosevelt: The Complete Correspondence*, vol. 3 (Princeton University Press, 1984), p. 140.
29. Kimball, *Churchill and Roosevelt*, vol. 1, p. 281.
30. Meacham, *Franklin and Winston*, p. 134.
31. Churchill, *The Second World War*, vol. 3, p. 615.
32. Churchill, *The Second World War*, vol. 4, *The Hinge of Fate* (Boston: Houghton Mifflin, 1950), p. 109.
33. Renwick, *Fighting with Allies*, p. 53.
34. Hastings, *Winston's War*, p. 182.
35. David Reynolds, *Summits: Six Meetings That Shaped the Twentieth Century* (New York: Basic Books, 2007), pp. 106–7.
36. Lord Moran, *Churchill Taken from the Diaries of Lord Moran: The Struggle for Survival, 1940–1965* (Boston: Houghton Mifflin, 1966), p. 88.
37. Lord Moran, *Churchill Taken from the Diaries*, p. 140.
38. Lord Moran, *Churchill Taken from the Diaries*, p. 141.
39. Churchill, *The Second World War*, vol. 5, p. 339.
40. Churchill, *The Second World War*, vol. 5, p. 360.

CHAPTER THREE: THE EMPIRE IS DEAD, LONG LIVE THE EMPIRE

1. John Bew, *Citizen Clem: A Biography of Attlee* (London: Riverrun, 2016), p. 432.
2. David McCullough, *Truman* (New York: Simon and Schuster, 1992), p. 447.
3. Bew, *Citizen Clem*, p. 352.
4. Bew, *Citizen Clem*, p. 383.
5. Dean Acheson, *Present at the Creation: My Years in the State Department* (New York: W. W. Norton, 1969), p. 594.
6. Hitchens, *Blood, Class, and Nostalgia*, p. 23.
7. Leebaert, *Grand Improvisation*, p. 49.
8. David S. McLellan, *Dean Acheson: The State Department Years* (New York: Dodd, Mead, 1976), p. 274.
9. Acheson, *Present at the Creation*, p. 478.
10. Bew, *Citizen Clem*, p. 494.
11. Acheson, *Present at the Creation*, p. 481.
12. Dean Acheson, *The Korean War* (New York: W. W. Norton, 1971), p. 91.
13. Leebaert, *Grand Improvisation*, p. 299.
14. Hugo Young, *This Blessed Plot: Britain and Europe from Churchill to Blair* (Woodstock, NY: Overlook Press, 1998), p. 24.

15. Wm. Roger Louis and Hedley Bull, eds., *The Special Relationship: Anglo-American Relations since 1945* (Oxford: Clarendon Press, 1986), p. 80.
16. Harold Nicolson, Marginal Comment, *Spectator,* June 30, 1950.
17. *New York Times,* June 16, 1950.
18. Young, *This Blessed Plot,* p. 37.
19. Winston Churchill, "The United States of Europe," *Saturday Evening Post,* February 15, 1930.
20. Acheson, *Present at the Creation,* p. 385.

CHAPTER FOUR: THE ROAD TO SUEZ

1. Lord Moran, *Churchill Taken from the Diaries,* p. 368.
2. Lord Moran, *Churchill Taken from the Diaries,* p. 377.
3. Acheson, *Present at the Creation,* p. 597.
4. David Dilks, *Churchill and Company: Allies and Rivals in War and Peace* (London: I.B. Tauris, 2012), p. 228.
5. Leebaert, *Grand Improvisation,* p. 301.
6. Leebaert, *Grand Improvisation,* p. 313.
7. Robert Rhodes James, *Anthony Eden: A Biography* (London: McGraw, Hill, 1987), p. 456.
8. Harry S. Truman, *Memoirs by Harry S. Truman: 1945 Year of Decisions,* rev. ed. (Saybrook, CT: William S. Konecky Associates, reissue edition, 1999), p. 275.
9. H. W. Brands, Jr., *Cold Warriors: Eisenhower's Generation and American Foreign Policy* (New York: Columbia University Press, 1988), p. 206.
10. Brands, *Cold Warriors,* p. 202.
11. Renwick, *Fighting with Allies,* p. 200.
12. Louis and Bull, *The Special Relationship,* p. 79.
13. Leebaert, *Grand Improvisation,* p. 413.
14. Acheson, *Present at the Creation,* p. 388.
15. Acheson, *Present at the Creation,* p. 600.
16. Jean Edward Smith, *Eisenhower in War and Peace* (New York: Random House, 2012), p. 619.
17. Smith, *Eisenhower in War and Peace,* p. 620.
18. Lord Moran, *Churchill Taken from the Diaries,* p. 587.
19. Lord Moran, *Churchill Taken from the Diaries,* p. 436.
20. Lord Moran, *Churchill Taken from the Diaries,* p. 529.
21. Lord Moran, *Churchill Taken from the Diaries,* p. 538.
22. Dwight D. Eisenhower, *Mandate for Change: 1953–1956* (New York: Doubleday, 1963), p. 247.
23. Rhodes James, *Anthony Eden,* p. 375.
24. Eisenhower, *Mandate for Change,* p. 247.
25. Rhodes James, *Anthony Eden,* p. 350.
26. Quoted to me by Hugo Young in a private conversation.
27. Young, *This Blessed Plot,* p. 83.
28. *The Poisoned Chalice,* BBC, broadcast on May 9, 1996. Presented by Michael Elliott, produced by John Bridcut.
29. *The Poisoned Chalice.*
30. Smith, *Eisenhower in War and Peace,* p. 695.
31. Rhodes James, *Anthony Eden,* pp. 505–6.
32. Peter G. Boyle, ed., *The Eden-Eisenhower Correspondence, 1955–1957* (Chapel Hill: University of North Carolina Press, 2005), p. 181.
33. Emmet John Hughes, *The Ordeal of Power: A Political Memoir of the Eisenhower Years* (New York: Atheneum, 1963), p. 213.

34. Christopher Sandford, *Harold and Jack: The Remarkable Friendship of Prime Minister Macmillan and President Kennedy* (Buffalo, NY: Prometheus, 2014), p. 19.

35. Smith, *Eisenhower in War and Peace*, p. 704.

CHAPTER FIVE: AN ANGLO-AMERICAN BOND

1. Richard Davenport-Hines, *An English Affair: Sex, Class and Power in the Age of Profumo* (New York: Harper Press, 2013), p. 44.

2. Alistair Horne, *Macmillan: 1957–1986*, vol. 2 (New York: Viking, 1989), p. 27.

3. Sandford, *Harold and Jack*, p. 109.

4. Horne, *Macmillan*, p. 27.

5. Douglas Hurd said this in 1993, at the Royal Institute for International Affairs (Chatham House).

6. Louis and Bull, *The Special Relationship*, p. 253.

7. Renwick, *Fighting with Allies*, p. 237.

8. Horne, *Macmillan*, p. 105.

9. Sandford, *Harold and Jack*, p. 96.

10. Sandford, *Harold and Jack*, p. 153.

11. Horne, *Macmillan*, p. 53.

12. D. R. Thorpe, *Supermac: The Life of Harold Macmillan* (London: Chatto and Windus, 2010), p. 394.

13. John Baylis, *Anglo-American Relations since 1939: The Enduring Alliance* (Documents in Contemporary History) (Manchester University Press, 1997), p. 102.

14. Renwick, *Fighting with Allies*, p. 254.

15. Young, *This Blessed Plot*, p. 118.

16. Horne, *Macmillan*, p. 229.

17. Horne, *Macmillan*, p. 231.

18. Julian Jackson, *Charles de Gaulle* (London: Haus, 2003), p. 96.

19. Jackson, *Charles de Gaulle*, p. 99.

20. Sandford, *Harold and Jack*, p. 52.

21. Lawrence Freedman, *Kennedy's Wars: Berlin, Cuba, Laos, and Vietnam* (Oxford: Oxford University Press, 2000), p. 301.

22. Horne, *Macmillan*, p. 292.

23. Freedman, *Kennedy's Wars*, p. 310.

24. Horne, *Macmillan*, p. 310.

25. Reynolds, *Summits*, p. 211.

26. Sandford, *Harold and Jack*, p. 104.

27. Horne, *Macmillan*, p. 375.

28. Horne, *Macmillan*, p. 378.

29. Renwick, *Fighting with Allies*, p. 251.

30. Renwick, *Fighting with Allies*, p. 260.

31. Sandford, *Harold and Jack*, p. 171.

32. Horne, *Macmillan*, p. 301.

33. Sandford, *Harold and Jack*, p. 264.

34. Ben Pimlott, *Harold Wilson* (London: HarperCollins, 1992), p. 296.

CHAPTER SIX: THE CLOSE RELATIONSHIP

1. David Farber, ed., *The Sixties: From Memory to History* (Chapel Hill: University of North Carolina Press, 1994), p. 19.

2. Sylvia Ellis, *Britain, America, and the Vietnam War* (Westport, CT: Praeger, 2004), p. 12.

3. Ellis, *Britain, America, and the Vietnam War*, p. 15.

4. Richard Crossman, *The Diaries of a Cabinet Minister,* vol. 1, *1964–66* (London: Bookclub Associates, 1976), p. 117.

5. Speech to the House of Commons, August 3, 1961, https://www.theyworkforyou.com/debates/?id=1961-08-03a.1665.1.

6. Ellis, *Britain, America, and the Vietnam War,* p. 184.

7. Jonathan Colman, *A Special Relationship?: Harold Wilson, Lyndon B. Johnson, and Anglo-American Relations "At the Summit," 1964–68* (Manchester: Manchester University Press, 2005), p. 48.

8. Colman, *A Special Relationship?,* p. 49.

9. Crossman, *Diaries of a Cabinet Minister,* vol. 1, p. 95.

10. Colman, *A Special Relationship?,* p. 56.

11. Colman, *A Special Relationship?,* p. 61.

12. Colman, *A Special Relationship?,* p. 77.

13. *New Statesman,* May 7, 1965.

14. Ellis, *Britain, America, and the Vietnam War,* p. 31.

15. Young, *This Blessed Plot,* p. 196.

16. Young, *This Blessed Plot,* p. 194.

17. Crossman, *Diaries of a Cabinet Minister,* vol. 1, p. 595.

18. Ellis, *Britain, America, and the Vietnam War,* p. 250.

19. Ellis, *Britain, America, and the Vietnam War,* p. 229.

20. Renwick, *Fighting with Allies,* p. 284.

21. Ellis, *Britain, America, and the Vietnam War,* p. 251.

CHAPTER SEVEN: TO EUROPE AND BACK

1. Richard Nixon, *RN: The Memoirs of Richard Nixon* (New York: Grosset and Dunlap, 1978), p. 270.

2. Nixon, *RN,* p. 371.

3. Kathleen Burk, *Old World, New World: Great Britain and America from the Beginning* (New York: Atlantic Monthly Press, 2008), p. 622.

4. Edward Heath, *The Autobiography of Edward Heath: The Course of My Life* (London: Hodder and Stoughton, 1998), p. 471.

5. John Campbell, *Edward Heath: A Biography* (London: Jonathan Cape, 1993), p. 342.

6. Young, *This Blessed Plot,* p. 217.

7. Young, *This Blessed Plot,* p. 218.

8. Young, *This Blessed Plot,* p. 238.

9. Henry Kissinger, *The White House Years* (New York: Little, Brown, 1979), pp. 95–96.

10. Campbell, *Edward Heath,* p. 344.

11. Baylis, *Anglo-American Relations since 1939,* p. 186.

12. Campbell, *Edward Heath,* p. 345.

13. Heath, *The Autobiography of Edward Heath,* p. 492.

14. Burk, *Old World, New World,* p. 621.

15. Burk, *Old World, New World,* p. 626.

16. Pimlott, *Harold Wilson,* p. 624.

17. Pimlott, *Harold Wilson,* p. 627.

18. Interview with Llew Gardner on Thames TV, May 15, 1975.

19. Young, *This Blessed Plot,* p. 278.

20. Kenneth O. Morgan, *Callaghan: A Life* (Oxford: Oxford University Press, 1998), p. 614.

21. John Dumbrell, *The Carter Presidency: A Re-evaluation* (Manchester: Manchester University Press, 1993), p. 138.

22. Peter G. Bourne, *Jimmy Carter: A Comprehensive Biography from Plains to Post-Presidency* (New York: Scribner, 1997), p. 398.

23. Dumbrell, *The Carter Presidency*, p. 131.
24. Dumbrell, *The Carter Presidency*, p. 133.
25. Dumbrell, *The Carter Presidency*, p. 131.
26. Jimmy Carter, *Keeping Faith: Memoirs of a President* (New York: Bantam Books, 1982), p. 113.
27. Morgan, *Callaghan*, p. 603.
28. Morgan, *Callaghan*, p. 619.

CHAPTER EIGHT: AN EXTRAORDINARY RELATIONSHIP

1. Margaret Thatcher, *The Downing Street Years* (London: HarperCollins, 1993), p. 611.
2. Baylis, *Anglo-American Relations since 1939*, p. 205.
3. Baylis, *Anglo-American Relations since 1939*, p. 207.
4. Baylis, *Anglo-American Relations since 1939*, p. 203.
5. George R. Urban, *Diplomacy and Disillusion at the Court of Margaret Thatcher: An Insider's View* (London: I.B. Tauris, 1996), p. 34.
6. Thatcher, *The Downing Street Years*, p. 87.
7. Thatcher, *The Downing Street Years*, pp. 68–69.
8. Thatcher, *The Downing Street Years*, p. 157.
9. Charles Moore, *Margaret Thatcher: From Grantham to the Falklands* (New York: Knopf, 2013), p. 322.
10. Charles C. Johnson, "Thatcher and the Jews," *Tablet*, December 28, 2011.
11. Urban, *Diplomacy and Disillusion*, p. 28.
12. Douglas Keay, "Aids, Education and the Year 2000," *Woman's Own*, October 31, 1987.
13. Thatcher, *The Downing Street Years*, p. 157.
14. Richard Aldous, *Reagan and Thatcher: The Difficult Relationship* (New York: W. W. Norton, 2012), p. 43.
15. Quoted in the *New York Times*, February 27, 1981.
16. BBC News, April 3, 2002.
17. R. Gerald Hughes, *The Postwar Legacy of Appeasement: British Foreign Policy Since 1945* (London: Bloomsbury, 2014), p. 92.
18. *New York Times*, January 5, 2013.
19. Moore, *Margaret Thatcher*, p. 738.
20. Thatcher, *The Downing Street Years*, p. 192.
21. Thatcher, *The Downing Street Years*, p. 193.
22. Aldous, *Reagan and Thatcher*, p. 91.
23. Thatcher, *The Downing Street Years*, p. 235.
24. Address to Parliament, June 8, 1982.
25. Aldous, *Reagan and Thatcher*, p. 156.
26. Speech in Parliament, October 26, 1983, Public Papers of the Presidents of the United States: Ronald Reagan, 1982, p. 745.
27. Thatcher, *The Downing Street Years*, p. 331.
28. Urban, *Diplomacy and Disillusion*, p. 86.
29. Urban, *Diplomacy and Disillusion*, p. 52.
30. Thatcher, *The Downing Street Years*, p. 442.
31. Thatcher, *The Downing Street Years*, p. 444.
32. Aldous, *Reagan and Thatcher*, p. 224.
33. Thatcher, *The Downing Street Years*, p. 445.
34. Thatcher, *The Downing Street Years*, p. 472.
35. Thatcher, *The Downing Street Years*, p. 473.
36. Thatcher, *The Downing Street Years*, p. 70.

37. Thatcher, *The Downing Street Years*, p. 727.

38. Thatcher, *The Downing Street Years*, p. 82. The poem, entitled "Norman and Saxon (A.D. 1011)," was first published in 1911.

39. Dominic Lawson, "Saying the Unsayable about the Germans," *Spectator*, July 14, 1990.

40. Thatcher, *The Downing Street Years*, p. 742.

41. Young, *This Blessed Plot*, p. 348.

42. Thatcher, *The Downing Street Years*, p. 744.

43. George Bush and Brent Scowcroft, *A World Transformed: The Collapse of the Soviet Empire, the Unification of Germany, Tiananmen Square, the Gulf War* (New York: Knopf, 1998), p. 151.

44. Bush and Scowcroft, *A World Transformed*, p. 187.

45. Thatcher, *The Downing Street Years*, p. 783.

46. Thatcher, *The Downing Street Years*, p. 791.

47. Thatcher, *The Downing Street Years*, p. 774.

48. Bush and Scowcroft, *A World Transformed*, p. 83.

49. Thatcher, *The Downing Street Years*, p. 783.

50. Aldous, *Reagan and Thatcher*, p. 290.

51. Charles Moore, *Margaret Thatcher: The Authorized Biography*, vol. 3, *Herself Alone* (New York: Knopf, 2019), p. 638.

52. Bush and Scowcroft, *A World Transformed*, p. 340.

53. Thatcher, *The Downing Street Years*, p. 769.

54. Thatcher, *The Downing Street Years*, p. 784.

55. *Los Angeles Times*, February 7, 1993.

Chapter Nine: Kinder, Gentler

1. Anthony Seldon, *Major: A Political Life* (London: Weidenfeld and Nicolson, 1997), p. 131.

2. Earl A. Reitan, *The Thatcher Revolution: Margaret Thatcher, John Major, Tony Blair, and the Transformation of Modern Britain, 1979–2001* (Lanham, MD: Rowman and Littlefield, 2002), p. 118.

3. Quoted in Timothy Garton Ash, "Why We Must Not Let Europe Break Apart," *Guardian*, May 9, 2019.

4. Seldon, *Major*, p. 231.

5. Bush and Scowcroft, *A World Transformed*, p. 383.

6. Seldon, *Major*, p. 153.

7. Jerry W. Sanders, "Retreat from World Order: The Perils of Triumphalism," *World Policy Journal* (L:1, Spring 1991).

8. *New York Times*, October 24, 1990.

9. Bush and Scowcroft, *A World Transformed*, p. 430.

10. *Washington Post*, April 17, 1991.

11. *New York Times*, January 30, 1991.

12. Baylis, *Anglo-American Relations since 1939*, p. 224.

13. Sanders, "Retreat from World Order."

14. Seldon, *Major*, p. 159.

15. Bush and Scowcroft, *A World Transformed*, p. 487.

16. Reitan, *The Thatcher Revolution*, p. 123.

17. Address to joint session of Congress, September 11, 1990.

18. Baylis, *Anglo-American Relations since 1939*, p. 225.

19. Renwick, *Fighting with Allies*, p. 385.

20. Seldon, *Major*, p. 165.

21. Seldon, *Major*, p. 244.

22. Young, *This Blessed Plot*, p. 443.

23. *Economist*, September 25, 1993.

24. Young, *This Blessed Plot*, p. 465
25. James A. Baker III, *The Politics of Diplomacy: Revolution, War & Peace 1989–1992* (New York: Putnam Adult, 1995), p. 645.
26. Baker, *The Politics of Diplomacy*, p. 637.
27. Brendan Simms, *Unfinest Hour: Britain and the Destruction of Bosnia* (London: Allen Lane, 2001), p. 5.
28. Simms, *Unfinest Hour*, p. 50.
29. Simms, *Unfinest Hour*, p. 40.
30. Simms, *Unfinest Hour*, p. 7.
31. *Daily Telegraph*, May 10, 2019.
32. J. F. McAllister, "Atrocity and Outrage," *Time*, August 17, 1992.
33. Simms, *Unfinest Hour*, p. 50.
34. Baker, *The Politics of Diplomacy*, p. 651.
35. Sidney Blumenthal, "The Order of the Boot," *New Yorker*, December 7, 1992, p. 62.
36. Blumenthal, "The Order of the Boot," p. 62.

Chapter Ten: Too Much Conviction

1. John Dickie, *"Special" No More: Anglo-American Relations—Rhetoric and Reality* (London: Weidenfeld and Nicolson, 1994), p. 250.
2. Seldon, *Major*, p. 364.
3. Peter Riddell, *Hug Them Close: Blair, Clinton, Bush and the "Special Relationship"* (London: Politico's, 2004), p. 55.
4. Seldon, *Major*, p. 364.
5. Seldon, *Major*, p. 365.
6. Simms, *Unfinest Hour*, p. 60.
7. Simms, *Unfinest Hour*, p. 96.
8. Young, *This Blessed Plot*, p. 465.
9. Seldon, *Major*, p. 726.
10. Seldon, *Major*, p. 723.
11. Blair's speech in his first party conference as prime minister.
12. Alastair Campbell, *The Blair Years: The Alastair Campbell Diaries* (New York: Knopf, 2007), p. 96.
13. Geoffrey Wheatcroft, *Yo Blair: Tony Blair's Disastrous Premiership* (London: Politico's, 2007), p. 28.
14. Blair said this in a speech at Sofia University in Bulgaria on May 17, 1999.
15. Tony Blair, *A Journey: My Political Life* (New York: Knopf, 2010), p. 139.
16. Sidney Blumenthal, *The Clinton Wars* (New York: Farrar, Straus and Giroux, 2003), p. 634.
17. Blumenthal, *The Clinton Wars*, p. 308.
18. Riddell, *Hug Them Close*, p. 83.
19. Young, *This Blessed Plot*, pp. 484–85.
20. Blair, *A Journey*, p. 722.
21. Riddell, *Hug Them Close*, p. 71.
22. John Kampfner, *Blair's Wars* (New York: Free Press, 2003), p. 32.
23. Kampfner, *Blair's Wars*, p. 16.
24. Blumenthal, *The Clinton Wars*, p. 156.
25. Riddell, *Hug Them Close*, p. 95.
26. Blair, *A Journey*, p. 392.
27. Blair, *A Journey*, p. 393.
28. Blair, *A Journey*, p. 400.
29. Blair, *A Journey*, p. 397.
30. Blair, *A Journey*, pp. 367–68.

31. Blair, *A Journey*, p. 402.
32. Kampfner, *Blair's Wars*, p. 56.
33. Blumenthal, *The Clinton Wars*, p. 635.
34. Blumenthal, *The Clinton Wars*, p. 639.
35. Blair, *A Journey*, p. 416.
36. Blair, "Doctrine of the International Community," Speech to the Chicago Economic Club, April 22, 1999, https://www.globalpolicy.org/component/content/article/154/26026.html.
37. Paul Berman, quoted in *Yo Blair*, p. 60.
38. Campbell, *The Blair Years*, p. 397.
39. Campbell, *The Blair Years*, p. 397
40. Blair, *A Journey*, p. 350.
41. Kampfner, *Blair's Wars*, p. 73.
42. Riddell, *Hug Them Close*, p. 135.
43. Christopher Meyer, *DC Confidential: The Controversial Memoirs of Britain's Ambassador to the US at the Time of 9/11 and the Run-Up to the Iraq War* (London: Phoenix, 2006), p. 1.

CHAPTER ELEVEN: THE FINEST MOMENT

1. Blair, *A Journey*, p. 722.
2. Meyer, *DC Confidential*, p. 59.
3. Blair, *A Journey*, p. 619.
4. George Tenet, *At the Center of the Storm: My Years at the CIA* (New York: Harper Collins, 2007), p. 174.
5. Riddell, *Hug Them Close*, p. 147.
6. Wheatcroft, *Yo Blair*, p. 84.
7. Speech to the Labour Party conference, October 2, 2001, https://www.americanrhetoric.com/speeches/tblair10-02-01.htm.
8. *Times* (London), January 1, 2002.
9. Bob Woodward, *Bush at War* (New York: Simon and Schuster, 2002), p. 107.
10. Blair, *A Journey*, p. 626.
11. Blair, *A Journey*, p. 626.
12. Tenet, *At the Center of the Storm*, p. 310.
13. Michael Isikoff and David Corn, *Hubris: The Inside Story of Spin, Scandal, and the Selling of the Iraq War* (New York: Crown, 2006), p. 3.
14. Kamfner, *Blair's Wars*, p. 167.
15. Campbell, *The Blair Years*, p. 612.
16. Blair, *A Journey*, p. 683.
17. Campbell, *The Blair Years*, p. 614.
18. "Bush's Brain Trust," interview by Sam Tanenhaus, *Vanity Fair*, July 2003.
19. *New York Times*, October 3, 2004.
20. Blair, *A Journey*, p. 659.
21. John Walcott, "What Donald Rumsfeld Knew We Didn't Know About Iraq," *Politico*, January 24, 2016.
22. Interview with Christiane Amanpour, at University of California, Berkeley, March 18, 2004.
23. *Financial Times*, January 7, 2003.
24. Blair, *A Journey*, p. 762.
25. Kampfner, *Blair's Wars*, p. 279.
26. Blair, *A Journey*, p. 1045.
27. Blair, *A Journey*, p. 1051.
28. Wheatcroft, *Yo Blair*, p. 107.

Chapter Twelve: After the Crash

1. *Washington Post*, August 2, 2007.
2. BBC, July 13, 2007.
3. *New York Times*, July 30, 2007.
4. Andrew Rawnsley, *The End of the Party: The Rise and Fall of New Labour* (London: Viking, 2010), p. 447.
5. Gordon Brown, *My Life, Our Times* (London: Bodley Head, 2017), p. 429.
6. Brown, *My Life, Our Times*, p. 425.
7. Brown, *My Life, Our Times*, p. 423.
8. *Christian Science Monitor*, September 14, 2009.
9. Mansion House Speech, June 21, 2007.
10. Mansion House speech, June 21, 2006.
11. *New York Times*, November 9, 2009.
12. Brown, *My Life, Our Times*, p. 339.
13. Barack Obama, *The Audacity of Hope: Thoughts on Reclaiming the American Dream* (New York: Crown, 2006), p. 309.
14. Brown, *Our Life, Our Times*, p. 329.
15. Rawnsley, *End of the Party*, p. 626.
16. Brown, *Our Life, Our Times*, p. 339.
17. *Independent*, March 25, 2010.
18. Brown, *My Life, Our Times*, p. 429.
19. Hillary Clinton, *Hard Choices: A Memoir* (New York: Simon and Schuster, 2014), p. 208.
20. Rawnsley, *End of the Party*, p. 345.
21. David Cameron, *For the Record* (New York: Harper, 2019), p. 151.
22. Speech at the Ninestiles School, Birmingham, July 2015. Published in the *Independent*, July 20, 2015.
23. Ben Rhodes, *The World as It Is: A Memoir of the Obama White House* (New York: Random House, 2019), p. 110.
24. *New York Times*, March 3, 2011.
25. Cameron, *For the Record*, p. 284.
26. Jeffrey Goldberg, "The Obama Doctrine," *Atlantic*, April 2016.
27. Goldberg, "The Obama Doctrine."
28. *Independent*, November 15, 2015.
29. Cameron, *For the Record*, p. 286.
30. *Washington Post*, August 18, 2011.
31. Barack Obama, "Remarks by the President in Address to the Nation on Libya," March 28, 2012.
32. Clinton, *Hard Choices*, p. 466.
33. *Guardian*, August 29, 2013.
34. Cameron, *For the Record*, p. 466.
35. https://twitter.com/paddyashdown/status/373339499868467201.
36. BBC News, August 30, 2013.
37. *Independent*, November 15, 2016.
38. Rhodes, *The World as It Is*, p. 383.
39. Rhodes, *The World as It Is*, p. 386.

Chapter Thirteen: Grand Illusions

1. Sam Knight, "Nigel Farage on the Story Behind His Friendship with Trump," *New Yorker*, November 30, 2016.
2. Ed Caesar, "The Chaotic Triumph of Arron Banks, the 'Bad Boy of Brexit,'" *New Yorker*, March 25, 2019.

3. *Daily Telegraph*, January 28, 2017.
4. *Daily Telegraph*, January 28, 2017.
5. *Daily Mail*, November 4, 2016.
6. Allison Pearson, "For Brexit to Work, We Need Dunkirk Spirit Not 'Naysaying Nellies,'" *Daily Telegraph*, August 1, 2017.
7. *Daily Telegraph*, November 14, 2008.
8. Teresa May, Speech to the Conservative Party Conference, October 5, 2016, https://www.youtube.com/watch?v=08JN73K1JDc.
9. Interview in the *Daily Mail*, September 14, 2019.
10. *Incredible Hulk* #227 (New York: Marvel, September 1978).

Index

A Note About the Author

Ian Buruma was educated in Holland and Japan. He has spent many years in Asia, which he has written about in *A Japanese Mirror*, *Bad Elements* and *A Tokyo Romance*. His other books include: *The Wages of Guilt*, *Murder in Amsterdam* (shortlisted for the Samuel Johnson Prize and winner of the Los Angeles Times Book Prize), *Anglomania*, *Year Zero* and *Their Promised Land*. He was awarded the Erasmus Prize in 2008 and was named as one of the 100 top global thinkers by *Foreign Policy* magazine in 2010. Buruma lives in New York, where he teaches at Bard College.